I0796805

ARTHUR'S MISCELLANY

ABOUT THE EDITORS

John Matthews is the author of over a hundred titles on myth, folklore, and ancient traditions. He has worked in the film industry as an historical advisor and won a BAFTA for his work on the movie *King Arthur* (2004). He has made a lifetime study of every aspect of the Arthurian legends, has edited international journal *Arthuriana*, and has contributed to a variety of other journals, including *Parabola*, *The Temenos Academy Review* and *Agenda*.

Stuart W. Pyhrr studied art history at the Institute of Fine Arts, New York University, while working under the direction of Helmut Nickel, Curator of Arms and Armor at the Metropolitan Museum of Art. He formally joined the department in 1977 and succeeded his mentor and friend as curator-in-charge in 1988. Following a four-decade career at the museum, Pyhrr retired in 2020 as Curator Emeritus. The author of numerous articles and exhibition catalogues focusing on European arms and armour, he continues to research and publish.

ARTHUR'S MISCELLANY

Aspects of King Arthur, from Shields of Power to the Questing Beast

HELMUT NICKEL

Edited by John Matthews and Stuart Pyhrr

AMBERLEY

Page 1: King Arthur from the Heroes Tapestries. South Netherlandish, *c.* 1400-1410. Wool warp, wool wefts, 168 × 117 in. (426.7 × 297.2 cm). (The Metropolitan Museum of Art, New York, Munsey Fund, 1932; Gift of John D. Rockefeller Jr., 1947 (32.130.3a; 47.101.4))

First published 2025

Amberley Publishing
The Hill, Stroud
Gloucestershire, GL5 4EP

www.amberley-books.com

British Library Cataloguing in Publication Data.
A catalogue record for this book is available from the British Library.

ISBN 978 1 3981 2439 4 (hardback)
ISBN 978 1 3981 2440 0 (ebook)

1 2 3 4 5 6 7 8 9 10

Typeset in 10.5pt on 14.5pt Sabon.
Typesetting by SJmagic DESIGN SERVICES, India.
Printed in the UK.

Contents

Acknowledgements

Special thanks must go to the editors of *Interpretations*, *Arthuriana* (Journal of the International Arthurian Society) and *Avalon to Camelot*, especially Freya Reeves, who shared their archives and allowed us to reprint the papers that Helmut had written for them over the years. Freya Reeves, publisher of *Avalon to Camelot,* remembers that 'It was both a joy and a privilege to publish a lively article by Helmut Nickel in each of the eight issues of the magazine.' Additional thanks go to the magazine's editor Alan Lupack and copyeditor Dan Nastali, for their contributions.

Introduction

The essays collected here were published between 1980 and 2012. We have also included several previously unpublished articles on related Arthurian themes. Some of these will be seen to overlap in places and there is a certain degree of repetition, inevitable over such a lengthy period. It was decided to keep these as they were, with only the lightest editing, rather than reduce their impact by cutting details. They are a further tribute to Helmut Nickel's extensive scholarship, a considerable contribution to the world of Arthurian studies.

Helmut's own description of his involvement in the topic of Arthurian literature and art, as well as his lifelong passion for heraldry, makes for interesting reading. It was written – somewhat reluctantly – for the journal *Avalon to Camelot*, to which Helmut was a regular and lively contributor:

> My interest in the professional field of arms and armor and in the Arthurian legends started at a very early age. In fact, I do not remember a time when I was not interested in these two subjects.
>
> It seems to have started on a family hiking trip when we passed a farmhouse in the village of Graupa near Dresden. Intriguingly, the house had two white swans wrought into its green-painted iron gate and two lengthy inscriptions chiselled on its sandstone pillars. I must have been about four years old, because I could not read yet, and asked my mother about them. She explained that this had once been the summer retreat of Richard Wagner, who had written Parsifal and Lohengrin in this house. She told me the stories of the Grail and the

Swan-Knight in condensed form (I was particularly impressed that the damsel rescued by Lohengrin was named Elsa von Brabant, as Else was my mother's name).

About the same time my father took me to Dresden to see the Rüstkammer, the famous ancient armory of the former Prince-Electors and Kings of Saxony. From that time on I was absolutely hooked. My first tin soldiers were, of course, a set of little knights from the renowned toy making company Heyde in Dresden, which manufactured them from about 1870 until WWII. From this you will have deduced that I grew up in and near Dresden, Germany, about sixty years ago.

I graduated from the Free University in West Berlin and I was lucky enough to become an art historian. My doctoral thesis about the development of the knightly shield in Western Europe was sufficiently off the beaten track to attract attention so that I was asked to join the department of arms and armor of the Metropolitan Museum of Art in New York in 1960.

During my student days in West Berlin I earned my thinly buttered bread as an illustrator, specializing as an adaptor for comic strips of classic adventure stories, such as The Three Musketeers, The Count of Monte Christo, and Robinson Crusoe. I worked also on homemade Westerns, such as the Western stories of Karl May, immensely popular in Europe. May, a late nineteenth-century writer, lived in Dresden. Alas, my truly great love, the Arthurian stories, were a field already pre-empted by Hal Foster's Prince Valiant ('Prinz Eisenberz' in his German editions), and thus I never had a chance to illustrate a romance of chivalry.

From this, as well as what follows, it will be seen that Helmut Nickel's interest in all things chivalric and Arthurian has extended throughout most of his long life. His involvement as a young soldier in the Second World War was also extraordinary and shows that personal courage and sense of chivalry would in an earlier time have made him a courageous knight. All illustrations are by Helmut Nickel unless otherwise stated. I am personally very proud to have been able to bring the work of our dear friend to the attention of a wider public.

John Matthews
Oxford, 2025

Above: Tournament armour at the Rüstkammer, Dresden – the inspiration for a lifelong study by Helmut Nickel. (Courtesy Pudelek, under creative commons)

Left: French plate armour before 1588 at the Rüstkammer, Dresden. (Courtesy Pudelek, under creative commons)

1

Notes on Arthurian Heraldry

The Retroactive System in the 'Armagnac' Armorial

Heraldry, as defined by Sir Anthony Wagner, Clarenceaux King of Arms, is 'the systematic use of hereditary devices centred on the shield' (Marks and Payne 11; Ailes 1).

The imaginary arms of Arthurian heraldry as codified by the roll of arms thought to have been compiled *c.* 1440-50 for and possibly even by Jacques d'Armagnac, due de Nemours (Sandoz 389-420), have been called a 'caricature du système heraldique véritable' by Michel Pastoureau, whose *Armorial des Chevaliers de la Table Ronde* constitutes the so far most comprehensive work on the subject (Pastoureau 12).[1] In it Pastoureau points out that the major heroes within a family group, such as Gawain, Lancelot, Palomydes and Perceval, tend to be 'chefs d'armes', who bear the basic arms from which the arms of other family members are derived. If the arms of a hero's father are identical to those of his son, as is the case with King Ban and his son Lancelot, King Lot and Gawain, King Uriens and Ywain, this is explained as meaning that as a parallel to the rules of *véritable* heraldry these heroes' fathers are seen as already deceased and therefore their oldest sons would become chefs d'armes of their families[2] (Pastoureau 70, 82, 95, 103-05).

However, this does not apply in all cases, and it seems that the system is somewhat more complicated. Though logical in its own way, the Arthurian heraldry in question is exactly the opposite of the definition by Sir Anthony. These arms are not inherited by sons from their fathers, but they were originally attributed to a knight of high reputation and then transferred back 'retroactively' to that knight's father, who is usually of lesser renown. Among the one hundred and seventy-odd Knights of the Round Table listed in the 'Armagnac' armorial there are twelve family groups that extend over two generations or more. The best-known group is the Orkney clan of King Lot and his sons, Sir Gawain and his brothers. This clan is also of special interest, because two entirely different sets of arms have been assigned to the princes of Orkney at different times.

In French literary and pictorial sources of the thirteenth and fourteenth centuries Sir Gawain is bearing a white shield with a red canton. His younger brother Gareth has the canton semy of gold or silver eaglets, while their half-brother Mordred bears a red shield with a white canton, and the arms of Gawain's son, Guinglain, *le Bel Inconnu*, are *Ermine, a canton gules* (Brault 40-44; Pastoureau 70, 73, 91; Jenkins 36). Though the arms of King Lot of Orkney are not actually documented in any of the sources, it is clear that all these shields are canting arms for the descendants of King Lot. Canting arms in Arthurian heraldry are usually puns in French; '*lot*' means 'section' and a canton can be considered to be a section of a shield.[3] These arms plainly follow the by then established rules of real-life heraldry.

By contrast, in the 'Armagnac' armorial the arms of King Lot are given as: *Purpure, a double-headed eagle or, beaked and membered azure.* Sir Gawain's arms in the armorial and also in miniatures of the fifteenth century (Brault 41-42; Loomis pi. 286; Scott-Giles VIII: 338-39 and Pastoureau 70, 84) are the same as his father's; his brothers bear these arms of the double-eagle in a purple field differenced in various ways. Agravaine has the eagle beaked and membered gules, with a *fess vert* over all, Gaheris's eagle is beaked and membered argent, within a border goutte gules, Gareth bears the eagle beaked and membered gules, with a bendlet gules over all, and Mordred bears the double-eagle under a chief argent[4] (Scott-Giles VIII: 334, 338, 389, IX: 32; Pastoureau 40, 67, 72-73,91) As mentioned above, Pastoureau suggests that the lack of any difference between King Lot's and Sir Gawain's arms is an indication that the armorial considered Lot as already dead, and Gawain therefore to be head of the clan and thus its '*chef d'armes*' (Pastoureau 70). It appears, though, as already recognized by Brault, that the arms of the golden double-eagle originally were those of Gawain (Brault 42n4), and were transferred to King Lot retroactively.

A possible reason for the radical change in the arms of the Orkney clan could be that the compiler of the 'Armagnac' armorial might have been offended by the fact that in the older tradition, the arms of the 'bad guy' Agravaine, did not share the canton gules of his brothers, but were: *Argent, a lion gules* (Brault 38; Pastoureau 40). Thus, they happened to be identical to the family arms of Armagnac. The compiler might have felt it to be well advised to search for an alternative design and found one in two – for his purposes – impeccable sources.

The first of these sources appears to be Geoffrey of Monmouth's *History of the Kings of Britain*, where it is said that Gawain at the age of twelve years had been given into the care of Pope Sulpicius, who in due time also gave him his knightly arms (Geoffrey ix: ii; Brault 41-42). These arms presented by the Pope in Rome would have included a shield, which could be assumed to bear a 'Roman' device. In another case of 'retroactive' heraldry the arms of the medieval Holy Roman Empire: *Or, a double-headed eagle sable, armed gules*, were generally considered to have been the arms of ancient Rome; for instance, in the iconography of the Nine Worthies, they were regularly attributed to Julius Caesar.[5] In the early thirteenth-century prose romance of the Grail, *Perlesvaus*, Gawain is associated with Pope Gregory the Great and receives for his own the red shield with a golden eagle that once belonged to Judas Maccabaeus (Brault 42n3). Therefore, it appears that Gawain's golden double eagle is a combination of the device of Judas Maccabaeus and the arms of the Roman Empire,[6] and became assigned to his father King Lot only in retrospect.

The most obvious case of retroactive heraldry is that of Ywain, the Knight with the Lion, whose canting arms were: *Azure, a lion or, armed gules,* and whose arms were promptly transferred to his father, King Uriens of Gorre[7] (Brault 49; Scott-Giles IX: 335; Pastoureau 103-06).

The common charges in the arms of the Benoic-Gannes clan are three red bendlets on white shields. Though these are borne in the Benoic family (King Ban of Benoic – Lancelot du Lac) over two and in the Gannes branch (King Bors of Gannes – Bors of Gannes – Helain le Blanc) even three generations, it is clear that these bendlets are all based on the traditional arms of Lancelot: *Argent, three bendlets gules,* as already established in the thirteenth century (Brault 46-47; Scott-Giles IX: 31; Pastoureau 82). The outward appearance of proper inheritance is maintained by projecting them back in time to King Ban, Lancelot's father (Scott-Giles IX: 35; Pastoureau 49). The arms of Lancelot's half-brother, Ector de Maris: *Argent, three bendlets gules, a sun azure over all* (Scott-Giles VIII: 335; Pastoureau 74), and those of the members of the

Gannes family, King Bors and his son Lionel: *Argent, semy of stars sable, three bendlets gules over all,* those of his other son, Sir Bors: *Ermine, three bendlets gules,*[8] and of Bors's son Helain le Blanc: *Argent, three bendlets gules, a label sable* (Scott-Giles VHL335, 336, 339; Pastoureau 52, 75, 83-84), as well as those of their cousins, Blamore and Blioberis: *Argent, semy of crescents sable, three bendlets gules over all* (Scott-Giles VHL335; Pastoureau 50-51), give the impression of correct and coherent inheritance, but in reality they all are ingeniously contrived variants of Lancelot's magic shield, given to him by the Damsel of the Dolorous Guard in one of the early episodes of the *Lancelot propre.* This damsel did offer to Lancelot the choice of three white shields, one with a single red bend that gave its bearer the strength of a single man, one with two bendlets that accordingly lent the strength of two men, and one with three bendlets that would impart the strength of three men to its lucky owner (Brault 46-47; Pastoureau 82). Not surprisingly, Lancelot chose the shield with the three bends.

Lancelot's son Galahad does not participate in the armorial system of the clan; he bears the Adventurous Shield destined for him. It was marked with a red cross by the blood of the dying Josephe or Josephus, son of Joseph of Arimathea (Brault 50n3; Pastoureau 67-68).

Among the arms of the four Saracen knights of the Round Table, those of King Esclabor of Babylon and his sons, Palomydes and Saphere, look at first glance as if they were following the rules of 'real' heraldry, but they are of the 'retroactive' kind too. King Esclabor bears: *Chequy, or and gules* (Scott-Giles VIII: 334-35; Pastoureau 62-63), his son Palomydes: *Chequy, argent and sable* (Scott-Giles DC: 33; Pastoureau 93-94), and Saphere: *Per pale vair and chequy or and vert* (Scott-Giles IX: 34; Pastoureau 99). Of these three worthies, Palomydes is by far most renowned. The black and white chessboard shield pattern assigned to him was probably inspired by the tradition that his namesake, the Greek hero Palamedes, had invented the game of draughts to beat the boredom of the siege of Troy. The chequy arms with different tinctures were subsequently transferred to his father and his brother.[9] The *vair* and *vert* in Saphere's arms are probably canting; they would be homophones to the second syllable in Saphere's name, if pronounced in French.

Among the members of the Listenois clan are to be found two basic blazons and various combinations thereof. King Pellinore bears: *Or, crusily azure* (Scott-Giles DC: 33; Pastoureau 94-95), but his brother, Lamorak of Listenois, as is not unusual among brothers in Arthurian heraldry, bears entirely different arms: *Purpure, a leopard argent, armed gules* (Pastoureau 81). Perceval, youngest of Pellinore's sons,[10] bears: *Purpure, crusily or* (Brault 48; Scott-Giles K:33; Pastoureau 95-96) and Tor filz Aries, Pellinore's illegitimate son by the wife of Aries the cowherd, bears: *Or, crusily sable* (Scott-Giles IX:34; Pastoureau 102-03), but Pellinore's two older sons, Agloval and Lamorak of Wales, bear a combination of the charges of their parent generation, crosslets and leopards, but on purple fields. Agloval bears: *Purpure, crusily or, a leopard argent* (Scott-Giles VIII: 334; Pastoureau 40), and Lamorak of Wales: *Purpure, crusily or, a leopard or, armed gules* (Scott-Giles IX: 30; Pastoureau 81).

Of this clan the most important member is without a doubt Perceval, and a shield semy of crosses would be a very appropriate cognizance for him as one of the achievers of the Grail. Perceval, as the Red Knight of the older traditions based on Chrestien de Troyes, would also be the one to whom the tincture purple in its original meaning of dark crimson red would have been applicable. Neither King Pellinore, the pursuer of the Questing Beast, nor Tor are known to have distinguished themselves in a religious way; the shield pattern semy with crosslets they share is likely to be a retroactive transfer from Perceval to Pellinore. Also, it seems that the colour purple is a transfer from Perceval's arms to those of his uncle Lamorak. Bastardy is not indicated in any special way in Arthurian heraldry, and therefore Tor can inherit the arms of his natural father, differenced only by the tincture of the crosslets.

The arms of both King Lac of Estregalles and his son, Erec (who is called Sir Harry Fitz Lake by Malory), are: *Or, three dragons' heads gules, langued vert.* Though King Lac and Sir Harry have only very minor roles in Malory's work, in the French tradition Erec is a major hero in the oeuvre of Chrestien de Troyes and his followers. For this reason, it can be suspected that the not readily explicable cognizance of the three dragons' heads was originally Erec's and became King Lac's by transfer (Scott-Giles VIII: 339, IX: 30; Pastoureau 62, 80). Interestingly, King Lac's other son, Brandiles de Vaulxsur, bears completely different canting arms: *Gules, three upright swords* (brands) *argent, hilted azure* (Pastoureau 52-53).

The most striking example of transfer of arms from son to father is the arms of King Bagdemagus of Gorre: *Gules, three sinister gloves fingers upward argent* (Scott-Giles VHL334-35; Pastoureau 49-50). These are canting arms derived from the name of Bagdemagus's miscreant son, Meliagant. '*Gant*' is French for 'glove', and the element *mel* = *mal* as 'bad' is indicated by the left-handedness of the gloves. A parallel in real-life heraldry is to be found in the arms of Henry Malemein: *Gules, three left hands fingers upward argent,* in the Dering (A) Roll, c. 1275 (Wright pi. 4). The arms of Meliagant are: *Azure, three gloves fingers downward argent (Gyron* fol. a iiii, verso; Scott-Giles IX: 32). Though it is not specified that the gloves in Meliagant's arms should be left gloves; their positioning with downward pointing fingers is probably meant to indicate graphically the baseness of the abductor of Queen Guinevere.[11]

Among the remaining four father-and-son groups there are three, Meliadus of Lyonesse – Tristram, Gyron le Courtoys – Gallinant le Blanc, Brunor Sans Peur – Dinadan and Brunor La Cotte Mai Tayle, that have a parent generation with plain shields of a single tincture that is repeated in the field colour of their sons' arms (Pastoureau 54-55; 56, 61, 73, 88, 103).

Tristram 'of Lyonesse' bears canting arms: *Vert, a lion or*; Pastoureau suggests that the *plain vert* of the shield of his father could have been created by '*soustraction*' of the canting lion. Interestingly, Tristram's cousin, Alixandre li Orphelin, bears: *Vert, a lion argent,* though he is not 'of Lyonesse' but is the son of Boudwin, brother of King Mark of Cornwall.

Gyron's son, Gallinant le Blanc, bears: *Or, a dragon gules, armed and langued sable.* These arms cannot be construed as canting or otherwise suggestive of Gallinant's personality. However, in the most comprehensive extant copy of the 'Armagnac' armorial, MS. 77 A10, Staatliche Museen, Berlin, it is explained how Gyron's kinsman, Seguran le Brun, once killed a particularly hideous dragon and therefore took as his arms: *Or, a dragon sable, armed and langued vert.* This memorable deed apparently was proudly reflected in the arms of Gallinant and also in those of that unsavoury relative, Brun Saunce Pitie, who bore: *Sable, a dragon argent.* Even the patriarch of the Le Brun clan, Seguran's uncle Brunor le Brun, who as *le vieil chevalier* is the hero of the first part of *Gyron le Courtoys,* was also known as *le chevalier au dragon (Gyron,* fol. xiii verso).[12]

Though they are distant kinsmen of the Le Brun clan, the sons of Brunor Sans Peur *with the argent shield,* Dinadan and his brother Brunor La Cotte Mal Tayle, have lions instead of dragons as their cognizances. Dinadan bears: *Argent, a lion sable, armed vert,* and Brunor La Cotte Mal *Tayle: Argent, a lion chequy gules and sable, armed vert.* Presumably the lion sable was assigned to Dinadan, Tristram's loyal companion, as a counterpoint to Tristram's golden lion, and the 'cut-up' chequy pattern of Brunor's lion is probably a hint at his surname La Cotte Mal Tayle.

Pastoureau sees these dragons and lions as brisures that difference the sons' shields from their fathers'. It looks, though, as if the three plain shields: *Vert* for Meliadus, *Or* for Gyron, and *argent* for Brunor le Chevalier Sans Peur, were not meant to be arms in the sense of family arms, but rather were personal devices of knight-errantry, which were neither in constant nor consequent use. In order to participate in a tournament incognito, Meliadus was known to have borne an argent shield and Gyron a sable one, and after one good fight Gyron and the Chevalier Sans Peur even exchange shields and ride that way to the confusion of their enemies *(Gyron,* fols. xix, xx ff., xxii ff.).

There is only one single family group, extending over three generations, that does not fit into the 'retroactive' pattern; it is the family of King Arthur himself, his father Uther Pendragon and his enigmatic son Artus le Petit. Their shield charges, two dragons for Uther Pendragon (derived from Geoffrey of Monmouth's story of the two dragon banners, made after the sign of the fiery dragon in the sky), thirteen crowns for King Arthur,[13] and a golden tree for Artus le Petit, are utterly unrelated to each other, though there are indications of relationship to be found in Arthur's *crest* of a dragon, his battle cry PENDRAGON TESTE DE DRAGON, and Artus's motto: C'EST POUR ARTHUR (Cooke and Foster 5; Pastoureau 46-47).

Outside of the 'Armagnac' armorial the standard rules of heraldic inheritance for Arthurian heroes are being observed, as seen in the older arms of the princes of Orkney. Another example is found in Wolfram von Eschenbach's *Parzival,* where Parzival's father, Gahmuret, discards his badge of knight-errantry, the Anchor, when he comes into his inheritance and has the panther sable 'that his father bore' mounted on his shield (Wolfram 61).

It is interesting to see that the early fifteenth-century heraldic handbook, *Traits de blason,* by Clément Prinsault, dedicated to Jacques d'Armagnac (Douet d'Arcq 257-74, 321-42; Dennys 214) is illustrated by seventy shields as examples for blazoning, and practically all of these have been used either directly or in adaptations as models for the arms in the 'Armagnac' armorial.[14] If Jacques d'Armagnac himself was the compiler of the armorial, to exploit a handy source like Prinsault's Treatise would have been the most convenient way of getting enough material for an ambitious project like this roll of arms for more than one hundred and seventy Arthurian knights, whose arms in many cases would have to be invented from scratch. If Prinsault was the compiler, it would have been even easier for him to borrow from his own work. Whoever the compiler was, he cleverly arranged a system by its nature a '*caricature du systeme veritable*', gave a credible impression of authentic and seriously researched heraldry.

Notes

1. There are probably close to one hundred manuscript copies of the 'Armagnac' armorial in existence. The most important copies in this country are: Harvard University Library, Houghton Ms typ 1312 (ex-Hofer1); Pierpont Morgan Library, Ms. 16 (this copy includes short biographies of the individual knights); and Walters Art Museum, Baltimore, Ms. 463 (supplies crests, supporters and devises in addition to shields and biographical data).
2. '*La notoriété semble primer le rang*' (Pastoureau 95).
3. Brault (42) points out that in German heraldry a canton, *Eck,* is often used as a canting device for armigers, whose names include the syllable '*-eck*' = 'corner', but he thinks that no such pun could be made in Gawain's case.
4. The arms of Gaheris were: *Argent, three eaglets gules.*
5. These arms of 'Ancient Rome' are found in countless medieval miniatures and paintings representing scenes from antiquity; in Christian iconography they are found in crucifixion scenes, etc. The arms attributed to Julius Caesar as one of the Nine Worthies were: *Or, a double-headed eagle sable, armed and beaked gules.*
6. Purpure was originally meant to be a dark crimson red; in the late twelfth century *De Ortu Walwanii*, Gawain was distinguished by his red surcoat; in *Gawain and the Green Knight* his shield with the pentangle is red.
7. The arms of Uriens's illegitimate son, Yvain le Aoutre, were: *Azure, a pale or* (Pastoureau 106). Though they are in the 'family colours,' blue and gold, the charge is totally different.
8. The *ermine* in Sir Bors's arms is partly to indicate not only his usual (with one exception) constant chastity, but also a close connection with Brittany; the arms of the duchy of Brittany were: *Plain ermine.* Sir Bors's crest is an ermine collared with a scarf of *ermine*. This is the main charge in the arms of the city of Vannes (Gannes!) in Brittany.

9. The arms of the fourth Saracen knight, Arphazar, the brother of Esclabor, are: *Sable, a saltire argent.* In the 'Armagnac' armorial it is not uncommon for brothers to have totally different arms. In some copies of the 'Armagnac' armorial Arphazar is called '*chevallier descosse*' therefore, his saltire might be derived from the St Andrew's Cross of Scotland.
10. Pastoureau calls Perceval the oldest son of Pellinore's, evidently because of his appearing to be '*chef d'armes*' of the clan. By Chrestien and his followers Perceval is considered to be the youngest son.
11. The arms of King Bagdemagus in the fourteenth century, as illustrated in the *Armorial des Tournois des Rois de I'Espinette* (Bouton pi. 3), were: *Vert, semy of crowns or.* The printed list in *Gyron le Courtoys* is the only one that incorporates the arms of Meliagant.
12. Branor le Brun also carries a shield '*Dore*', and on another occasion one *per pale argent and sable (Gyron,* ii verso; v).
13. King Arthur's best-known arms are: *Azure, three crowns or.* The thirteen crowns are the result of erroneously reading *treize* for *trois* in a written French source without illustrations.
14. See for instance Douet fig. 52: *Argent, three crosses fitchy sable,* and the same arms for Herrois le Joyeux; Douet fig. 58: *Sable, an escarbuncle or,* and the same for Abilan du Desert; Douet fig. 65: *Gules, a point or* as the arms for Friadus le Gay (Pastoureau 39, 67, 75).

Select Bibliography

Ailes, Adrian. 'Heraldry in Twelfth-Century England: The Evidence', in *England in the twelfth century: Proceedings of the 1988 Harlaxton Symposium.* Harlaxton College, 1990.

Bouton, V. *Armorial des tournois: jouste faicte a Tournay l'an mil trois cents trente.* Paris, 1870.

Brault, Gerard J. *Early Blazon. Heraldic Terminology in the twelfth and thirteenth Centuries, with Specific Reference to Arthurian Literature.* Oxford, 1972.

Cooke, Robert, and Joseph Foster. *Two Tudor Books of Arms,* London, n.d.

Dennys, Rodney. *The Heraldic Imagination.* New York: Clarkson N. Potter, Inc., 1975.

Douet d'Arcq, L. 'Un Traité du Blason.' *Revue Archáeologique*, first series, XV, 1858.

Geoffrey of Monmouth. *The History of the Kings of Britain*. Trans. Lewis Thorpe. New York: Penguin Classics, 1966.

Gyron le Courtoys. Intro. by C. E. Pickford. Facsimile ed. London: Scolar Press, 1977.

Jenkins, Elizabeth. *The Mystery of King Arthur.* New York: Coward, McCann & Geoghegan, Inc., 1975.

Loomis, Roger Sherman. *Arthurian Legends in Medieval Art.* London: Oxford UP, 1937.

Marks, Richard, and Ann Payne. *British Heraldry from its Origins to c. 1800*. Exhibition catalogue. London: British Museum Publications, 1978.

Pastoureau, Michel. *Armorial des Chevaliers de la Table Ronde*. Paris: Le Leopard d'or, 1983.

Sandoz, Edouard. 'Tourneys in the Arthurian Tradition'. *Speculum* 19 (1944), pp 389-421.

Scott-Giles, C.W. 'Some Arthurian Coats of Arms.' *The Coat of Arms* VIII, 64 (October 1965); IX, 65 (January 1966). Pp 332-339

Wright, C. E. *English Heraldic Manuscripts in the British Museum*. Exh. cat. London: British Museum Publications, 1973.

Originally published in *Quondam et Futurus* Vol 3 No. 3. Autumn 1993 pp. 1-23.

2

About Arms and Armour in the Age of Arthur

In Geoffrey of Monmouth's *History of the Kings of Britain* (*c.* 1135), Chrestien de Troyes' *Erec et Enide* (*c.* 1170) and *Sir Gawain and the Green Knight* (*c.* 1370) we find detailed descriptions of the arming of a knight. Those of Erec and of Sir Gawain are accurate accounts of their contemporary armour and even of the correct sequence of how these armour elements were put on. The arming of King Arthur, however, as Geoffrey (IX, 4) describes it at the eve of the Battle of Badon, mentions armour elements quite different from those in use during the early twelfth century.

Geoffrey has Arthur don

> ... a leather jerkin *(lorica)* worthy of so great a king. On his head he placed a golden helmet with a crest carved in the shape of a dragon; and across his shoulders a circular shield called Pridwen, on which was painted a likeness of the Blessed Mary, Mother of God... He girded on his peerless sword, called Caliburn, which was forged in the island of Avalon. A spear called Ron graced his right hand: long, broad in the blade and thirsty for slaughter.

None of these elements are even close to those worn by knights of Geoffrey's own days; those would have been in essence the same as described in Erec's arming: a mail shirt of interwoven steel rings, mail leggings *(chausses)*, a conical or semi-globular helmet with nose-guard, but without any crest, and finally a large almond-shaped or triangular shield, of wood covered with leather and painted with the beginnings of heraldry. On the other hand, Geoffrey's description of the circular shield, the Roman-style leather lorica, and – most important – Arthur's dragon-crested helmet, corresponds in all details to the actual armour found in the Sutton Hoo ship burial. This is another definite indication that Geoffrey did not rely solely on his fertile imagination, but must have had some earlier source, perhaps even a 'very ancient book in the British language'.

It has been said repeatedly that Arthur must have been a Romanized British warleader, who revived half-forgotten Late Roman cavalry tactics in order to repel the hit-and-run raids of sea-borne Saxon pirates. Interestingly enough, among the names of the twelve battles mentioned in Nennius' battle-list (*c.* 800 AD) of victories attributed to 'Arthur, dux bellorum', there are eight names of rivers (where encounters with pirates are to be expected), but three of the remaining four are names of towns that were garrisons of Late Roman heavy cavalry. The Roman cavalry in Britain was particularly strong; in fact, in the fifth century the only two existing regiments of heavy armoured cavalry *(cataphractarii)* in West Rome were stationed in Britain, together with a sizable troop of 'Sarmatian veterans', whose ancestors had been brought to Britain (originally to fight the Picts) about 250 years earlier, and had been settled in Lancashire. The Sarmatians were horse nomads from the Eastern European steppes, armoured with scale armour of horn, iron or bronze, including armour for their horses, and wearing *spangenhelms* constructed from a framework of bronze or iron straps (*Spangen* in German) with iron or horn fillings. Their Eastern style armour actually was the prototype for that of the *cataphractarii* of the Late Roman and Byzantine armies. They fought with long lances *(contus)* and double-edged swords *(spatha);* their battle-standard was a dragon on a pole, and their tribal god of war was worshipped in the form of a naked sword planted upright in the ground or a platform. It is not impossible that these Sarmatian troopers were the cavalry arm of the 'historical Arthur'.

After four hundred years of Roman occupation, it is inevitable that there was a considerable amount of Roman influence on British armour, though – this being the Dark Ages – we have very little documentation about it. Significantly enough, Geoffrey states that when the Romans withdrew from Britain (allegedly 410 AD), they left behind armour and weapons as models for the Britons to copy for their self-defence (VI, 3). This means probably that whoever among the tribal warriors was wealthy enough would equip himself with a Roman-style helmet *(cassis* or *galea)*

Sarmatian from a 2nd-century mausoleum. (Courtesy Linda Malcor and John Matthews, from *Artorius: The Real King Arthur*)

and possibly a mailshirt *(lorica hamate)*. The main defence, carried by practically every warrior with the possible exception of archers, who needed both hands for drawing their bows, would have been the large oval or circular shield (Lat. *scutum;* Welsh *ysquit)*. These shields were of half-inch thick wood, covered with leather, and reinforced with bronze or iron mountings; its central handgrip was specially protected by a large metal boss *(umbo)*.

Shields were probably painted in tribal colours, with distinctive marks for individual warriors. The image of the Virgin Mary on Arthur's shield has equivalents in the portrait medallions of emperors on the shields of high Roman commanders, such as represented on the consular diptych of Stilicho, preserved in the Cathedral Treasury of Monza. The cross, assigned to Arthur as his shield device by the *Annales Cambriae,* would have been most natural for a Christian warrior, and was doubtlessly used by others too.

The arms and armour of the Saxons was not much different from that of the Britons, though here the Roman influence was naturally less strong. The standard defence of a Saxon warrior was a round shield with a central boss; the shields were usually painted red. Legend has it that the Saxon war leaders bore the tribal totem animal, the White Horse, as a shield emblem (Hengist – 'stallion', Horsa!). Warriors who could afford them would have worn mail shirts; helmets are known to have been used by prominent heroes. These helmets might have been of the cross-strap construction of the Sutton Hoo helmet, sometimes with a visor mask (*grim*), or they might have been of the Gothic *spangenhebn* type. In any case, there is no known Saxon (or Viking) helmet designed for battle that had horns!

The name of the Saxons is derived from that of the *seax,* a machete-like long knife, which was one of their favourite weapons; the Angles, in turn, seem to have received their name from *ango,* a barbed harpoon. Another favourite weapon was the axe; like the *seax* it was also a tool, and handy on shipboard. Swords with beautifully pattern-welded blades – probably made in the Rhinelands, where the Solingen cutlery centre is still flourishing – were highly treasured; richly decorated with gold and silver mountings they are found in graves (the Saxons were pagans, who buried their fallen warriors with their weapons; the Britons were Christians, and did not believe in grave goods, which makes it difficult for the archaeologist to assess their material culture) and also, more significantly, in ritual deposits in sacred lakes, such as in Nydam in the homeland of the Angles, the province Angeln at the Danish-German border. On an occasion such as this, a sacrificed sword might be retrieved by the priestess in charge of such a sacred lake, to be given to a hero and to be returned to the lake after his death...

Select Bibliography

A.V.B. Norman and Don Pottinger, *Warrior to Soldier:* English Weapons *and Warfare, 449-1660*; London, 1966.

J.W. Eadie, 'The Development of Roman Mailed Cavalry' in *Journal for Roman Studies,* 57 (1967), pp.161-173.

H. Russell Robinson, The Armour *of Imperial Rome*; London/New York, 1975.

William Reid, Arms *through the Ages*; London, 1976.

Ortwin Gamber, 'Some Notes on the Sutton Hoo Military Equipment' in *The Journal of The* Arms *& Armour Society,* X, no. 6 (Dec. 1982), pp. 208-216.

Rupert Bruce-Mitford, 'The Sutton Hoo Helmet-Reconstruction and the Design of the Royal Harness and Swordbelt' in *The Journal of the Arms & Armour Society,* X, no. 6 (Dec. 1982), pp. 217-280.

Originally published in *Avalon to Camelot* 1, no. 1 (Autumn, 1983), pp. 19-21.

Merowingian seaxes at the Württembergisches Landesmuseum, Stuttgart. (Courtesy of Bullenwächter under Creative Commons)

3
The Arms of King Arthur

In the tenth-century *Annales Cambriae,* which possibly goes back to contemporary sources, the entry about the Battle of Badon Hill (516 A.D.) mentions that Arthur 'carried the Cross of our Lord Jesus Christ on his shoulders for three days and three nights'. It is likely that this Latin quote is based upon a Welsh source, in which the words for 'shoulder' *(ysqwyd)* and 'shield' *(ysqwyt)* were close enough in spelling to get mixed up quite easily. Since a full-sized cross on the shoulder of a fighting man would have been a totally unacceptable encumbrance, it has been suggested that this cross was made of fabric sewn onto Arthur's coat, in the manner of eleventh- and twelfth-century crusaders. On the other hand, a cross, painted on a shield, would be an almost natural device for a Christian warrior fighting against pagan foes.

The same is true for the image of the Virgin Mary, which according to Nennius' battle list (*c.* 800), Arthur, *dux bellorum,* carried 'on his shoulders' during his fight at Castle Guinnion. It has been suggested that this image was either on an enamelled brooch or an icon attached to Arthur's tunic. More likely, though, is the possibility of an image on a shield. High-ranking officers in the late Roman army would bear a portrait of the emperor as special decoration on their shields – perhaps the most significant example would be the representation of the West Roman commander-in-chief, Stilicho, on his consular diptych, now in the cathedral treasury of Monza, Italy. Geoffrey of Monmouth (*c.* 1136) describes 'Saint Mary, Mother of God' as being painted on the inside of Arthur's shield, so 'that many a time and oft did [he] call her back into his memory' (IX. 4). The outside of the shield was presumably decorated with the cross; after all, Geoffrey liked to have the best of both worlds, if possible.

Geoffrey also mentions Arthur's helmet crest of a golden dragon, the device he had inherited from his father, Uther Pendragon. In Geoffrey's time, helmet crests were not yet worn by knights in real life, though dragon crests as integral parts of the reinforcing ridges of Dark Age helmets are known from surviving examples of much earlier helmets, such as the one found in the Sutton Hoo ship's burial, now in the British Museum. This detail about the dragon crest can be considered as affirmation of Geoffrey's claim that he took his material from an older source.

Originally published in *Avalon to Camelot* II No. 2 (1986) pp. 22-3.

4

The Enigmatic Arms of Erec, Fils du Roy Lac

The very first description of a full armorial achievement – shield charge and helmet crest – of a Knight of the Round Table, is given by Hartmann von Aue in his *Erec* (*c.* 1190-92), the earliest Arthurian epic in German. It is a rather free adaptation of Chrétien de Troyes' seminal *Erec, fils du Roy Lac* (*c.* 1170), that itself is the very first Arthurian fantasy story of them all. Hartmann, in his second Arthurian epic, *Iwein (*adapted from Chrétien's *Yvain au le Chevalier au Lion* (*c.* 1180), directly identifies himself as the author and proudly presents his qualification:

Ein riter so geleret was,	There was a knight so learned
daz er in den buochen laz	that he could read in books
swaz er dar geschriben vant.	whatever he found written there.
Der waz Hartmann genant.	He was called Hartmann,
Dienstman waz er von Owe.	he was in service at Aue.

The scholarship of which Hartmann is so proud includes a good knowledge of French that would enable him to translate both *Erec* and *Iwein* directly from his French sources.

One of the highpoints of Hartmann's *Erec* is the wedding of Erec et Enide at King Arthur's court. As a finale to its long, lavish celebration a splendid tournament was to be held, and Erec, fiz du Roy Lac, felt obliged as the groom of this Cinderella-type dream wedding – a king's son marrying a poor vavassour's daughter – to show up looking as splendid as possible. His helmet crest was an angel wrought of finest gold, and he had three splendid shields made along with three matching horse couvertures:

driu schilte gelich	three shields alike
Und driu gereite alsamelich	and three matching caparisons
mit einem wafen garwe,	with one sole elegant charge,
doch schiet si diu varwe.	but differing in tinctures
Der eine hurtllch gnuoc was.	One was pretty enough.
Uzen ein liechtes spiegelglas	On the outside a bright mirror glass
Vil verre glaste der schin.	that shone so far away.
Dar uf ein mowe guldin	On it there was a golden *mowe*
Zuo der maze so si solde.	of the right proportions.
Innen gar von golde.	Its inside was all of gold.
Derander was zinnober rot.	The other one was cinnabar red.
Dar uf er slahen gebot	He ordered to nail upon it
Ein mowen von silber wiz	a white *mowe* of silver
...also wart der drite var	...and then there was the third one
Von golde uzen und innen gar,	of gold outside as well as inside,
Daruf ein mowe zobellin	with a *mowe* of sable pelt.
Daz diu niht bezzer mohte sin.	You might not find one better.
Dariuber ein buckel geleit.	On top of it was a shield boss.
Vil silber schone zerbreit.	of silver and spread out very beautifully.
Diu ris ze breit noch ze smal	The straps were neither too wide or too narrow
Si bevienc daz bret uberal.	and covered the board all over.
Des bestuont diu mouwe.	This is how the *mouwe* was made.
Inerhalp ein frouwe	On the inside [was the image of] a Lady
an dem vordern orte.	at the dexter point.

This image of a lady on the inner side of this shield equals the icon of the Holy Virgin Mary 'inpictus' on the inside of King Arthur's shield Pridwen, as described by Geoffrey of Monmouth (*c.* 1135), and later in the shield of Gawayne at his quest for the Green Chapel (*c.* 1350). Here, though, on Erec's shield, it would be a portrait of Enide herself.

Presumably, the three shields and matching couvertures of different colours were ordered so that Erec could stage his quasi-incognito appearances on three different days – on the first day as the Knight of the Golden Sleeve, on the second Day as the Knight of the Silver Sleeve, and finally as the Knight with the Sleeve of Sable Pelt. Erec bore his device on the three shields without paying any attention to the later basic rule of heraldry against placing metal on metal, such as the gold on silver in the first shield, but also the silver '*buckelris*' on the golden shield.

The description of the three shields and their three matching couvertures has baffled generations of scholars and has evoked much controversy. The word 'mouwe' is variously interpreted as 'sleeve', 'wrap' or 'cover'. They were thought as protections for the precious gold and silver charges in inclement weather. Such a cover, though, would defeat the very purpose of a heraldic device, instant recognition at a distance, at least a bowshot away.

One of the main problems is that *mouwe* is neither a German nor a French word; rather, it is found in Middle Dutch and indeed means, 'sleeve'.

In the early fourteenth century Flemish chivalric romance, *Die Riddere metter Mouwen* (The Knight with the Sleeve) an unnamed and unproven youth comes to King Arthur's court, while King Arthur and all the knights of the Round Table are abroad on the Hunt of the Stag with the White Foot. Queen Guinevere, accompanied by a damsel, Clarette, observes from a window of her chamber how a caitiff knight mistreats a damsel right in front of the castle. In her rage, Guinevere asks the newly arrived youth, as the only man at hand, to stop and punish the miscreant knight. She gives him black armour and a sword, and Clarette hands him, blushing, one sleeve of her white dress, as *Minnepfand,* token of her love at first sight, and ties it to his lance. The freshly made Knight of the Sleeve promptly defeats the miscreant knight and sallies forth on the usual quest to right wrongs, help damsels in distress, fight robber knights and other evildoers, as well as a dragon or two.

While the *Riddere metter Mouwen* postdates Hartman's romance by many years, the adoption of a lady's sleeve as a shield device is strikingly similar. It would seem that the erudite and polyglot Ritter Hartmann quite deliberately chose a fashionable Flemish term for a – for Germany – bizarre and apparently newly introduced device. The French equivalent for the English heraldic term *maunch* is '*manche mal taillée*', i.e. 'badly tailored sleeve'. An antiquarian who did not understand the complicated cut of a lady's elegant hanging sleeve probably created this rather disdainful term. Such sleeves were separately attached at the shoulder of a lady's dress and could be torn off in a fine show of spontaneity and handed to her champion as a *Minnepfand*. Aside from its symbolic value, such a daring gesture would display the lady's arm deliciously bare for all to see and leave her rivals to eat their hearts out. If the enigmatic *mouwe* is indeed a lady's elegant sleeve, it could be a hint at the first meeting of the newlyweds, when Enide, as daughter of an impoverished nobleman, had her elbows showing through holes in the sleeves of her threadbare dress.

However, there is another possible explanation: the *mouwe* might not have been a sleeve at all. *Mouwe* in this case could be a ghost word that led Ritter Hartmann astray, because of his learning: Hartmann probably had as his source a now lost manuscript that would have contained a description of the preparation for the tournament. (Chrétien, in the published texts, gives the preparation for the tournament rather short shrift, and thus Hartmann had to invent it out of the whole cloth.)

There is a French heraldic term *coupé émanché* for a zigzag dividing line of partition; its English equivalent is *per fess dancetty*. Relying on his French source, Hartmann might well have mistaken the component *manch* in *émanché* as an alternate French word for 'sleeve', and in order to make sense out of the description, he had to elaborate on it, such as nailing the 'mouwe' on the shield board. By using dancetty lines of partition on parti-coloured shields, even the otherwise awkward *buckelris* could be accommodated without much trouble. The following illustrations demonstrate the very different appearance of Erec's tournament equipment according to the different interpretations of *mouwe*.

In spite of the fame and popularity of the Erec romance, the name of the hero varies not only from country to country but even from scribe to scribe. It can be found as Erik (in the Norse saga), as Heret filz du Roy Lac in later French tradition, in Italy as Arrecco della Tavola Ronda, as Arrake filz Lake in *The Awentyrs of Arture*, and barely recognizable as Malory's Harry Fyse Lake in *Le Morte d'Arthur*.

The same thing happened to Erec's arms. The mysterious *mouwe* of Ritter Hartmann is not mentioned again, and totally different charges appear instead. In the voluminous *Romance de Durmart le Galois* (*c.* 1230-40) Erec's shield and banner display: *lozengy of Or and gules*, but in the 'authentic' *Armorial des Chevaliers de la Table Ronde* compiled for Jacques d'Armagnac, duc de Nemours (*c.* 1450), the full achievement of arms of 'Heret filz du Roy Lac' are: *Or, three dragon heads vert* (sometimes gules or even sable), his crest is a dragon's head vert, and the supporters are two dragons vert. His battle cry is SORTES SORTES! (Sally Forth!)

Previously unpublished. The author's last Arthurian article, completed in 2019. Illustrations, based on the author's sketches, by Stephen Bluto.

5

The Arms of Sir Yvain, The Knight with the Lion, and those of his Kin

The two earliest surviving Arthurian romances are *Erec et Enide* (*c.* 1170) and *Yvain, le Chevalier au Lion* (*c.* 1175-80) by Chrétien de Troyes. Both were translated into German – as *Erek* and *Iwein* – by Hartmann von Aue, between 1180 and 1200. They were also incorporated into the Welsh *Mabinogion*, with the names of the heroes changed into Gereint ab Erbin and Owein. Malory knows them as Sir Harry le Fitz Lake and Sir Uwayne.

Chrétien's intention was to use the stories of these two champions to demonstrate how a knight by trial and error could find the right measure for the two qualities that make up the perfect knight: courtly love and adventurous spirit. Erec is shown to succumb to love for his Enide to such a degree that he completely neglects his chivalrous duty to seek out adventure and to right wrongs; he later overdoes it in the opposite sense when he drags long-suffering Enide along on his quests, until he finally manages to achieve the right balance. Yvain, on the other hand, starts out as a reckless adventurer who finds love but forgets it, and who has to be brought back to his lady and to fulfilment of true chivalry through gruelling tests.

In one of his adventures, Yvain rescues a lion from a fire-breathing dragon; the grateful animal becomes his loyal companion, and for the rest of the story Yvain is known as the Knight with the Lion. His most famous adventure, however, is that of the magic fountain in the forest of Brocéliande. Pouring water from the fountain onto a stone slab nearby produces a terrible thunderstorm; this misdeed is to be avenged by the guardian of the fountain, who is also the lord of the surrounding country. Yvain provokes the storm, the guardian challenges him, and in the ensuing fight Yvain chases his opponent back to his castle, only to have his own horse cut in half by the descending portcullis of the castle gates.

After the guardian has died of his wounds, Yvain becomes the guardian in his stead and succeeds also as the husband of the Lady of the Fountain, who is the true owner of the miraculous well. Eventually, Yvain has to fight Gawain, who also comes to undertake the adventure of the magic fountain. This fight is a draw, and Gawain persuades Yvain to accompany him on further quests. Yvain promises to return within three months to his Lady of the Fountain, but forgets to come back in time, which leads to numerous complications before the happy ending.

Though Chrétien de Troyes gave Yvain his surname, 'le Chevalier au Lion', he does not mention any heraldic charges for him at all. Later authors and illustrators quite naturally attributed to Yvain a lion as his shield emblem, sometimes even anachronistically in events that took place before the fateful meeting with the grateful lion. Once in a while, an author seems to have wondered whether Yvain should not have had a shield device other than a lion in the early part of his career. The author of the French verse romance *Hunbaut* (c. 1250-1275), for instance, attributes to 'li fius de roi Urien' (the son of King Urien) a red shield with pheasants! This puzzling and highly unusual charge, though, might be a scribe's error, when he read *feasanz*, 'pheasants' for *feassauz*, 'small fesses', or narrow horizontal stripes.

The tale of the Lady of the Fountain in the *Mabinogion* insists that the lion rescued by Owein was pure white, but there is only one example in medieval art where Yvain is portrayed with a white lion on his shield. This is in a mural at Castle Rodeneck, Tyrol (*c.* 1200-1210), representing the fight at the fountain. The guardian is wearing a red surcoat, and Yvain is shown with a blue shield. The thirteenth-century French verse romances *Durmart* and *Escanor* describe Yvain's shield as golden with a red lion thereon, while in a wall hanging embroidered with stories of famous lovers made in the early fourteenth century for a wealthy burgher of Freiburg/Breisgau, Yvain is pictured in the adventure of the fountain with a black lion on a white shield, and with a black lion's head as his helmet crest.

In the only surviving illustrated manuscript of Chrétien's poem (*c.* 1325) one miniature shows Yvain's surcoat and horse trappings as blue, embroidered with a golden lion. This colour scheme of gold on blue subsequently becomes the standard version of Yvain's arms. His crest is a golden lion's head, his shield supporters are two golden lions, and his battle cry is: C'EST POUR MORGUEN (This is for Morgan) in honour of his mother, Morgan le Fay. In addition to being called the Knight with the Lion, Yvain was also known as 'Yvain aux blanches mains' (of the white hands). However, this surname was not exploited heraldically, neither was the mysterious reference to Owein's ravens in 'The Dream of Rhonabwy' in the *Mabinogion.*

Yvain's father, King Urien of Gorre, is also given a blue shield with a golden lion in the fifteenth-century armorial rolls, clearly a transfer from the arms of his famous son. King Urien's helmet crest is also a golden lion's head, but his shield supporters are two white swans and his device is: A TOUT. King Urien had a second, illegitimate son with the wife of the seneschal of Carmelide. This son was also named Yvain, but he was called Yvain le Avoultre (the Other One) This surname seems to have puzzled translators and adaptors of the story, who thus made him variously into Yvain the Adventurer or even Yvain the Adulterer; Hartmann von Aue apparently took it for a place name and calls him Iwan von Lafultere.

As an illegitimate son of the King of Gorre, Yvain le Avoultre bears in the fifteenth-century armorial rolls a shield in the family colours of blue and gold, but not with the prestigious lion. In its stead he bears: *Azure, a pale Or.* Interestingly, in the *Second Continuation of Perceval* there appears a knight Yvain, whose golden shield is *paleté* or *paillé,* strewn with red lioncels. *Paillé* was a curious charge, imitating the pattern of a brocade fabric with figure-filled medallions, in this case with small lions. Originally it was probably meant to be a shield cover of real fabric instead of simply painted designs.

In the lists of knights of the Round Table given by Chrétien de Troyes (in *Erec*) and in the fifteenth-century armorial rolls, there are mentioned also an Yvain d'Ussenel, an Yvain de Loenel (Losenel), and an Yvain de Cameliot. It is possible that all three of them originally were other names for Yvain le Avoultre, who hailed from Carmelide (Cameliot). D'Ussenel and de Loenel could be garbled forms of the same name. In any case, only Yvain d'Ussenel is known by arms assigned to him. They are sometimes: *Or, two bars gules,* sometimes: *Or, paillé with lioncels gules,* and also: *Or, two bars paillé with eaglets sable and lions gules,* which brings us right back to the early forms of Yvain's arms in *Hunbaut* – small fesses or bars – and those of Yvain le Auoultre in the *Second Continuation,* with his shield *paillé.* Yvain d'Ussenel's crest is a red lion's head, and his device is in Breton: TEYNEICT (Shut up!).

In 1330 the burghers of Tournay in Flanders, now Belgium, decided to arrange a travelling show of tournaments. Part of the pageantry was that the jousters assumed the names and armorial bearings of champions of the Round Table, such as King Ban de Benoic, King Boors, King Baudemagus, King Pelleas de Chastel Périlleux, le Roy des Cent Chevalliers (the King of the Hundred Knights; you will notice that the challengers simply *had* to be kings at least), and also 'le Roy Lyonneaux,' whose arms were: *Argent, semi with lioncels gules.* This looks very much like another version of the Yvain arms strewn with lions and was probably meant to be the disguise of King Urien of Gorre. The reason that Urien was not called by his real name might have been that in Flemish/French bilingual Tournay it sounded objectionable; 'Urian' is one of the names for the Devil in Germanic tongues.

The adventure of the magic fountain in the forest of Brocéliande was first brought to the attention of King Arthur's court by one of Yvain's cousins, Sir Calogrenant de Vindesores. Calogrenant's arms are: *Gules, a viper Or,* with the self-same viper as his crest. The guardian of the fountain, who first defeats Calogrenant and then is slain by Yvain, is called Esclados the Red by Chrétien and King Ascalon by Hartmann; in the *Mabinogion* he is a nameless Black knight. There are only four medieval representations of the fight at the fountain surviving; one of them is French and the other three, interestingly enough, are of German origin. The French example is in the illuminated manuscript of *c.* 1325 already mentioned; Esclados the Red is pictured bearing a red shield, true to his name. The German examples are two series of murals: one at Castle Rodeneck, Tyrol, the other at the manor house Hessenhof at Schmalkalden, Thuringia (*c.* 1250), and the third example is the embroidered wall hanging at Freiburg (*c.* 1325), also mentioned above. In the fight scene on the wall hanging, King Ascalon wears a crowned helmet and also has a golden crown on his red shield. In the Rodeneck murals, 'Aschelon's' shield is turned away from the viewer, but in the Schmalkalden series the guardian of the fountain bears a dark-coloured shield – probably once red – with a light-coloured eagle on it. In the following scenes, when it is Yvain's turn to act as the guardian, he carries the same eagle-shield!

Yvain's adventure of the hapless horse cut in two by the portcullis has been painted in the Schmalkalden murals and was carved on choir pews at Lincoln, Boston, and Oxford. It also served as the explanatory legend for the city arms of Pardubice in Czechoslovakia: *Gules, the forepart of a horse argent, bridled sable,* and was the prototype for one of the more believable stories, including a clever twist of the fountain motif, of the redoubtable Baron von Munchausen. In the Pardubice legend the city's liege lord, Jesek of Hostynec, had his horse cut in half by the portcullis of the city gate of Milan during the siege of 1158, a date twenty years earlier than Chrétien's *Yvain*. The fabulous Baron Munchausen, as is to be expected, does considerably better.

As an officer in Russian service during a campaign against the Turks in the 1740s, he was chasing a horde of enemy cavalry so far ahead of his own troopers that he pursued the fleeing Turks into a nearby walled town and out again through the opposite gate, barely noticing the dropping portcullis of the first gate that almost trapped him. The Turkish riders having disappeared into the hills, the Baron turned his black Lithuanian charger back towards the town, and he watered him at the fountain in the market square. The horse did not stop drinking, and Munchausen suddenly realized that its hindquarters were cut off and the water was simply running out of the break. When his dragoons finally turned up, they dragged along with them the rather unwilling rear part, which they had found outside in a pasture among a herd of mares. Fortunately, the farrier of the troop was a skilled veterinarian who spliced the two halves together, using for the suture flexible twigs from a laurel tree close by. Within a short time, these twigs took root and sprouted out from the horse's back, creating a lofty bower. Thus the worthy Baron and his famous Lithuanian were able to finish the campaign in style, resting in the shadow of their own laurels!

Select Bibliography

Bouton, V. *Armorial des Toumois: Jouste faicte a Tournay l'an mil trois cent trente*. Paris, 1870.

Brault, G. J. *Early Blazon: Heraldic Terminology in the Twelfth and Thirteenth Centuries with special Reference to Arthurian Literature*. Oxford, 1982.

de Blangy, A. *La forme des tourneys au temps du roy Uter et du roy Artus, suivie de Armorial des chevalliers de la Table Ronde*. Caen, 1897.

Loomis, R. S., and L. H. Loomis. *Arthurian Legends in Medieval Art*. New York, 1937.

Pastoureau, M. *Armorial des chevalliers de la Table Ronde*. Paris, 1983.

Sandoz, E. 'Tourneys in the Arthurian Tradition', *Speculum* 9 (1944), pp. 389-420.

Scott-Giles, C.W. 'Some Arthurian Coats of Arms', *The Coat of Arms* 8 (1965), pp. 332-339, and 9 (1966), pp. 30-35.

Originally published in *Avalon to Camelot* 1. no. 4 pp. 12-15.

6

The Arms of Sir Perceval and his Kin

One of the characteristics of a medieval knight was his use of heraldic devices to identify him when the visor of his helmet hid his face. These devices were the blazon on his shield, the crest on his helmet, and the designs displayed on his horse trappings and on his surcoat, worn over his mail armour; from the latter use, the entire set became known as the 'coat-of-arms'.

In order to be tactically efficient, a shield's cognizance should be easily identifiable from a distance, at least a bowshot away. For this reason, the basic rule of heraldry is that a shield should have charges of strongly contrasting colours, light and dark. The light tinctures were called 'metals': 'gold' for yellow (called *or* in proper terminology, which is heavily influenced by French) and 'silver' for white (*argent*). The dark tinctures were 'colours': red *(gules* from Persian *gûl*, a rose, a term brought back from the Crusades); blue *(azure,* from Arabic *azx-aq,* 'sky'); black *(sable,* after the fur of the Siberian mink); green *(vert);* and purple. Vert and purple are relatively rare in actual heraldry but became popular in fictitious arms. It was only natural for an author of chivalric romances or an illuminator of manuscripts to assume that every fighting man, even back to Biblical times, must have had such armorial devices, just like the knights he could see every day. The arms of Arthurian heroes are mentioned occasionally in the epics and romances themselves and were depicted in the miniatures illustrating many of these manuscripts.

From the fourteenth century on, there were attempts to regulate and collect these arms in armorial rolls and lists, to make sure that poets and painters could assign 'authentic' arms to their heroes. There must be more than a hundred copies of these manuscript rolls in existence. As mentioned in the notes to Chapter 1, the three most important ones in the United States are in the Harvard University Library, Cambridge, (Ms. 1 typ 1312), in the J. Pierpont Morgan Library, New York City (Ms. 16), and in the Walters Art Museum, Baltimore (Ms 463). The Harvard manuscript, considered the earliest of these (*c.* 1450), lists just the shields of the knight with names attached. The Pierpont Morgan Library copy (*c.* 1500) is the artistically most accomplished; it also gives a brief description of the knight's valour, accomplishments, and character – even the colour of his hair and eyes. The Walters Art Museum copy (*c.* 1510) is the most elaborate; in its miniatures the shields are accompanied by helmet crests, mantlings, supporter figures, and bandscrolls inscribed with the mottoes and battle cries of the knights.

(Fig. 1) Sir Perceval's arms. A purple shield scattered with his crest, a golden cross. Supported by two white griffins and his motto: CHRIST'S CROSS.

In the earliest complete epic that tells the Grail story, Wolfram von Eschenbach's *Parzival* (*c.* 1200), Parzival is known as the Red Knight because he wears arms that are all red, without distinctive charge on his shield. These red arms he had captured from the previous Red Knight, Ither von Gaheviess, who was challenged and slain by the newcomer Parzival after insulting King Arthur and the Round Table.

Although raised in Wales, Wolfram's Parzival is the son of Gahmuret, Prince of Anschouwe (Anjou), who has spent most of his life roaming the world as a knight-errant. At one time Gahmuret was even in the service of the Baruch of Baghdad (an exotic ruler styled after the Khalif Haroun-al-Rashid, but not recorded in history) and, as his champion, had borne the Baruch's arms – *Vert, an anchor ermine* (Fig. 2) – instead of his own Angevin arms, which he took up again when messengers arrived with the news that his father had died and that he was now the head of the principality. Wolfram skilfully turns this into a heraldic play upon words when he has Gahmuret exclaim: 'My anchor has now found land!' With this he drops the Baruch's anchor emblem and has 'the pantel, that his father wore' nailed on his shield instead. This 'pantel' is usually interpreted as a panther, but the panther as a heraldic emblem is nowhere else connected with Anjou. Wolfram, a knight himself, shows considerable knowledge of outlandish heraldry; it is not likely that he would have treated such an important motif lightly. Possibly 'pantel' is meant to be a 'little ribbon', from medieval German *band, pant,* and indeed, the arms of 'Anjou Ancient' were *a label gules,* i.e., a red ribbon, across a field *fleurdelysé* (Fig.3).

Parzival never uses the Angevin arms himself. When he becomes the Grail King, he will adopt the badge of the Grail Knights: the turtledove of the Holy Ghost (Fig. 4). Parzival's son, Lohengrin the Swan-Knight, bears a swan, of course (Fig. 5).

During his wanderings as a knight-errant, Gahmuret had fathered another son, Feirefiz, with a princess of 'India'. When Feirefiz in his turn sets out on knight-errantry, he bears as his emblem on shield and helmet 'Ecidemôn das reine tier.' So far this 'pure animal' has escaped classification by zoologists; presumably it was meant to be the 'Indian' equivalent of an ermine, the symbol of purity in medieval Europe.

In the French and English tradition, best known from Malory, Sir Perceval is the son of King Pellinore of Listenoise, who bore a shield: *Or, semé with crosslets azure,* and had a black eagle as his crest, and two black eagles as supporters to his shield; his motto was PAR LA CROIX,

For the Cross. His oldest son, Perceval, changed the colours of the family arms, according to Continental custom, and bore as a difference: *Purple, semé with crosslets Or,* and had as his crest a golden cross; his supporters were two white griffins, and his motto: CRUX CHRISTI, Christ's Cross (Fig. l). Perceval's younger brothers, Sir Aglovale and Sir Lamorak, bore almost identical arms. Sir Aglovale's shield was: *Purple, semé with crosslets Or, a leopard argent overall,* and Sir Lamorak's was: *Purple, semé with crosslets Or, a leopard Or overall.* Correspondingly, Sir Aglovale's crest was a silver leopard's head, and Sir Lamorak's a golden one. Their supporters were two leopards each, silver for Sir Aglovale, and golden for Sir Lamorak. Sir Aglovale's motto was DE GALLES DE GALLES, Of Wales of Wales, and Sir Lamorak's SOIES SEUR, Be Sure. The leopards in the younger brother's arms were taken from the arms of their uncle, Pellinore's brother Sir Lamorak de Listenoise: *Purple, a leopard argent.* His crest was a purple leopard's head, his supporters, two purple leopards, and his motto TOST OV TARD, Early or Late. Finally, there was Sir Tor, the natural son of King Pellinore, who differences his father's arms: Or, *semé with crosslets sable* (these little black crosses were probably styled after the black eagles in King Pellinore's crest and supporters), and had as his crest the long-necked head of a crane, with two cranes – symbols of vigilance – as supporters. His motto was FORT COMME UNG TOR, Strong as a Tower, an obvious pun on his name (Tor = tour = tower).

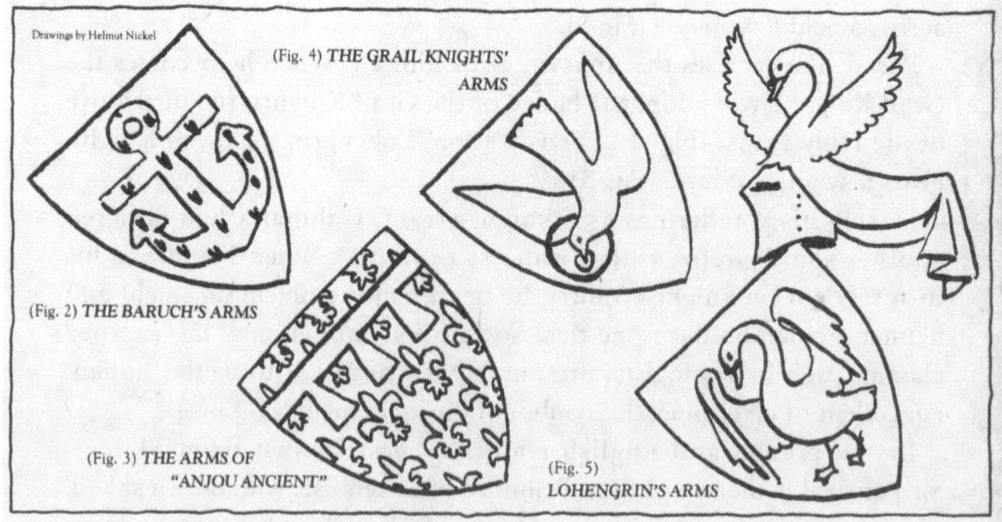

Figs 2-5: The Arms of the Grail Knights.

Select Bibliography

A. de Blangy. L*a forme des toumois au temps du roy Uter* et *du roy Artus, suivie de l'Armorial des chevaliers de la Table Ronde*. Caen, 1897.

E. Sandoz. 'Tourneys in the Arthurian Tradition.' *Speculum* 19 (1944), pp. 389-420.

C. W. Scott-Giles. 'Some Arthurian Coats of Arms.' *The Coat of Arms* VIII (1965) pp. 332-339 and IX (1966) pp.30-35.

M. Pastoureau. *Armorial des chevaliers de la Table Ronde*. Paris, 1983.

Originally published in *Avalon to Camelot*, I. no. 3 (Spring 1984) pp. 11-12.

7

The Arms of Sir Kay and Sir Bedivere

King Arthur's oldest companions were Kay and Bedivere. Kay was Arthur's foster brother and became his seneschal, an office that today would translate as Chief of Administration and Operations. Originally, Kay was a great warrior; in the Welsh archaic epic *Culhwch and Olwen* even supernatural feats are attributed to him, such as being able to hold his breath underwater for nine days and nights, and to go nine nights without sleep. If he wished, he could be as tall as the tallest tree in the forest, and his body heat was so great that whatever he held in his hand stayed dry even in the heaviest rain, and in the bitterest cold he could kindle a fire for his comrades. However, in the same epic it is also said that Kay's heart will always be cold, that nobody could see any burden he was carrying, whether great or small, though there would be never another official or servant as loyal or efficient as him.

This spell of non-appreciation of his efforts is probably at the bottom of the increasing denigration of Kay's character, which goes from bad to worse in practically all romances following after Chrétien de Troyes' *Erec* (*c.* 1170), where all that is left of his former heroic stature is his surname Kay the Tall.

Kay was the son of Sir Ector (Antor), the foster father to whom Arthur was entrusted by Merlin. Sir Ector's arms, though he was a knight, are not known; Kay's arms were originally, as mentioned in *Durmart le Galois* (*c.* 1230-50): *Sable, a chief argent*. Later, in the rolls of arms of the Knights of the Round Table composed in France in the fifteenth century, these arms are changed into: *Azure, two keys argent*, and even to: *Azure, two wings argent*. The original arms were probably meant to be 'canting', i.e. a graphic representation of Kay's position as 'chief' of Arthur's household. The arms with the keys – though they too could be seen as an indication of Kay's office as seneschal, who held the keys to store rooms and treasury – were most likely the result of a misunderstanding, when in a French roll of arms without illustrations the word *chef*, 'chief' was read as *clef*, 'key'. This in turn could be misread as ailes, 'wings' in some scribe's crabbed handwriting. In the same rolls Kay's crest is a silver key (or a pair of white wings), but his shield supporters are, strangely enough, two green greyhounds, and his devise is: HORS DE BUISSONS (Out of the Bushes), which might hint at a sneaky attack from ambush.

In Chrétien's *Erec*, the son of Kay the Seneschal is mentioned, 'Gronosis, versed in evil', but no attributed arms are known for him. Also listed in *Erec* as the fifth and sixth among the ten foremost knights of Arthur's court are 'the Handsome Coward' (*Le Beau Couard*) and 'the Ugly Brave' *(Le Lait Hardi*). The latter was the nephew of Kay the Seneschal but was also a cousin of Erec's. Le Beau Couard and Le Lait Hardi are possibly the same characters that appear in *Culhwch and Olwen* as Sandde Angel-face and Morfran, son of Tegid. They were two of the three survivors of the battle of Camlann (the third was Cynwyl the Saint, who rode Hengroen, the fastest horse in Arthur's host). Sandde was so beautiful that everyone thought him to be an angel, and therefore would not raise a weapon against him, while Morfran was so ugly, 'with hair on him like the hair of a stag', that everyone thought him a devil, and would not put a spear into him either.

Le Lait Hardi, as mentioned in *Durmart*, bears: *Sable, a chief argent with a lion passant gules in the dexter point.* These charges are clearly derived from those of his uncle Kay. In the fifteenth century rolls of arms, however, he bears: *lozengy of argent and sable*, which pattern corresponds to the arms of his cousin Erec: *lozengy of Or and gules*, but retains the black-and-white colour scheme as an indication of his relationship to Kay. Le Lait Hardi's crest is a golden rake, his shield supporters are two wildwomen 'au naturel' (doubtlessly a hint at his hairiness), and his devise is: MAUGRE FORTUNE! (In Defiance of Fate!).

It is rather surprising that someone with a nickname like 'Handsome Coward' should be listed as the fifth of the ten best knights of the Round Table, but it is easily explainable as a misunderstanding of his true surname, *Le Beau Courant* (the Handsome Runner), which is also reflected in his arms: *Sable, a horse argent, with horseshoes Or*. Evidently his original fleetness of foot was turned into cowardice through his contrasting association with the Ugly Brave.

Sir Bedivere (Bedwyr, Bedguerus, Bedoier) is always closely linked to Kay in the early sources. The very first time he is mentioned, in the *Life of St. Cadoc*, the legend of a Welsh saint by Lifric of Llancarfan (*c.* 1075), Bedivere is sitting with Arthur and Kay on a hillside playing at dice, when they get interrupted by an eloping pair of lovers, whom they then protect against their pursuers. In *Culhwch and Olwen* Bedivere is praised for his fighting skill of delivering nine counter thrusts for each single thrust received, though he would be one-handed, and for never shrinking from any enterprise for which Kay was bound.

In Geoffrey of Monmouth's *Historia Regum Britanniae* (*c.* 1135) it is Kay and Bedivere whom Arthur selects to accompany him in the adventure of the dreadful Giant of Mont St. Michel. Later, Bedivere is killed in the battle against the Romans, and Kay dies avenging his friend's death. In contrast to this, later sources, best known from Malory's *Morte d'Arthur*, show him as the last surviving knight after the battle of Camlann, who is entrusted with throwing Excalibur into the mere.

Sir Bedivere is the butler (*pincerna*) of Arthur's court in the *Historia*, but later sources consistently make him Arthur's *connétable*, 'Master of the Stables', i.e. Commander of Cavalry. His court office of butler is then transferred to his brother, Lucan the Butler, a figure probably created for the purpose. Though Bedivere the Bold is one of Arthur's oldest companions, who can always be counted on to be there, where and whenever needed, he plays a very minor role in most romances, and did not become a main hero of a story before George Finkel's *Twilight Province* (1967) and Catherine Christian's *The Pendragon* (1979). Rosemary Sutcliff in *Sword at Sunset* (1963) makes Bedwyr the lover of Guinevere instead of Lancelot; this is followed by Mary Stewart in *The Last Enchantment* (1979) and by Gillian Bradshaw in her *In Winter's Shadow* (1982).

Bedivere's arms are: *Or, a gonfanon gules, fringed vert.* This old-style battle-banner (OHG. *gund*, 'battle', *fanun*, 'banner') is an allusion to his office as the cavalry commander. His crest is a white glove (perhaps a hint at the arm clad in white samite that retrieved Excalibur); his shield supporters are two white doves, and his devise is: PREIST A VOLER (Ever ready to fly), which refers both to the doves and to the gonfanon of his arms. Some illustrators of armorial rolls misread their sources and gave Sir Bedivere a griffin, instead of a gonfanon.

Sir Bedivere's brother, Lucan the Butler, bears: *Or, a lynx gules party with sable.* His crest is a red lynx's head, and two red lynxes are his shield supporters; his devise is: JE PARVIENDROI (I shall succeed). In an earlier romance, *Escanor*, by Girart d'Amiens (*c.* 1275), Lucan is given different arms, allusive to his office as butler: *Gules, five wine tuns argent.*

One of their cousins is Sir Girflet, fils de Dô, who in some French tales of the death of King Arthur is the last surviving knight, tasked with throwing Excalibur into the lake. Sir Girflet bears: *Or, semé with thistles sable*; his crest is a red flaming fire, two wildcats are his supporters, and his devise is: PRES OU LOING (Sooner or later). The thistles (*chardon*, 'card') are canting for Carduel, the dukedom of Girflet's father, while the wildcats might indicate a connection with the lynxes of his cousin Lucan.

Select Bibliography

A. de Blangy, *La forme des tournois au temps du roy Uter et du roy Artus, suivie de l'Armorial des chevaliers de la Table Ronde*, Caen, 1897

E. Sandoz. 'Tourneys in the Arthurian Tradition,' *Speculum* 19 (1944); pp. 389-420, ill.

C. W. Scott-Giles. 'Some Arthurian Coats of Arms', *The Coat of Arms* VIII (1965); pp. 332-339 and IX (1966); pp. 30-35, ill.

G. J. Brault. *Early Blazon: Heraldic Terminology in the Twelfth and Thirteenth Centuries with special Reference to Arthurian Literature.* Oxford, 1972

M. Pastoureau, *Armorial des chevaliers de la Table Ronde*, Paris, Le Leopard d'or, 1983

Originally published in *Avalon to Camelot* 2. no. 2 pp. 21-22.

8

The Arms of Sir Tristram, his Kin and Friends

Though originally Tristram or Tristan was the hero of an epic cycle independent from the Arthurian legends, he became associated with Arthur's court at an early date. Chrétien de Troyes in his *Erec* (1170) lists already 'Tristan, who never laughed' in the roll call of Arthur's knights, and Malory names him as one of the two best knights of the Round Table, with only Lancelot possibly being his better.

The basic story of the tragic love-triangle between King Mark of Cornwall, Yseult la Blonde and Tristram is fairly consistent in all its versions and retellings. On the other hand, Tristram's family data, such as his parents' names, his homeland, and also his armorial bearings as 'one of the best knights of the world' vary greatly from case to case; the only consistent feature is that he always is the nephew of King Mark, his sister's son.

In the Welsh triad of the Three Powerful Swineherds of Britain, Tristram appears as 'Drystan son of Tallwch', who sends the swineherd of his uncle, 'King March son of Meirchyawn', with a message to March's queen, 'Essylt'. While the swineherd is away on his errand, Drystan takes his place, and protects his charges so well that even King Arthur himself, assisted by Kay and Bedivere, fails to 'obtain' a single piglet. The name Drystan is taken from a historical person, Drust son of Talorc, a king of the Picts, who reigned in the North of Scotland, *c.* 780 AD.

It is interesting to see that 'a boar black as sable' is Tristan's shield device in Gottfried von Strassburg's *Tristan und Isolt*. The boar was probably on a white field, because white is the colour of Tristan's surcoat and horse trappings, as described by Gottfried. Here Tristan is the son of Riwalin, an exiled prince from Parmenie (Brittany), who took service as a knight with King 'Marke von Kurnewal', and was betrothed to Marke's sister, Blanscheflur, but was killed before the proper wedding. This flaw in Tristan's birth, as well as his illicit love affair with Isolt, will have been represented in the boar as a symbol of both unchastity and sexual potency. On the other hand, in the ambivalence of medieval animal symbolism the boar also signified force and courage.

Significantly, Tristan's friend at Marke's court, the seneschal Marjodo, has a dream of a wild boar that comes running from the forest right into the king's palace and straight into the king's bedchamber, where it demolishes the bed and soils the sheets with the foam from its snout. On awakening from this dream, Marjodo finds his roommate Tristan missing; he gets up to look for him and finds footprints in freshly fallen snow. Following them to a little building in the compound, he finds Tristan and Isolt in bed together. One version of the 13th century *Prose-Tristan* tells of a similar dream forecasting the death of Tristan: immediately before her landing in Brittany, where she was summoned to heal the fatally wounded Tristan, Yseult dreams that she holds the head of a huge boar in her lap, which bespatters her clothes with its blood. This dream convinces her that she will be too late; clearly, she identified the boar as an alter ego of Tristan's.

In most other French and English sources, however, Tristan/Tristram bears a lion as his shield device. This is an obvious canting for Lyonesse, his fictitious home country west of Cornwall, which has since sunk below the sea. In the Anglo-Norman Tristan poem by Thomas D'Angleterre (*c.* 1155-85) Tristan is described as having red horse trappings embroidered with a golden lion. In the armorial roll of Jacques d'Armagnac (*c.* 1450) and in numberless illustrations in romance manuscripts he bears a green shield with a golden lion. The colour green is probably derived from the tradition that he was the son of Meliadus/Meliodas, King of Lyonesse, who was known as the Knight of the Green Shield, because he used to bear a plain green shield without any other devices. Tristram's cousin, Alisandre l'Orphelin, bears a green shield with a silver lion.

Malory has Sir Tristram wearing green as 'his colour' on the road to Lonezep and on the first day of the tournament; on the second day he changes to red, and on the third to black, in order to hide his true identity. At the Tournament at the Castle of Maidens he bears a black shield, and at the Tournament at the Castle Roche Doure Morgan le Fay makes him bear a golden shield showing

> ...a kynge and a quene therein paynted, and a knyght standynge aboven them with hys one foote standynge uppon the kynges hede and the othir uppon the quenys hede. Hit signifieth Kynge Arthure and quene Guenyver, and a knyght that holdith them bothe in bondage and servage.

Meaning, of course, Lancelot.

On other occasions Malory has Sir Tristram bearing the 'arms of Cornwall'. This is heraldically quite proper, because Sir Tristram was not only a liegeman of King Mark's but also a close kinsman as the son of Mark's sister, Elizabeth. However, there is a slight problem in considering what the 'arms of the Kingdom of Cornwall' might be. In Malory's time there was a Duchy of Cornwall (no Kingdom), and its arms were (and still are): *Sable, fifteen bezants Or, arranged 5, 4, 3, 2, 1*. On the other hand, there were also the arms of Richard of Cornwall, who was elected King of the Romans in 1256: *Argent, a lion gules, crowned Or, armed azure, in a bordure sable, bezanté Or*. Most likely Malory had these more 'royal' arms in mind for King Mark and the royal house of Cornwall, as more appropriate than mere ducal arms. King Mark's son, Merangis, 'who was quite different from his father, except for body size', is credited with arms: *Argent, a bordure gules*.

As a newly made knight, Sir Tristan's first deed of arms was his famous duel with Sir Marhalt, the champion of Ireland, who was an uncle of Yseult's, and also a knight of the Round Table. After having defeated and killed Sir Marhalt, Tristan takes the shield and sword of his slain foe and boasts that he will carry these 'in all placis where I ryde on myne adventures, and in the syght of kyng Arthure and all the Round Table'. This shield of Sir Marhalt's was, according to the d'Armagnac armorial roll: *barry of argent and azure, a lion gules over all*, though early fourteenth century representations, both French and German, show a blackamoor's head as a canting device for Morhault/Morold, alternative spellings for Marhalt.

Sir Tristan's loyal friend, Sir Dinadan, the 'merry japer', serves as a comic relief to melancholy Tristram, 'who never laughed'. Sir Dinadan's arms were: *Argent, a lion sable*. His brother, Sir Breunor le Noir, surnamed 'La Cotte Mai Tayle', bore: *Argent, a lion checquy sable and gules*.

Both were the sons of Brunor le Noir, King of Estrangorre, known as 'le bon chevallier sanz paour' and also as the Knight of the Silver Shield, because he belonged to the earlier generation of famous heroes, like Meliadus of Lyonesse, who bore shields of only one colour.

The other great friend of Sir Tristan's is Sir Palomydes the Saracen, who changed from a fierce competitor for the favours of La Beale Isoude to a faithful companion in arms in many an adventure. He bore: *checquy of argent and sable*, sometimes augmented by two scimitars gules, to indicate his Near Eastern origin (he was the son of the King of Babylon). Interestingly, *checquy of argent and sable, two scimitars gules over all* are the actual arms of the distinguished Burgundian family Pot, who adopted this device after a member had played Palomydes' role in a Round Table tournament.

Select Bibliography

A. de Blangy. *La forme des tournois au temps du roy Uter et du roy Artus, suivie de 1'Armorial des chevaliers de la Table Ronde*, Caen, 1897

E. Sandoz. 'Tourneys in the Arthurian Tradition', *Speculum* 19 (1944); pp. 389-420

C. W. Scott-Giles. 'The Heraldry of Romance', *The Coat of Arms* II, 15 (1953); pp. 257-260

C. W. Scott-Giles. 'Some Arthurian Coats of Arms', *The Coat of Arms* VIII, 64 (1965); pp. 332-339 and IX, 65 (1966); pp. 30-35

M. Zips. 'Tristan und die Ebersymbolik', *Genealogica et Heraldica (Proceedings of the 10th International Congress of Genealogical and Heraldic Sciences)*, Vienna, 1970; pp.445-450

M. Pastoureau. *Armorial des chevaliers de la Table Ronde*, Paris, 1983

Previously unpublished.

9

The Arms of Lancelot du Lac

Morgan holds unfaithful lovers prisoner in the Val without return. Lancelot must lift the spells and face the two dragons guarding the entrance of the valley, his arms *Argent, three bendlets gules*. Illumination of a 15th-century French *Lancelot-Grail* manuscript. (Reproduced under creative commons)

Lancelot, also called Sir Lancelot of the Lake, was the son of King Ban of Benoic or Benwick, a kingdom in France not to be found on any map. He got his cognomen 'of the Lake', because he was abducted as a child by the Lady of the Lake and raised in her magical underwater realm. Lancelot was also known as the Knight of the Cart, because once when he had ridden his horse to death in pursuit of the abductors of Queen Guinevere, he had climbed into a pillory cart to keep up the chase. Later, he crossed the Sword Bridge guarded by two enchanted lions, in order to get into the Land of No Return, where Guinevere was held captive.

Lancelot's arms are: *Argent, three bendlets gules*; his crest is a golden falcon, and the supporters are two wildmen. His devise is DU LAC MADAME. He is described as the best knight in the world, with the sole exception of his son Sir Galahad. He also has been called one of the best-looking men in the world, tall and well built in body and limbs. His full hair was in between of blond and brown, but with a clear reddish tint. His complexion was also not too red and not too pale; his mouth relatively small but well formed, with white teeth, small and very even. His nose was rather long and had a high ridge. His eyes were green and gentle, but when he was enraged they would become blood-shot and flash like a glowing ember, and then he also would snort like a maddened war-horse and gnash his teeth fiercely. But when he calmed down, he would not remember anything he did in his rage.

The three bendlets in Lancelot's shield indicate that he had the strength of three ordinary men. The falcon of his crest was a well-known symbol of courtly love, because the falcon returns to his master's fist not through coercion, but affection. This, together with his devise DU LAC MADAME, hinted at his role as champion and lover of Queen Guinevere. The wildmen are possibly suggestive of Lancelot's temporary bouts of insanity, when he, as Malory puts it, 'ever ran wylde woode from place to place'.

Lancelot was a relative late-comer to the Companionship of the Round Table. Not yet mentioned in Geoffrey of Monmouth's *Historia Regum Britanniae* (*c.* 1135), he appears first in Chrétien de Troyes' *Erec et Enide* (*c.* 1170), where he is ranked third, after Gawain and Erec, son of Lac, in the roll call of Arthur's knights. His role in Chrétien's *Cligès* (*c.* 1176) is not very distinguished either; there he is just another champion to be defeated for the greater glory of the hero of the tale, Cliges. However, in *Le Chevalier de la Charrette* (*c.* 1180) he is without question the best knight in the world. It is not likely that Chrétien himself was responsible for this change of status. It must have been at least in part the expressed wish of his patroness, the Countess Marie de Champagne, who gave him the story outline, apparently a now lost earlier poem.

Though Malory does not mention Lancelot's arms of the three red bends at all, he gives a detailed description of the shield Lancelot carried in his guise as *Le Chevalier Mai Fet*: 'All of sable, and a quene crowned in the myddis of sylver, and a knyght clene armed knelynge afore her'. As mentioned above, Malory also tells how at the Tournament at the Castle of Hard Rock, Morgan Le Fay made Tristram bear a shield on which a knight is portrayed, 'hys one foote standynge vpon the kynges hede and the other ypon the quenes'. This graphic representation of the fateful triangle was maliciously designed by Morgan because of her jealous feelings for Lancelot, and to make Arthur aware of the illicit love between his queen and his foremost knight.

Previously unpublished.

10

The Arming of Sir Gawain

Parzival's Gawain in a capital relief at the Church of Saint-Pierre, Caen.

Sir Gawain's arming, before setting out to meet the Green Knight at the Green Chapel, has been of interest to Arthurian scholars mostly for the interpretation of his enigmatic shield emblem. It is of greater interest to students of arms and armour for its straightforward and detailed 'professional' description of how a knight should be armed in the second half of the fourteenth century:

[A carpet is spread on the floor]
Fyrst a tule tapit, ty3t ou*er* þe flet,
& miche wat3 þe gyld gere þat glent þer alofte;

[and he steps thereon.]
Þe stif mon steppe3 þeron, & þe stel hondole3,
[He is dubbed in a doublet of Tarsic silk, and a well-made hood]
Dubbed i*n* a dublet of a dere tars,
& syþen a crafty capados, closed aloft,
Þat wyth a bry3t blau*n*ner was bou*n*den w*ith*-i*n*ne;
[They set steel slices on his feet, and lap his legs in steel greaves]
Þe*n*ne set þay þe sabatou*n*3 vpon þe segge fote3,
His lege3 lapped i*n* stel w*ith* luflych greue3,
W*ith* polayne3 piched þer-to, policed ful clene,
Aboute his kne3 knaged wyth knote3 of golde;
[Fair cuisses enclose his thighs]
Queme quyssewes þe*n*, þat coyntlych closed
His thik þrawen þy3e3 w*ith* þwonges to-tachched;
[and afterwards they put on the steel habergeon]
& syþen þe brawden bryne of bry3t stel ry*n*ge3,
Vmbe-weued þat wy3, vpon wlonk stuffe;
[well-burnished braces, elbow pieces, and gloves of plate]
& wel bornyst brace vpon his boþe armes,
W*ith* gode cowters & gay, & gloue3 of plate,
& alle þe godlych gere þat hy*m* gayn schulde
Þat tyde;
[Over all this is placed the coat armour]
Wyth ryche cote armure,
[His spurs are then fixed]
His gold spore3 spend w*ith* pryde,
[and his sword is attached to his side by a silken girdle.]
Gurde wyth a bront ful sure,
W*ith* silk sayn vmbe his syde.[1]

Here we are shown how at first a red blanket (*tuly tapit*) is spread out on the floor, on which the armour elements *(gere)* are laid out systematically for easy assembly and a final check by Gawain, who wears a tight-fitting padded jacket *(dublet)* of expensive *(dere)* fabric imported from Tharsia (*tars*), and a fur-lined hood *(capados),* both as shock-absorbers under his armour and as protection against the wintry cold.

A knight had to be armed standing up due to the overlapping construction of the armour elements. To avoid top-heaviness, arming began at the feet. His iron shoes *(sabatouns)* were the first armour put on; it is understood that this was done with the help of squires or pages. Next came the greaves *(greves),* which enclose the lower legs, then the knee-cops or poleyns *(polaynes),* and finally the thigh-defences or cuisses *(quyssewes)* to complete the leg-armour.[2]

After the arming of Gawain's legs was completed, his body armour, the mail shirt or byrnie *(bruny,* cognate with German *Brünne*) of interlinked steel rings, was put on over the rich fabric *(wlonk stuffe)* of his doublet. A mail shirt was wrought in rows of rings *(brayden)* similar to the knitted meshes of a sweater, and it was pulled on like a sweater over the head. It could consist of up to a quarter of a million rings; the smaller the rings were, the more supple was its texture and the more comfortable it was to wear. Mail was very resistant against sword cuts, but would yield under a crushing blow. For this reason, a padded under-garment as shock absorber and a shield as shock-breaker were absolutely necessary. A generic term for mail armour, as differentiated from plate armour, was *paunce* (ll: 2018: Both *his paunce and his plates…*), cognate to German *Panzer.*[3]

The next step was to attach the arm-defences (*brace*),[4] including *cowters* for the elbow joints, and steel gauntlets *(gloves of plate*).

Over his mail, Gawain donned his *cote-armure,* while his spurs were fastened *(spend);* he girted on his sword *(bronde)* by means of its sword-belt (*saynt,* from French *ceinture*). The *cote-armure* was a sleeveless vest – by the second half of the fourteenth century, fashionably form-fitting – developed from the surcoat originally introduced by Crusaders in the Holy Land as a protection against the burning sun that heated the steel rings of the mail shirt until they were too hot to touch. In time, heraldic designs were emblazoned on these coats, thus creating the *coat-of-arms,* which once was a real coat. The sword-belt was worn very low on the hips; it was studded with heavy metal mountings and helped to keep the skirts of the cote-armure from riding up.

Interestingly, though Gawain's arms and legs are encased in plate armour, there is no mentioning of a breast or backplate. The first plate armour elements introduced, in the late thirteenth century, were poleyns and greaves, designed to protect legs and knees in the crush of battle or tournament, when horses might collide with bone-shattering force. Arm defences followed in the first half of the fourteenth century, but plate armour for the torso did not appear for another generation or so. Apparently, it was felt to be too confining, and as long as the shield was still used as a shock-breaker, most knights seem to have considered a stout mail shirt adequate protection.[5]

The final armour element Gawain put on was his helmet:

Þe*nn*e hentes he þe holme, & hastily hit kysses,
Þat wat3 stapled stifly, & stoffed wyth-i*nn*e:
Hit wat3 hy3e on his hede, hasped bihynde,
Wyth a ly3tli vrysou*n* ou*er* þe auentayle,
Enbrawden & bou*n*den wyth þe best ge*m*me3,
On brode sylkyn borde....

...Þe cercle wat3 more o prys,
Þat vmbe-clypped hys crou*n*,
Of diamau*n*te3 a deuys,
Þat boþe were bry3t & brou*n*.[6]

This description has caused considerable confusion, leading to the notion that a strap *(urysoun)* was attached to the back of the helmet (*hasped bihynde*) across the mail hood (*over the aventayle*), to 'attach it to the collar of the shirt of mail'[7] or to be 'bolted to the back plate'.[7] Neither of these suggested methods would be technically feasible; instead the text describes quite graphically the construction of a fourteenth-century basinet with an all-round mail curtain, the camail or aventail, protecting neck and shoulders.[8] The bowl of such a basinet was of domed conical shape coming to a tall point (*high on his hed*). Its camail was attached around the rear from temple to temple in a most ingenious way, but in front the camail was deeply scooped out, leaving the face above the mouth free.

The camail was attached by means of a broad strap sewn along its top edge; a row of perforations throughout the entire length of this strap was fitted over a corresponding row of staples on the back of the helmet. Each of these staples was pierced by an eyelet; a wire threaded through the entire row of staples kept the strap from slipping off. These basinets could be worn with or without a visor; Gawain's helmet must have been of the visorless type because it was adorned – befitting his status as a son of the king of Orkney – with a coronet or circlet (*cercle*), against which a visor would get jammed when raised. The priceless circlet was studded with diamonds arranged in the shape of Gawain's *devys*, his personal badge.

This devys was a golden pentangle, the Seal of Solomon: *the pentangle depaynt of pure golden hewes* [1.621]; *a syngne that Solomon set* [l.625] *an Englych hit callen ... the endeless knot* [ll.629-630], which Gawain carried as cognizance on his shield, but also embroidered on his cote-armure (ll.636-637). His shield was red (l.619: *gules*, the heraldic term for 'red', as mentioned earlier, from the Persian gûl, a rose, a term brought back by the Crusaders). His cote-armure was also red, as mentioned when he ties the green love-lace over it (l.2036). The significance of the pentangle is explained at length (ll.620-664) as a symbol to show Gawain's perfection in specific ways (see chapter 29). On the inner side of his shield, he had the Queen of Heaven's image painted to look at her even in battle that his boldness should not fail. This detailed explanation makes it clear that this pentangle was a strictly personal badge, and as such, quite different from inherited family arms.

In the thirteenth & fourteenth century rolls of arms describing the fictitious heraldry of Arthurian heroes, Sir Gawain was given a shield *argent, a canton gules,* i.e. silver, with a red quarter in the upper left corner. In the fifteenth century, this was replaced by *purple, a double-headed eagle Or.* Both these arms are shared by his entire family, according to proper heraldic usage. Gawain's father, King Lot of Orkney, bears the family arms (canton as well as double-eagle) undifferentiated, as does Gawain as the oldest son (presumably after his father's death), but the younger brothers, Agravaine, Gaheris, Gareth, and Mordred, bear the family arms with marks of difference.

It seems that the early arms: *argent, a canton gules*, were chosen as 'canting arms,' i.e., a rebus on the name of King Lot, derived from courtly French *lot*, 'section.' Therefore, it is likely that Gawain's *devys* of the golden pentangle hides such a rebus, too. The golden *endeles knot* could be a word play with the heraldic term for 'gold' – *Or*, and *knit* (ll.1831; 1849), as verb from 'to knot', to make up 'Or-kney', the name of Gawain's home country. In fifteenth-century rolls of arms, Gawain's war cry is 'Orcanie'.

In arming, the shield and lance were handed to the knight only after he had mounted his horse (ll.2061); if a squire were accompanying a knight, he would be acting as the knight's shield-bearer (*squire* is derived from French *écuyer,* which in turn is derived from *écu,* 'shield'). Shields of the fourteenth century were made of linden wood, about three-quarters of an inch thick, overlaid with glued-on leather, tough enough to hold the wood together even after it had split under a heavy blow. This layer of leather was also the base for the painted heraldic design. The shield was held by the left arm by means of a fist-grip and a loop for the forearm.

In addition to these, the shield also had an adjustable sling (*bauderyk*, l.62) attached to its top; this sling could be thrown around neck and shoulders.

At the time of the Norman Conquest and during the early Crusades, shields were very long and almond-shaped. The elongated lower point covered the left knee of the knight when in 'braced' position, but after the introduction of poleyns and greaves, the shield could be made shorter, and thus handier and – most important – lighter. When visored helmets were introduced, the curved top of the shield could be cut straight, and thus the shield became triangular, which was then interpreted as symbolizing the Holy Trinity (similarly meaningful was the cross-shape of the sword).

For tournaments, however, a completely different type of shield became popular in the later part of the fourteenth century: it was oval to squarish in outline, with a cutout for the lance on its dexter side. This new shield was the *targe,* also called the *shield for peace*. It became customary after about 1350 for knights to have two shields, for war and for peace as a garniture. The *shield for war* was of the traditional triangular shape and bore the knight's family arms; the *shield for peace* usually was a targe and displayed his badge or personal device. Since Gawain's shield bore his *devys,* not his family arms, it was presumably his *shield for peace,* proper to carry on a quest, not on campaign.

All in all, the description of Sir Gawain's armour corresponds in every detail to surviving representations of English knights (such as on tomb brasses) datable to the second half of the fourteenth century; and most significantly, it is the exact counterpart of the famous effigy of Edward Plantagenet, the Black Prince (d. 1376), in Canterbury Cathedral. Hung up above his tomb were the arming doublet, the jousting helm, the sword, and the two shields for war and for peace of the Black Prince. Doublet, helm, sword scabbard, and shield for war still survive. The shield for war is triangular and bears the royal arms of England. The shield for peace is lost, but we know that it was black and displayed the three silver ostrich feathers, the Black Prince's personal badge.[9]

Notes

1. Text from: *Syr Gawayne: A collection of Ancient Romances*, Ed. Sir Frederic Madden, London, 1839. ll 568-589

2. Incidentally, the Spanish term for these thigh-defences was *quixotes*!
3. While Gawain was resting at Castle Hautdesert, his armour, which had suffered much during his winter journey, was cleaned by the efficient staff of Sir Bertilak's household: 'His other harnays, that holdely was keped, Both his pounce and his plates piked ful clene, The rynges rokked of the roust of his rich bruny, And all was fresh as upon first' (ll. 2017-2019.) Cleaning of plate armour was done with patience and an oily rag, but a squire entrusted with cleaning his master's armour was holden to always brush in one direction for a fine, matte sheen; scouring in circular motion would result in a spotty shine. Mail armour could not be cleaned by hand; it was 'rokked', i.e. tumbled in a rotating wooden barrel together with a few shovelfuls of sawdust sprinkled with oil. The friction of the rings against each other rubbed the rust and dirt loose, to be absorbed by the sawdust.
4. The *braces* were sub-divided in *vambrace* for the forearm and *rerebrace* for the upper arm.
5. General literature: Claude Blair *European Armour* (London: 1958); Vesey A. B. Norman, *Arms and Armour,* series: Pleasures and Treasures (4), New York: 1964); Vesey Norman, *Warrior to Soldier, 446-1660* (London: 1964); Paul Martin, Arms *and Armour from the 9th to the 17th century* (Rutland, VT: 1968); Helmut Nickel, *Warriors and Worthies* (New York: 1969); Richard Barber, *The Knight and Chivalry* (New York: 1970); William Reid, *Arms through the Ages* (London, 1976); *The Complete Encyclopaedia of Arms & Weapons* (New York, 1979).
6. Madden, ll 605-10 and 615-618
7. *Urysoun* is defined as 'a strap attaching the helmet to the collar of the shirt of mail'.
8. George Cameron Stone, *A Glossary of the Construction, Decoration and Use of Arms and Armor* (Portland, Maine: 1934), p. 158 defines *Camail:* 'The camail was sometimes held down at the back by a strap bolted to the back plate.'
9. Gerard J. Brault Early *Blazon,* (Oxford: 1972), Chapter 13: Arthurian Heraldry, pp. 37-52.

Originally published in *Avalon to Camelot* I no. 2, Winter 1983/4, pp. 16-19.

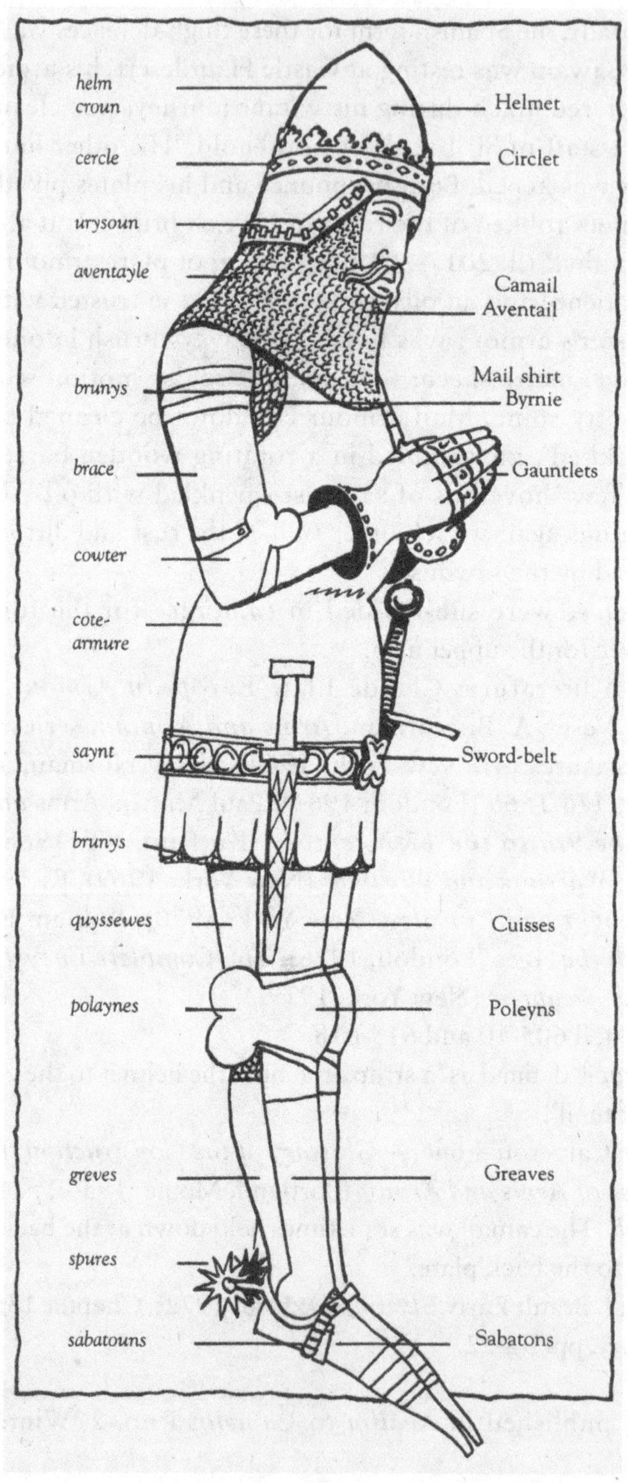

Armour of Edward II.

11

Why Was the Green Knight Green?

From the original manuscript of *Sir Gawain and the Green Knight*. The Green Knight is holding up his severed head in his right hand. (Reproduced under creative commons)

Among the many uncanny beings found in Arthurian stories the Green Knight holds pride of place. The vexing question of his identity has been convincingly answered by Richard R. Griffith's brilliant detective work in his landmark study *Bertilak's Lady: The French Background of Sir Gawain and the Green Knight* (249-66), but another puzzle remains: Why were the Green Knight and his horse green not only in their dress and trappings, but also in their bodies?

There are, of course, any numbers of knights of diverse colours, and usually with matching steeds, to be found in the epics of chivalry (Brault 31-35). In Malory's Tale of Sir Gareth of Orkney, for instance, there appear the four brothers, Sir Perarde the Black Knight, Sir Pertholepe the Green Knight, Sir Perymones the Red Knight, and Sir Persuante of Inde the Blue Knight; in addition to them there is another Black Knight, Sir Gryngamoure, and Sir Ironsyde, the Red Knight of Red Laundes. While all their armour, shields, banners, and horse trappings are of the appropriate colours, their skins and hair are of normal human hues.

Sirs Perarde and Gryngamoure ride black horses; Sirs Perymones and Ironsyde are mounted on red chargers (Vinaver 1.303.3; 1.305.24; 1.309.5; 1.311.30-1; 1.321.18)[1] The colours of the horses of the Blue Knight and the Red Knight are not mentioned; presumably they would have to be content with mounts of conventional colouring, as was the case with Sir Gareth himself, when at the tournament at Castell Perelus he changed his colours by the magic of the ring given him by the maiden Lioness from course to course, but rode a conservative bay (Vinaver 345-51).

In setting out on his search for the identity of the Green Knight, Richard Griffith makes it clear that the denouement of the plot as given by the Green Knight at the Green Chapel is not like that in a third-rate detective story 'in which the murderer turns out to be somebody you never heard of', as has been felt by most modern readers and interpreters who were disappointed by this apparent flaw in an otherwise undisputed masterpiece. Likewise, it looked to many readers that the driving force of the bad guys in this story was a 'motiveless malignity'. Quite to the contrary, as Griffith shows, when the Green Knight reveals himself to be Gawain's host, names himself as 'Bertilak de Hautdesert I hat in this londe,' and declares that the old lady at his castle is actually Morgan le Fay, who staged the entire complicated ploy of the Challenge and the Beheading Game out of enmity against the Round Table and also in order to scare Queen Guinevere to death, he supplies important clues that point to characters and episodes in a French romance, the *Merlin-Continuation*, which links the Vulgate *Merlin* to the Vulgate *Lancelot* (Micha 319-24).

In the *Merlin-Continuation* one reads of the controversial deeds of a once renowned knight, Bertelak le Rous, a vassal of King Leodegrance, the father of Queen Guinevere. This Sir Bertelak, who would have qualified to be one of the hundred knights who – together with the Round Table itself – were Guinevere's dowry, commits a blood-feud slaying on the eve of Arthur and Guinevere's wedding. For this he is exiled by a court of judges, which includes Leodegrance, Arthur, and Gawain. In his exile Sir Bertelak secretly marries a beautiful maiden, Guinevere, who is the illegitimate daughter of King Leodegrance, conceived and born on the same day as his legitimate daughter, the future Queen Guinevere. The two Guineveres are exact look-alikes, with the exception of a crown-shaped birthmark which graces what might be delicately called the hip of the trueborn daughter.

In the course of events King Arthur is persuaded that he has been tricked into marrying the wrong sister; he takes the false Guinevere to his throne and bed and sends away the true Guinevere who thus is justified to join her exiled lover, Lancelot. When at long last this evil conspiracy is uncovered and the true Guinevere reinstated, both the false Guinevere and her husband Bertelak le Rous are banished forever from Arthur's court.

On hearing the name 'Bertelak' a fourteenth-century connoisseur of Arthurian romances would recognize this clue and realize that the fearsome Green Knight and Gawain's jolly host in the wilderness castle are disguises of the exiled and disgraced knight Bertelak le Rous, and that the amorous Lady of the Castle could be none other than the false Guinevere. Therefore, far from being driven by a 'motiveless malignity', both the Green Knight and his lady have ample reason to feel vengeful against King Arthur, Queen Guinevere, and Gawain.

Even Morgan le Fay, the standard arch-villainess of Arthurian stories who here has to supply the magic necessary for the transformation of Sir Bertelak into the Green Knight and for the Beheading Game itself, has an old grudge against Queen Guinevere, who once thwarted her in her love affair with the knight of Avalon, Sir Grygamour.

The identification of the Green Knight with a questionable, but unquestionably human, character from a French romance invalidates all the learned interpretations of the Green Knight as a vegetation demon, solar deity, representative of the Old Religion, the Devil or

Death personified, which have been brought forth over the last seven decades following George Lyman Kittredge's fundamental *Study of Gawain and the Green Knight* (Kittredge; Krappe 206-15). However, the identification with Bertelak *le Rous* leads to another vexing question: Why did Bertelak le Rous turn into a Green Knight and not a Red Knight, as could be expected from his surname? His magically bestowed power to play the Challenger in the Beheading Game seems unconnected with his colouring.

The Beheading Game itself has its closest parallel and possible prototype in an episode in the Irish tale of *Bricriu's Feast* (written down before 1106) in which a giant *bachlach* (churl) clad in a shaggy black fur cloak invites the assembled champions of Ireland to an exchange of head chopping. The *bachlach,* who is actually the wizard Curoi mac Dairi in disguise, has been gladly accepted by believers in the purely Celtic origins of Arthurian motifs as the source for the name of the lord of the Castle Hautdesert in its earlier – unfortunately erroneous – reading 'Bercilak'.

Similar beheading games appear in four French romances. In *La mule sanz frein* (c.1210) and *Hunbaut* (1250-75) the challenger is a gigantic 'vilain', black as a moor and clad in a shaggy black hide, wielding a huge axe; in *Perlesvaus* (1225-50) the challenger is a knight richly dressed, but carrying an axe; in the *Livre de Caradoc,* an interpolation into the First Continuation of Chrétien de Troyes's *Perceval,* he is a tall knight in an ermine robe, armed with a long sword and riding a tawny steed. Again, neither in the Irish nor in the French sources is the challenger in the Beheading Game in any way connected with the colour green.

Green as a *Verfremdungseffekt* is found on another supernatural horse from an Arthurian story. In Chrétien de Troyes's *Erec et Enide* (Comfort 69) the King of the Dwarves, Guivret le Petit, presents Enide with a palfrey of striking colours: its body is sorrel, but its head is half white and half black; between the two halves there runs a line greener than a grapevine leaf (Comfort vv.5173-366).[2] The Minnesinger Hartmann von Aue, who translated Chrétien's *Erec* into German, describes Enide's palfrey as blindingly white on its left side, and raven black on its right, but where the two colours meet, there is a grass-green stripe of half a finger's width, as if it were painted with a fine brush, starting at the horse's mouth, running up between the ears and along its back all the way to the tail, which is half black and half white, too. The colours of the palfrey's ears are counter changed, black on the left side and white on the right (7290). This baffling colour scheme led Alwin Schulz, one of the erudite and meticulous German *Kulturhistoriker* of the nineteenth century, to the conclusion that it must have been a medieval custom to paint horses in bright colours to improve their appearance.

However, it must be kept in mind that Enide's palfrey was from the stables of the dwarf king, and clearly not an ordinary animal (Comfort 6713-809).[3] Pied and spotted horses have been regarded as special long before pintos became 'medicine-horses' among the Plains Indians; pied horses are conspicuous among the grave figurines of the Tang dynasty; spotted spirit-horses *(bura)* bore the souls of Siberian shamans in trance on their travels through the heavens (Potapov 486; Nickel 179-83), and in Europe cavalry regiments' pied horses were the distinctive mounts of trumpeters, who in civilized warfare during the seventeenth through nineteenth centuries enjoyed diplomatic immunity as carriers of messages, such as truce offers or surrender proposals, between the combatants.

With the French background of *Sir Gawain and the Green Knight* firmly established by Richard Griffith's identification of Sir Bertilak, the key to the green disguise of the Green Knight is likely to be found in this French background, too. Again, the strange colouring of his horse should be of help in the search for this key. As seen above, Enide's palfrey had some green in its hide; interestingly enough, Enide had another palfrey, given to her earlier by her cousin, whom Roger Sherman Loomis sees as a sorceress, 'Morgain and Niniane, the Lady of the Lake, blended into one' (105-07). This other palfrey, too, was piebald (ver); in the easiest available translation, however, in that by W. W. Comfort in Everyman's Library (18), this palfrey is called 'dappled,' which rather blurs the image. *Ver* – 'piebald' – is a homophone to vert, 'green' *(OED* 12:146), which makes it easy to see how a piebald horse of a special nature could turn into an even more extraordinary green horse in a French text.

When translated into other languages, such as Hartmann's Middle High German in which *ver* would be *bunt* and *vert* would be *grüne,* the connection cannot easily be recognized if one is unaware of the French derivation. The same would be the case with a translation into English. A parallel to this confusion of sound-alike words is the story of how Cinderella got her glass slipper. Originally this extravagant footwear was a French *pantoufle de vair* (a slipper lined with fur), which became a *pantoufle de verre* (glass slipper) when the word *vair* – 'miniver' – became obsolete except as an esoteric heraldic term and was no longer readily understood.

In this group of homophones (ver, 'piebald,' vert, 'green,' *vair*, 'fur', *verre*, 'glass') it seems that the third set *(vair*, 'fur') might supply the key. The common features of the Green Knight, the Irish *bachlach,* the French 'vilains' and the knight on the tawny steed are that they are very hairy and/or bushy bearded and wear fur cloaks or shaggy hides. This might indicate that in the hypothetical French prototype (which is assumed to have served as immediate source for *Sir Gawain and the Green Knight*) the terrifying Green Knight on his green steed was originally an *homme sauvage,* clad all over in *vair* and riding an otherworldly piebald (*ver*) horse. Besides obvious features, such as the Green Knight's long hair, bushy beard, and fur cloak, there is another significant clue that he originated from a wildman: he sits his mount *scholes,* i.e. without shoes, though he wears gilt spurs, the class distinction of a knight. One of the characteristics of a wildman, aside from his hairiness, is his bare feet; though occasionally he might dress in cloaks, hats, or other garments, his feet are invariably without shoes (Loomis 331).[4]

On his quest for the Green Chapel Sir Gawain encounters manifold dangers from dragons, wolves, bulls, bears, and other denizens of the wild, including *wodewose* (wildmen). These, however, are the real wildmen of the woods; by contrast, Sir Bertilak assumes his guise only temporarily. This corresponds with a wildman episode in the Vulgate *Merlin* (Husband), when Merlin – who loved to act the shape-shifter – enters the emperor's court first as a wild stag and, later, as a wildman who prophetically unmasks the infidelity of the empress. In this episode of the temporary wildman on a mission to embarrass a ruler's court and his wife, there is probably the inspiration for the appearance of the Green Knight at Arthur's court. From what seems to have been a disappointingly simple misunderstanding of a French prototype, the *Gawain*-Poet's power of imagination and skill as a wordwright created the awesome image of the Green Knight on his green charger riding into King Arthur's hall to challenge the flower of chivalry.

Notes

1. In the description of Sir Persaunte's company '... men and women and horsis, trapped shyldis and sperys, was all of the color of inde,' a comma seems to be misplaced; it would make better sense as '... men and women and horsis trapped, shyldis and sperys...'

2. In addition to that, the fact that Enide's mount is a palfrey (from the Latin *paraveredus)* might have favoured a false etymology between *verdus* (post horse) and *viridis* (green).
3. Enide's robe was lined with the fur of the 'strange beasts from India, named "barbiolets"' whose heads were all white, and whose necks are mulberry black with red backs and green bellies. These four colours, incidentally, are those of the four cardinal directions of Far Eastern cosmology: red – south; black – north; green or blue – east; white – west.
4. Apparently worried about the shoelessness of the Green Knight in midwinter season, the text has been improved upon in the translation by Roger S. Loomis and Laura H. Loomis (*Medieval Romances*, New York: The Modern Library, 1957) to read 'with long green shoes', a good example of the caution with which translations have to be approached.

Select Bibliography

Brault, Gerard J. *Early Blazon: Heraldic Terminology in the Twelfth and Thirteenth Centuries with Special Reference to Arthurian Literature.* Oxford: Clarendon, 1972.

Comfort, W. W. *Chrétien de Troyes: Arthurian Romances.* Introduction and notes by D. D. R. Owen. London: Everyman's Library, 1975.

Griffith, Richard R. 'Bertilak's Lady: The French Background of *Sir Gawain and the Green Knight,' Annals of the New York Academy of Arts* 314 (1978): 249-66.

Husband, Timothy. *The Wild Man: Medieval Myth and Symbolism.* New York: The Metropolitan Museum of Art Exhibition Catalogue No. 8, with an illustration from L'y*stoire du Saint Graal et du Merlin,* ms. 207 Pierpont Morgan Library, New York. New York: 1980.

Kittredge, George Lyman. *A Study of Gawain and the Green Knight.* Cambridge: Harvard UP, 1916.

Krappe, A. H. 'Who was the Green Knight?' *Speculum: A Journal of Medieval Studies.* 13 (1938): 206-15.

Loomis, Roger Sherman. *Arthurian Tradition & Chrétien de Troyes.* New York: Columbia UP, 1949.

Micha, Alexandre. 'The Vulgate *Merlin.*' *Arthurian Literature in the Middle Ages.* Ed. Roger S. Loomis. Oxford: Clarendon, 1961.

Nickel, Helmut. 'And behold, a White Horse ... Observations on the Colors of the Horses of the Four Horsemen of the Apocalypse.' *Metropolitan Museum Journal* 12 (1977): 179-83.

Potapov, Leonid P. 'Über den Pferdekult bei den turksprachigen Volkern des Sajan-Altai-Gebirges.' *Abhandlungen und Berichte des Staatlichen Museums für Volkerkunde Dresden* 34 (1975): 485.

Schulz, Alwin (San-Marte). *Zur Waffenkunde des älteren deutschen Mittelalters.* Quedlinberg: Basse, 1867.

Vinaver, Eugene, ed. *The Works of Sir Thomas Malory.* 3 vols. Oxford: Clarendon Press, 1967.

Originally published in *Arthurian Interpretations* Vol. 2., No. 2. Spring, 1998, pp. 68-74.

12

Merlin, Magic and Swords of Power

Among the weapons in early man's arsenal are some that were originally designed for the survival economy of the hunt, such as the spear and the bow and arrow, or else were developed from household tools, such as the knife and axe; only the sword was created for the sole purpose of killing men. It is probably for this rather sinister reason that the sword has been universally regarded as the most noble of weapons and was surrounded with an aura of superstitious awe long before it acquired almost mystical significance in pious Crusaders' eyes because of the cross-shape of its guard.

The same superstitious awe and not a little suspicion of magic was also directed towards the sword's creator, the smith. Even his practical working methods, such as labouring preferably at night, because the temperature of the iron could be controlled only by closely observing the changing colours of the glowing metal, or his timing the quenching of a blade during the tempering process by reciting a verse or two, smacked strongly of magic to the medieval mind.

All metalworking had to be done by taming the divine element, Fire. Therefore, in classical antiquity, the fire-god Hephaistos/Vulcan was also a smith, who fashioned the sword of his brother Ares/Mars, the god of war, as well as the most beautiful jewellery for the goddesses and amazing technical contraptions. He is also set apart from the other Olympians by being afflicted by a bodily deficiency: he is lame. In compensation for this, he was wed to Aphrodite/Venus, the goddess of Love and Beauty, although sadly, she betrayed him with his brother Ares/Mars. In the medieval heroic epics of Northern Europe there appears a legendary smith of unequalled skill, Wayland (German Wieland, Norse Volund,

French Galan), who was also lame and married to a lovely swan maiden till she recovered her feather shirt and flew away. The most renowned smith in the Arthurian legends is Master Trebuchet, who made the sword of the Grail King. His name is clearly derived from French *trébucher* ('to stumble'), which suggests that he is yet another personification of the lame smith of mythology.

The most famous of all swords in legend is of course King Arthur's Excalibur. (In some texts the name Excalibur is given to both of Arthur's swords; in others, including Malory, only the sword received from the Lady of the Lake is called Excalibur.) Merlin's feat of planting it into a steel anvil mounted on a marble block implies that he also fashioned the sword itself. Like the other master craftsmen, Merlin has an unfortunate love affair, with Nimue, but he is never described as being lame. However, he is regarded – at least since Robert de Boron's Old French verse romance *Merlin* (*c.* 1200) – as the son of a devil, and the Devil in European folklore is traditionally recognized by his limp.

After Arthur has proved himself to be the rightful king of all England by drawing Excalibur from the stone, he offers it on the (stone) altar of St Paul's Cathedral, but he also carries it into battle against the six kings who challenge his authority. At the crucial moment of this battle, on the advice of Merlin, Arthur draws Excalibur, and it is 'so bryght in his enemyens eyen that it gaf light lyke thirty torches, and therwith he put them on bak.' Though this wonder weapon is without doubt a magic sword, it nevertheless breaks in Arthur's first true chivalric adventure, the duel he fights with King Pellinore because of the wounding of his youngest knight, Sir Grifflet. Helpfully, when the sword breaks, Merlin is at hand to save Arthur in the nick of time by casting an enchantment on Pellinore as he lifts his sword for the killing stroke, and 'he felle to the erthe in a grete slepe'.

Later, Merlin guides Arthur, who worries that he is now without a sword, to the lake, where an arm clothed in white samite and holding a fair sword in its hand rises out of the water. This is the wonderful sword Excalibur that King Arthur is to wield until the last grim battle of Camlann. When he receives this sword from the hands of the Lady of the Lake, Merlin explains to Arthur that the scabbard is even more valuable for a fighting man than the sword itself, because the scabbard has the magic quality that its wearer would not lose any blood, be he 'never so sore wounded'. Of course, as is often the case with magic objects, it doesn't take long for the scabbard to be stolen by Morgan le Fay, and Arthur becomes as vulnerable as any other man. At the end, when he is mortally wounded at Camlann, Arthur bids his last surviving knight to take Excalibur and throw it into a nearby body of water. Twice this knight hesitates; but he throws it the third time and an arm shoots out of the water, catches the sword in mid-flight, 'and shoke hit thryse and braundysshed, and than vanysshed with the swerde into the watir'.[1]

It is interesting that in the earlier versions of this story, such as that told in the thirteenth-century *Vulgate Cycle* (now known as the *Lancelot-Grail*), Sir Grifflet, whose defeat and wounding by King Pellinore was ultimately the cause for Arthur's acquiring the Sword from the Lake, is also the knight who has to return Excalibur to the water. In the much better-known version of Sir Thomas Malory's *Morte D'Arthur,* however, it is Sir Bedivere, Arthur's oldest follower and the last survivor, who performs this final task.

In the Vulgate cycle Arthur also has a sword named Sequence; this might be an alternative spelling (at a time when spelling was mostly phonetic and typically erratic) of *sécante* ('the Cutting One'). This suggests a parallel to Excalibur, whose name, as interpreted by the Lady of the Lake, means 'Cutte Steele.' Geoffrey of Monmouth is the first to give Arthur's sword a name – Caliburnus – though it should be pointed out that he has it neither drawn from a stone nor taken from a lake, but hints at its magical origin by mentioning that it was 'forged in the island of Avalon'. The name Excalibur/Caliburnus has been explained as being derived from Welsh *Caledfwlch* (Irish *Caledbolg),* meaning 'Lightning Sword,' or else from Latin *chalybs* ('steel') and *eburnus* ('white as ivory'). Considering the Lady of the Lake's explanation, a derivation from a word meaning 'steel' seems to be the more plausible one. *Ebumeus* as 'ivory' is also a poetic synonym for 'scabbard', which in turn makes one think of the magic value of Excalibur's scabbard as pointed out by Merlin.

Another magic sword connected with both Merlin and the Lady of the Lake is the sword of Sir Balin. It is brought to Arthur's court by a damsel sent by the Lady Lyle of Avilion; under her cloak she is girt with this sword that only a knight 'without velony other trechory and withoute treson' could deliver her from. Among all the assembled champions of the Round Table only Sir Balin can rid her of this unusual chastity belt. Sir Balin had just been released from the dungeons – he had slain a cousin of Arthur's – and before he leaves Arthur's court, he also slays the Lady of the Lake, who shows up to demand his head ostensibly as payment for Excalibur but actually as part of a blood feud between her and Balin's family. In spite of the damsel's well-meant warnings that this sword will be the cause of the undoing of Balin and of the best friend he has, he decides to keep it in addition to his own and is thereafter known as the Knight with the Two Swords.

Though with the help of his brother, Sir Balan, he defeats and captures King Royns (Ryance), who has invaded Arthur's realm, his other adventures are dismal mishaps. Proceeding on a road strewn with the corpses of damsels and knights whom he tried in vain to protect, he comes to the Castle of the Grail where he smites the Dolorous Stroke and must fight to the death a Red Knight. Mortally wounded by the last blow of the Red Knight, the damsel's prediction comes true as he recognizes in his dead opponent his brother Balan.

At this point Merlin comes wandering along and plants Balin's sword in a marble block, which later will float downriver to Camelot.[2] Merlin also takes off the sword's pommel and replaces it with another, on which he writes the prophecy that only the best knight in the world could draw this sword from the marble stone, and this should be either Lancelot or his son Galahad, and further, that Lancelot shall kill with this sword his best friend, who will be Gawain.

Very much the same set of adventures is found in the French verse romance *Meriadeuc, le Chevalier aux Deux Epees*, from the first half of the thirteenth century. It, too, has a damsel burdened with a belted sword that can be removed only by the best knight. There is also a blood feud and a complicated subplot that culminates in a duel with Gawain, whom Arthur had sent out to quest for the Knight with the Two Swords. In this case, however, both combatants survive in order to have Meriadeuc united in wedded bliss to the damsel he delivered from the sword. Strangely, neither Balin's nor Meriadeuc's magic swords seem to have personal names, though in *Meriadeuc* there is the motif of the sword that alone can heal the wound it has inflicted.

Similar magic is in Julius Caesar's sword, named *Crocea Mors* ('Yellow Death') according to Geoffrey of Monmouth, because nobody could survive a wound from it, and also in Sir Priamus' sword, with which he wounded Gawain in the fight at the border of Tuscany during Arthur's Roman campaign, as reported by Malory. Wounds made by Sir Priamus' blade would bleed forever, unless staunched by a special balm and washed with water from the four rivers that flow from the Earthly Paradise. Thoughtfully, Sir Priamus carried a box of the balm and a vial of the waters, just in case he should cut up someone who might turn out worth saving (as was the case with Gawain).

Somewhat more rationalized is the story about the sword of the Morholt of Ireland, whose blade was steeped in poison by his sister, the witch-queen Isolt, mother of Isolde the Fair. Isolt knew the only antidote. When Tristram slew the Morholt in their duel over the slave tribute the Morholt was to gather from Cornwall, and he himself had been wounded by the Morholt's venomed sword, a splinter broke off Tristram's sword edge and remained stuck in the Morholt's hard skull. It was retrieved by his sister, Isolt, and was almost Tristram's undoing when he came asking to be healed of his festering wound. The name of Tristram's sword was Curtana, and in 1207 Sir Tristram's sword is mentioned as one of the swords of state among the crown regalia of England. This sword had a blunted tip (the chip broken off in the Morholt's skull), and was also called the Sword of Mercy, symbolizing the power of just punishment tempered by mercy. The Curtana or Sword of Mercy that can be seen today among the regalia in the Tower of London, alas, is only a replacement made in 1661 for the original sword that was lost at the time of Cromwell's Protectorate.[3]

In the *Mabinogion* story of *Rhonabwy's Dream*, King Arthur's sword is described as having two dragons decorating its blade. This could refer to the two dragons in Nennius' report of the finding of Ambrosius Merlinus, as well as to the dragon banner and dragon helmet crest Arthur inherited from his father, Uther Pendragon. It could, however, also be a concrete description of a sword blade of pattern-welded steel. In order to produce a blade that would be shock-resistant but would still hold a keen edge, the smiths of the Dark Ages were forced to solve a seemingly insurmountable problem. As steel is forged harder and harder, it becomes brittle as glass; but untempered iron is soft and easily bent out of shape. (Caesar reported that Iron Age Celtic swords would be bent after a few heavy blows and had to be straightened out underfoot.)

As a compromise that turned out to be extremely effective, the ancient bladesmiths painstakingly hammer-welded together alternate strips of iron and steel of varying hardnesses and laboriously added separate edges of very hard steel. The core strips were often twisted and/or braided for extra cohesiveness; after polishing the finished blade showed a surface pattern of light and dark spots, reflecting the steel and iron strips. The prized 'dragon-skin' pattern, or twisted and curled-up fighting serpents, has been described in numerous examples from Norse sagas and Germanic epics.[4]

This structural difference between the extra-hard steel edges and the flexible core of the blade would stop a crack in the edge at the core and leave the sword perfectly serviceable in spite of this flaw. Such must have been the case with Tristram's sword, when a sliver was chipped out of one of its edges but left the sword unbroken.

Many sword smiths did their best to enhance their products by inscribing signs of power on their blades (those who wanted to play it safe used religious symbols, such as crosses or the sacred monograms IHS, INRI or SM representing Christ and Mary) or by decorating their hilts with silver, which was a sure repellent of any blunting spells an enemy might cast. The very oldest sword known, from the royal tombs of Ur in Chaldea (*c.* 2500 B.C.), has a gold blade – this was made even before the working of bronze, let alone iron, was properly established – signed with the ideogram of a locust as the symbol of 'utter destruction'. Marks in the shape of boars and crescents with human faces have been stamped on Celtic blades of the Late La Tène Period (first century B.C.); and similar crescents were stamped on the celebrated blades of the sword smiths of Toledo, Spain.

Wolf-marks were chiselled and inlaid in gold or brass by the famous smiths of Passau, a small town on the banks of the Danube on the border between Austria and Bavaria. These smiths succeeded in convincing their customers that their blades were not only of superior quality (which they definitely were), but also loaded with magic to a degree that they could protect their wearers against harm in battle from steel and iron (later this was extended to the lead of bullets, but not to silver, which is why the werewolf can be shot only with a silver bullet). The wolf-mark was widely imitated by smiths at Solingen in the Rhineland (who also turned out high-quality blades, but apparently thought that a little extra could not hurt), at Hounslow in England (where it was called 'the Fox'), and even Toledo (where it was called *el perillo* or 'little dog'), and was used for centuries, up to the 1700s. A fine sword was a treasured possession and could be handed down for generations. A good example is one of the swords in the collection of the Metropolitan Museum in New York, which was picked up on the battlefield of Omdurman during the uprising of the Mahdi (1898), and which has a silver hilt of local Sudanese workmanship but a fifteenth-century Passau blade with the wolf-mark!

Aside from the practical value of a good sword, its ideal value could be even higher, as can be seen from the swords of state that are part of the regalia of practically every realm in the world. One of the Three Treasures of the Emperor of Japan is the sacred Heavenly Precious Sword of the Gathering Clouds, which Susa-no-o, the brother of the Sun-goddess, retrieved from the tail of a dragon he slew, and one of the most sacred relics of Islam is the Sword of the Prophet, *D'hul-faqar.* As collectors' items, famous swords were avidly sought after and cherished; Richard Lionheart owned a sword said to have been Lancelot's (ultimately this would have been Balin's magic sword, if we trace it through Malory), which in 1190 he presented to Tancred of Lecce in order to cement their more than shaky alliance and to secure a Sicilian base for his crusade. (Other accounts say it was Excalibur itself.) Three hundred years later, the sword of Lancelot is listed in the armour collection of King Charles VIII of France, at Amboise, together with the sword *Victoire* of Joan of Arc.

Among the regalia of the Holy Roman Empire kept at Vienna is a silver-mounted sabre, said to have been a gift to Charlemagne by Khalif Haroun-al-Rashid of Arabian Nights fame, but there is also a tradition that originally it was the sword of Attila the Hun. Attila's sword, in turn, according to the Gothic-Alanic historian Jordanes (*c.* A.D. 550), was said to have been the sword of Mars himself, found thrusting out of the ground by a herdsman and handed to Attila in fulfilment of a prophecy about the World Conqueror. This is an echo of the ancient tradition of the horse-nomads of the Eastern steppes – Scythians, Alani, Sarmatians and Huns – who worshipped tribal war gods in the shape of a naked sword set upright in the ground or on a platform. This is also, according to one theory, the root of the motif of the Sword in the Stone.[5]

The motif of the Sword thrown into the Lake, too, may have been based on an Eastern tradition. As mentioned earlier, the name Excalibur/ Caliburnus is probably derived from *chalybs,* a Latin word for 'steel', which in turn was borrowed from the name of the Kalybes, a tribe of Sarmatian smiths in the Caucasus Mountains. The last speakers of a Sarmatian tongue today are the Ossetians in the Caucasus, who still preserve a sizeable repertoire of heroic epics about the Narts, a mythical tribe of superheroes. Their principal champion, Batradz, owned a magic sword that was bound up with his life. After his last battle, mortally wounded, he could not be relieved from his sufferings until his sword was thrown into the nearby sea. His last surviving follower did this only at the third attempt, after having deceived him twice.

Batradz and several other Nart heroes have bodies of steel (remember another 'hero' from the Caucasus, a certain Joseph Dzugashvili, who called himself *Stalin* or 'the Man of Steel'?) and thus they would belong to that interesting group of heroes who are actually swords personified.

Some of them show this clearly by being apprenticed to smiths in their youth, like Siegfried and Fionn/Finn Mac Cool, who both wrought their own swords as extensions or alter egos of themselves. Some served smiths, as did Cuchulainn. Some – even more transparently – were sons of smiths, such as Wittich the son of Wayland, who carried *Mimmung*, his father's masterpiece and the best of swords in Germanic legend, and who leaped to his death into the sea in order to keep his precious sword from falling into enemy hands. Even Arthur himself, by virtue of his life's being tied to Excalibur, and by his retiring to Avalon (the place of origin of Caliburnus), has acquired features of this sword-hero.

Sometimes the very name of the hero identifies him as the personification of a sword, as is the case with *Scherp-fe* ('Sword Edge') and Ort ('Sword Point'), the two sons of King Etzel, the historical Attila in German epics. In the epics about Dietrich von Bern (the historical Theoderic, King of the Ostrogoths who reigned A.D. 490-526), in Germanic legend roughly the equivalent of King Arthur, Dietrich has a tutor and master-of-arms by the name of *Hildebrand* ('Battle Sword'), son of *Heribrand* ('Campaigning Sword'), and father of *Hadubrand* ('Fighting Sword'), of the clan Wülfing, recalling the wolf-mark. Hildebrand, incidentally, has to kill his son Hadubrand very much as Arthur kills Mordred. This sword-hero equation is valid also for Lancelot, who was not only raised and trained in the magic lake, but was originally baptised *Galahad,* as Merlin points out; and of course, it also applies to his son, also Galahad, who draws the enchanted sword from Merlin's floating marble stone and mends the broken sword of the Grail King with his bare hands. Their name, Galahad, looks suspiciously like a variant of a common root like Latin *gladius,* Welsh *caled,* Gaelic *claidh,* or even Turkish *kilidj,* all of them meaning 'sword'.[6]

Besides the folklore and historical motifs surrounding the swords in the Arthurian legend, they also suggest an archetypal psychological symbolism. The workings of magic in the Arthurian legends are based on two opposing principles: the male principle, as represented by Merlin, and the female, as represented by Morgan le Fay, the Lady of the Lake, Nimue, the Lady Lyle of Avilion, and other damsels, all of them more or less thinly disguised aspects of one and the same supernatural figure associated with the Island of Avalon. Much of this magic, both male and female, is tied to the three swords of power we encounter in the legend: the Sword in the Stone, the Sword from the Lake, and the Sword of Balin, which passes on to Galahad and Lancelot.

Looking at these three swords with the hindsight of modern psychology after Freud, we can easily perceive that the first Excalibur, which Merlin planted into the anvil on the stone and used as a test to prove Arthur's calling and authority, embodied purely male magic. Therefore its powers must have been felt to be somehow incomplete (originally it even lacked a scabbard, the female component of a complete sword), and thus it failed Arthur at its first challenge, the duel with King Pellinore.

The Sword of Balin, on the other hand, is the subject of both female and male magic. First delivered by a damsel of Lady Lyle of Avilion (l'Isle d'Avalon), it causes the death of the Lady of the Lake, and after the end of Balin's unhappy adventures Merlin takes it from his dead hand and sets it into a marble block, there to wait for the best knight in the world who will kill his best friend with it. Balin's own death and the killing of his brother was foretold by the damsel girt with the sword; the tragedy of the best knight, who will pull the sword from the marble stone, was prophesied by Merlin. Because of these separate and un-coordinated magic actions, the history of Balin's sword became an example of magic gone wrong.

By contrast, the second Excalibur, the Sword from the Lake, was given to Arthur by both the Lady of the Lake and Merlin together; it also came to Arthur complete in its scabbard, perfect in its unity, a male/female symbolism that leaves nothing to be desired in explicitness. Because of this balance of male and female magic powers, this second Excalibur (the male principle) lasted until the end of Arthur's life, though the scabbard (the female principle) had been seized and cast into a lake by Morgan le Fay shortly after Merlin was imprisoned under the stone by Nimue. After Camlann, Excalibur had to be thrown into the mere, thus magically uniting it with the scabbard sunk into the deepest waters so many years earlier by Morgan, and then at long last Morgan reappears to guide Arthur to Avalon.

Notes

1. Iron ore was either quarried from mines in mountains or recovered as leached-out deposits from watery bogs. For this reason, swords like Excalibur are often extracted from rocks or water and also must be returned to their origins by being buried in caves or hollow hills, or tossed back into a lake.

2. A sword set into a marble block actually exists. This is the sword of the knight Galgano Guidotti, who was born in 1148 and according to tradition became a hermit in 1180 and died a year later as a saint. A chapel was erected on the site of his hermitage on Mount Siepi, near Siena, Italy, in 1180, and the sword set into the stone is well documented from that time on. Interestingly, the knightly saint's name, Galgano, is an Italian form of Gawain.
3. Tristram's sword, accidentally laid between himself and Isolde when they are discovered sleeping in their cave hideout, convinces Mark that their love is actually innocent – though in other versions it is Mark himself who places the sword there as a sign that he has been there and witnessed them together. In Le *Chevalier à L'Epée* (c. 1210), Gawain is subjected to a chastity test, not unlike the one presented by the Green Knight's lady, with a magic sword hovering above the bed. In the Nibelung epics, Siegfried places his sword between himself and Brunhild after he releases her from the sleeping spell within the Wall of Flames, because he is already betrothed to Kriemhild; Brunhild's misunderstanding of this gesture ultimately leads to his doom.
4. In the *Prose Edda,* Snorri Sturluson uses the simile of the sword as a serpent that leaves its scabbard like the snake sloughs off its skin. In the epic *Helgakvida* of the *Poetic Edda* the sword of the hero has 'along the edge a blood-dark serpent, / and at the guard a dragon turns against it, / twisting its tail.' Similar descriptions are given of the swords *Ekkisax* ('Knife Edge') in *Thidriks Saga* and *Skofnung* in *Cormac's Saga.* The technical term for pattern-welded blades in German is *wurmbunt* ('patterned like a snake').
5. The horse-nomads shared a uniform cultural pattern in spite of ethnic and linguistic differences, rather like the Plains Indians of the nineteenth century. Scythians, Alani and Sarmatians were members of an Indo-European Iranian language group; Huns were non-Indo-European Proto-Turks. In A.D. 175, Emperor Marcus Aurelius sent 5500 Sarmatian tribesmen to Britain as auxiliary cavalry to reinforce the Legion VI Victrix, which at that time had as its praefectus a certain Lucius Artorius Castus. The Sarmatians and Alani were heavy armoured cavalry. Aside from worshipping swords stuck in the ground, they also burned hemp leaves in sacred cauldrons to induce religious visions. Alani and Sarmatians were settled all over Central and Western Europe in Late Roman and Early Medieval times, either

as mercenaries of the Romans or as allies of the invading Germanic tribes – especially the Visigoths and Vandals – of the Migration Period.

6. The same applies to Lancelot's friend, *Galehault* (French Galiot, Italian Gaieotto), and to minor characters like *Gahalantyne, Galahalte, Galyhodyn* and *Galyhud,* found in Malory and elsewhere. The name of Gawain's sword, *Galatine,* plainly means 'the sword.' Considering the fact that an area in central Asia Minor is called *Galatia,* after Celtic invaders who settled there in the third century B.C., it becomes evident that even the very name *Celts (Galatae)* comes from the same root and would mean 'swordsmen'.

Further Reading

Davidson, Hilda R. Ellis. The *Sword in Anglo-Saxon England.* Oxford: Clarendon Press, 1962.

Grisward, Joel H. 'Le motif de l'épée jetée au lac: la mort d'Artur et la mort de Batradz.' *Romania* 90 (1969), pp. 289-340.

Reid, William. *Arms through the Ages.* London, 1976.

Twining, Lord. European *Regalia.* London: Batsford, 1967.

Vinaver, Eugène. 'King Arthur's Sword or the Making of a Romance.' *Bulletin of the John Rylands Library,* vol. 40, no. 2 (1958), pp. 513-526.

Originally published in *Avalon to Camelot* II No 4 (1987) pp. 28-34.

13

Ladies' Service and Ladies' Favours

The rescue of a damsel in distress – with or without a dragon-slaying – is generally considered one of the foremost duties of a knight, and chivalric literature, particularly its Arthurian branch, is full of examples of knights' services to ladies. Such service was often demanded, as well as performed, in extravagant ways. Though it is highly debatable how far harsh reality was mirrored in romance, enough real-life cases are documented to show that this ladies' service was an integral component of the perfect knight's education and career.

The earliest example of service in Arthurian literature is a rather ludicrous episode in – of all places – a Welsh saint's legend, the *Life of St Cadoc,* by Lifric of Llancarfan (*c.* 1075). In that part of the story leading up to the saint's birth, his future parents (a king of Glamorgan and the daughter of the king of Brecknock) are eloping with the princess's father hot on their heels. During their flight, they run into Arthur, Cei, and Bedwyr, who are playing at dice while relaxing on a hillside. In a display of emotion remarkably different from those that make up his later image, Arthur wants to snatch the girl away from her lover, but his companions remind him that their knightly custom is to aid a lady in distress. Thus, when the enraged father comes galloping over the hillcrest, he is confronted by the three champions defending his daughter's happiness, which helps temper the royal wrath rather quickly.

When Geoffrey of Monmouth, in his *Historia Regum Brittanniae*, describes Arthur's sumptuous Whitsuntide Feast, he tells us that ladies were wearing gowns matching the livery colours of their knights, and that no lady would accept the services of any knight unless he had proved himself three times in battle (IX, 13). This way, as Geoffrey puts it, 'the womenfolk became chaste and more virtuous and for their love the knights were ever more daring.'

In the first true Arthurian romance, Chrétien de Troyes' *Erec et Enide* (*c.* 1170), it is told how, in the adventures of the White Stag and of the Sparrowhawk, knights are willing to fight to the death to uphold their ladies' claims of surpassing beauty. Ladies, on the other hand, as shown by the long-suffering Enide, were ready for considerable sacrifices, too. In striking contrast to this, we find in Chrétien's *Lancelot* (*c.* 1180) an example of the extravagant standards of service expected by a lady, which were to dominate courtly literature for centuries. This is Queen Guinevere's capricious and shockingly ungrateful rejection of her rescuer Lancelot, who had braved mortal foes and magical obstacles, such as the lion-guarded Sword-bridge, but had failed by a hair's breadth when utter selflessness was demanded. Lancelot had hesitated for mere seconds before mounting the pillory cart, which during his pursuit of the abducted queen was his only available means of transportation. This hesitation to sacrifice his personal honour, an otherwise indispensable element of knightly virtue, was accepted as justification for the queen's scorn. It is significant that Chrétien found it necessary to inform his audience that the material for *Lancelot* was supplied by the lady who commissioned the work, the Countess Marie de Champagne, daughter of Eleanor of Aquitaine, Queen of England.

Eleanor was the daughter of William IX the Open-handed, Duke of Aquitaine, himself a gifted poet credited with being the founder of the courtly civilization represented by the literature of the troubadours, which celebrated ladies' service and the enjoyments of love. Eleanor and her daughter Marie did more than anyone else for the propagation and elaboration of what became known as courtly love (though the 'courts of love' attributed to them seem to be a romantic fiction). However, a clerk at Countess Marie's court, Andreas Capellanus, wrote a handbook of love, *De arte honeste amandi,* an adaptation of Ovid's *Ars amandi,* in which the correct relationship between a knight and his adored lady is codified and exemplified in detail.

The class culture of chivalry was an international phenomenon; a French *Chevalier* would have had much more in common with an English knight or a German *Ritter,* in spite of the language barriers, than with a burgher from the next town, let alone a peasant in one of his own villages. The German troubadours were called *Minnesinger,* pointing clearly to the supreme subject of their poetry (Middle High German *minne* = love). The songs of 138 *Minnesingers* (out of more than 300 known by name) are collected in the *Manesse Codex* (named after its compiler, the knight Rüdiger Manesse of Zürich (*c.* 1320), now in the library of Heidelberg University. Every *Minnesinger* in the codex is portrayed in a full-page miniature; the codex thus comprises a goldmine of information about costume, armour, games and pastimes, and practically all other aspects of everyday medieval life. Conspicuously frequent are scenes related to falconry; the falcon, who returns to his master's – or mistress's – fist compelled by affection, was a favourite symbol in German medieval love poetry.

It was customary that a boy aspiring to knighthood was sent for his education to the household of a great noble, usually his father's feudal overlord (this was also a convenient way to ensure the father's unswerving loyalty). Since he would first be a page boy, to be trained in the finer points of civilized life, he would be under the tutelage of the lady of the castle, and perhaps her grown-up daughters. Under these circumstances, it was easy for such a boy to develop an affection for sometimes only slightly older, usually married women of a social standing higher than his own.

One of the outstanding champions of courtly love was the Austrian knight, Herr Ulrich von Liechtenstein (*c.* 1200-1276), who won fame for himself by his *Artusfahrt* of 1227, a quest of knight-errantry in Arthurian disguise, complete with tournaments and Round Table banquets, in which he wended his merry way through Lombardy, Carinthia, Styria, Austria, and Bohemia. In his miniature from the Manesse Codex, Ulrich is shown in full tournament attire, his horse caparisoned in green (the colour of *minne)* and with Lady Love as his helmet crest; she holds an arrow and a flaming torch, indicating love's pains and burning desire.

Ulrich also wrote an autobiography, *Frauendienst* (ladies' service), a main source on the subject, describing in detail the rituals (and follies) of courtly love in real life, which sometimes seems more extravagant than the romances. Already, at age twelve, as page at the court of the duke of Austria, he fell in (fashionably) hopeless love with his lady, the Duchess Agnes. When in summertime he picked a bunch of wildflowers for her, he almost swooned when her fingers touched the stems where he had held them only moments before. Her lily-white hands held such a fascination for him that he secreted away her finger bowl after dinner, and drank the water she had rinsed her fingers in. When he was dubbed a knight, he dared to declare his devotion; not openly, of course, because Rule VI in Andreas Capellanus' handbook of love demands extreme secrecy in declaring one's love.

Portrait of Ulrich von Liechtenstein from the Manesse Codex, the most comprehensive source of Middle High German *Minnesang* poetry, produced in Zurich *c.* 1304. (Public domain)

Ulrich let his lady know through his cousin, who happened to be one of the duchess's ladies-in-waiting. Unfortunately, the lady not only rejected him (at least temporarily, as was part of the game), but also made a remark about his all-too-thick lower lip, which was duly reported to him by his concerned cousin. Ulrich promptly went to a famous surgeon in Graz, who cut the offending lip down to a hopefully more pleasing size. In tilt and joust Ulrich broke scores of lances for the honour of his lady, but to no avail; only when in one tournament he got one of his fingers badly mangled, the cold heart of *la belle dame sanz merci* warmed somewhat in pity. However, as soon as the finger was well again, she was as unapproachable as ever. To get her attention back, Ulrich had the finger cut off, put it in a pretty box of worked gold, and sent it to her together with one of his more glowing poems.

Though this extreme demonstration of devotion failed (not surprising for us with 20th-century hindsight, remembering Van Gogh's ear), Herr Ulrich had at least the consolation that the lady read the poem and kept the box.

Another *Minnesinger,* Duke Heinrich von Breslau, is portrayed in the Manesse Codex as receiving a wreath of flowers as a tournament prize from the hand of one of the ladies on the balcony. Duke Heinrich's dappled steed has caparisons patterned lozengy of gold and green; the golden fields bear his heraldic device, a black eagle with a silver crescent on its breast, while the green lozenges are embroidered with letters spelling out AMOR. The eagle in his shield has fastened to its wing a fluttering red ribbon, doubtlessly a token given to him by a lady – and judging from the looks being exchanged on the balcony, it was not the one who hands him the wreath!

Duke Heinrich's ribbon is one of the earliest representations of a lady's 'favour'; in literature, of course, many such love tokens are mentioned from the times of Queen Eleanor onwards. These favours usually were items of personal attire, such as a veil or a hair ribbon, that the knight could tie around his arm, thus 'carrying his heart on his sleeve'; It also could be the sleeve from the lady's gown, such as Princess Obilot gave to Gawain in Wolfram von Eschenbach's *Parzival,* or the Fair Maid of Astolat gave to Sir Lancelot. A sleeve, torn off in a fine show of spontaneity and leaving the damsel's arm deliciously bare (medieval costume included detachable sleeves) was of course one of the sexier items, as was a garter (the most prestigious order of chivalry, the Order of the Garter, owes its origin precisely to such an occasion – HONI SOIT QUI MAL Y PENSE).

Sometimes rival beauties might get carried away in their understandable desire to outstrip each other, to a degree that scandalized duennas or masters of ceremony, who had to intervene. One of the more sublimely obvious ways of bestowing such a signal token was to let the knight wear his lady's shift over his armour (in this case it would have to be delivered beforehand); after the tournament she would wear it again with its rents and tatters showing his prowess.

This cult of ladies was naturally deeply interlinked with the cult of the greatest lady of them all, Our Lady, the Virgin Mary. Already in the earliest Arthurian sources, in Nennius' *Historia Brittonum* (*c.* 800) and Geoffrey's *Historia Regum Britanniae,* King Arthur is described as wearing as his emblem an image of the Virgin Mary. Nennius mentions it as carried on his shoulder' (probably, as discussed earlier, a scribal error for 'on his shield' in a Welsh source, where *ysgwid* = 'shoulder', *ysgwit* = 'shield'); Geoffrey has it painted on the inside of Arthur's shield, 'that many a time and oft did he call her back unto his memory.' In the same way Sir Gawain bears a picture of the Virgin on the inside of his shield when he sets out to meet the Green Knight, 'so that when he beheld her, his heart did not fail.' On the other hand, we find that Erec, in Hartmann von Aue's German retelling of Chrétien's *Erec et Enide,* has a shield with 'a woman' on the inside in the corner right before his face, when he braces the shield in fighting position; in this case, the picture is not a sacred icon, but an image for secular *minne* devotion.

An actual shield with such a *minne* scene has survived in the Cathedral of Marburg, where it was hanging above the tomb of Landgrave Konrad of Thuringia (died 1241). On its front, it bears the landgrave's arms: *Azure, a lion barry argent and gules,* but on its inside is painted a knight in the Thuringian colours (presumably Konrad himself) kneeling before a lady. The court of Thuringia, under Konrad's father, Landgrave Hermann, was the most important German centre of courtly culture (best known from Richard Wagner's *Tannhäuser),* second only to the court of Marie de Champagne. A late fifteenth-century tournament shield, probably from Burgundy and now in the British Museum, shows as its emblem a lady standing behind him, under a scroll inscribed: '*vous ou la mort*'. This shield was presumably made for a Round Table tournament because designs like this are mentioned as carried by Sir Lancelot and Sir Tristram when they wanted to joust incognito.

Tournaments were the prime occasion where a knight could show off his prowess as well as his devotion to his lady. As an enhancement of the pageantry surrounding it, a Queen of Beauty might be chosen, sometimes after heated preliminary battles between the champions of the rival claimants; as a special spectacular, a Storming of the Castle of Love could be staged. These castles were structures erected right on the tournament field or wheeled in like a parade float; they were garrisoned by bevies of beauties, who defended it from the attack of amorous knights with weapons of *courteoisie,* such as baskets of flowers instead of slingstones, and rosewater instead of boiling pitch. The assault troops in their turn shot long-stemmed roses instead of arrows, and brandished flowering branches in place of swords and lances.

After an appropriate exchange of missiles and possibly hand-to-hand combat the garrison was expected to surrender, to be ransomed with kisses, or 'favours'. On one occasion, at a tournament held in 1214 in Treviso, North Italy, the garrison held out stubbornly and refused to capitulate until a group of Venetian knights among the assault forces exchanged their flower missiles for gold ducats. This wonder-weapon broke the resistance immediately, but the rest of the besiegers felt cheated; in particular the contingent from Padua, who started a brawl that eventually led to a real war with real sieges.

In general, though, these joyous occasions remained under control, not the least because of the civilizing influence of the ladies present. At a formal tournament, incidentally, it was the ladies who judged whether the applicants qualified in chivalry. The prizes fought for were usually of symbolic rather than great monetary value: a ring, a wreath of flowers, or quite spiritually, a kiss from the Queen of Beauty. A 'favour', however, could also on occasion be taken quite literally. In 1281, a tournament was held in Magdeburg, complete with Round Table, a 'Gral,' and a 'Dame Feie', a poor but beautiful girl who was willing to give her hand to the victorious champion. Fortunately for her, this was a rich patrician from Goslar, who was already married, and generously gave her a handsome sum as dowry that she might marry her true love.

Select Bibliography

Andreas Capellanus. *The Art of Courtly Love.* Translated by John Jay Parry. New York: F. Ungar, 1941.

Barber, Richard W. *The Reign of Chivalry.* New York: St. Martin's Press, 1980.

Loomis, Roger S. 'Arthurian Influence on Sports and Spectacle', in *Arthurian Literature in the Middle Ages*. Oxford: Clarendon Press, 1959, pp. 553-559.

Rudorff, Raymond. *Knights and the Age of Chivalry*. New York: Viking Press, 1974.

Schultz, Alwin. *Das höfische Leben zur Zeit der Minnesinger*. Leipzig: S. Hirzel,1889.

Warre Cornish, Francis. Chivalry; London, S. Sonnenschein & Co.; New York, Macmillan & Co., 1901.

Originally published in *Avalon to Camelot* I, no. 4 (Summer 1984, pp. 31-3.

14

Arthurian Animals

Of Cats and Dogs, Horses and Barking Beasts

Among the earliest pictorial representations of King Arthur to survive is a strange figural scene laid out in the mosaic floor of the cathedral of Otranto, at the very heel of the boot of Italy.[1]

This floor mosaic is a sprawling composition, extending for more than two hundred feet through the entire length of the nave, into the transepts and around the cathedral's apse. As a dedication inscription right at the entrance indicates, this work was created by the Presbyter Pantaleon, on the orders of Archbishop Jonathan, in 1165. The complicated iconographical programme of the mosaic is arranged around a huge Tree of Life, picturing Biblical scenes, such as Adam and Eve in Paradise, the Tower of Babel, Noah's Ark, Samson and the Lion, Jonah and the Whale, and assorted mythological subjects. These are not only taken from pagan classical mythology, such as shown by a representation of Diana the Huntress, but also from pseudo-classical traditions, as in the scene of the griffin flight of Alexander the Great, and – even more significantly – also from medieval legends. There is at least one scene showing King Arthur, though two others might be also episodes from the Matter of Britain. These rambling Biblical and mythological scenes are interspersed with series of medallions representing the Labours of the Months and the symbols of the Zodiac, more Biblical personages, and an entire Bestiary of animals, real, imaginary and whimsical – among the latter is an ass playing the harp and what is probably the earliest representation of Puss-in-Boots.

Between the Expulsion from the Garden of Eden and the Story of Cain and Abel, there is a crowned figure holding a ball-topped club or sceptre and riding a horned animal. This rider is clearly identified by an accompanying inscription: REX ARTVRVS. Next to this inscription is a naked man looking down on Arthur with hands raised in an imploring gesture. Confronting Arthur is a large spotted feline, and directly below the hind feet of Arthur's mount is a secondary scene showing the feline mauling a man lying on the ground. This double scene is believed to represent the Fight with the Chapalu or Palug's Cat. (Fig. 1)

The Otranto mosaic was created about thirty years after Geoffrey of Monmouth's bestseller, which presented King Arthur to a delighted broader public, and about fifty years after the very first representation of ARTVS DE BRETANIA in the famous relief of the liberation of WINLOGEE (Guinevere) on one of the archivolts of Modena Cathedral.

Fig. 1: King Arthur battling the monster cat Cath Palug/ Chapalu. Floor mosaic in Otranto Cathedral, Italy, dated 1165.

Interestingly, the Modena relief, executed some twenty years *before* the publication of Geoffrey's 'History', has as its subject already the abduction episode, one of the basic elements of the Arthurian legend, but the later Otranto mosaic shows a motif outside of the mainstream of Arthurian traditions.

The monstrous cat to be fought by a champion appears in Poem XXXI of the *Black Book of Caermarthen*, a collection of Welsh poetry compiled between 1154 and 1189, now one of the treasures of the National Library of Wales, at Aberystwyth. In this poem, which by believers in Welsh oral traditions is thought to have its origin in the sixth century rather than the twelfth, it is told that 'Cai the Pair went to Mon (Anglesey) to kill lions; his shield was polished against Cath Palug,' referring to what was apparently a major and well known adventure.[2]

The monstrous cat – though not directly connected with Arthur – is also to be found in the much-quoted triad of the Three Powerful Swineherds, recorded in the famous compilation by Edward Williams (Iolo Morganwg), that was first published in 1801, but claimed to be part of ancient Welsh bardic lore. In this triad is mentioned – somewhat cryptically, because of the terseness of the text – that a kitten, deposited at Maen Du in Arvon by the sow of Dallwaran Dalben, was thrown into the Menai by the sow's swineherd Coll, son of Collvrewi, 'and this was the glossy smooth cat that became a molestation to the Isle of Anglesea.'[3]

By contrast, in the *Livre d'Artus* of the *Vulgate* cycle there is an episode in which Arthur has to fight the 'Chapalu of Losan' (present-day Lausanne at the Lake of Geneva in Switzerland), when he is passing through Savoy on his campaign against Rome. Of this Chapalu we learn that four years earlier a fisherman throwing out his nets on Ascension Day made a vow to dedicate his first catch to the Lord. However, when he caught a surpassingly beautiful fish, he changed his mind, and vowed his second catch instead. Again he caught a prize, and changed his vow to his third catch.

This time he caught a black kitten, which he took home to rid his hovel of the mice and rats infesting it. The kitten, however, grew to a monstrous size, ate the fisherman and his family, and terrorized the entire countryside for the years to come. Arthur, accompanied by Merlin, sought out the Chapalu in its mountain lair. In a desperate fight Arthur killed the monster, but only when he managed to hack off its paws, after its claws lodged fast in his shield.[4] The site of the fight was renamed by Arthur from Mont du Lac to Mont du Chat.

It seems even that there existed a divergent tradition about Arthur's death, in which he would have met his end not at Camlann, but in the fight with the Chapalu. In a Latin elegy by Henricus Septimellensis, *c.* 1193, it is said that Arthur fought and killed a monstrous beast, but did not come back from the fight, and the Bretons therefore still hope for his return. Also, in Andre de Courtance's *Romanz des Francais*, composed before 1203, reference is made to stories current among the French, telling that Arthur was killed by the Cat 'Capalu', and the same story is retold by the Provencal troubadour Pèire Cardenal.[5]

Obscure as this motif of the fight with the monstrous cat is, it has a way of cropping up in strange places. In the Spanish fourteenth-century romance of chivalry, *The Knight Zifar*, it is mentioned as one of the more memorable deeds of King Arthur that he fought with *el Gato Paul*, 'Paul the Cat'![6] A very faint echo of this tale seems to have been strangely distorted into an Italian ballad of the late thirteenth century that has a wandering minstrel by name of Gatto Lupesco encountering two knights from 'Bretangna' on their way back from Sicily, where they were on a quest to find out whether 'lo re Artù' was truly staying in 'Mongibello' (Mount Etna) waiting for his return to England one day. The minstrel's name, Gatto Lupesco, translates as 'Wolfish Cat'.[7]

The spotted cat in the Otranto mosaic looks rather like a leopard and one of the explanations offered for the Cat of Anglesea is that it might actually have been a leopard, perhaps the descendant of escapees from a former Roman menagerie. On the other hand, it is possible that the entire story originated from a misinterpretation of the Welsh word *cath*, 'battle' as 'cat' and thus the Cath Palug might have been just another a battle with a human adversary by name of Palug.[8]

As already mentioned, among the profusion of figural scenes in the Otranto mosaic there are two more that could be illustrations of Arthurian motifs. Among the nave scenes is one showing the construction of a battlemented building; this is usually interpreted as the story of the Tower of Babel. However, prominently below this building scene there are two fighting dragons, one swallowing the other. This looks suspiciously as if this tower-construction scene might also double as an illustration of the episode of Vortigern's castle built on top of the cave with the two dragons, which led to the discovery of Merlin's powers. Ever since Geoffrey's ingenious publication, Merlin was highly regarded for his prophecies, which acquired almost the status of Holy Writ, and therefore such an alternative meaning of the tower scene is not to be rejected out of hand. This interpretation becomes even more likely, if the figure of a naked man in the scene of 'Rex Artvrvs' and the cat would be Merlin in his shape of a wildman.

The apse mosaics illustrate the stories of Samson and of Jonah, but right in the centre between these two pictorial complexes is a boar hunt, with a boar being pursued by hounds and speared by a huntsman on horseback. Here, too, it is very tempting to see this as the representation of another early exploit of Arthur's, the Hunt of the boar Trwch Troynt, as reported by Nennius. In the Mabinogion's 'Culhwch and Olwen' this story is interwoven with the hunt of another mighty boar, Ysgithyrwyn.

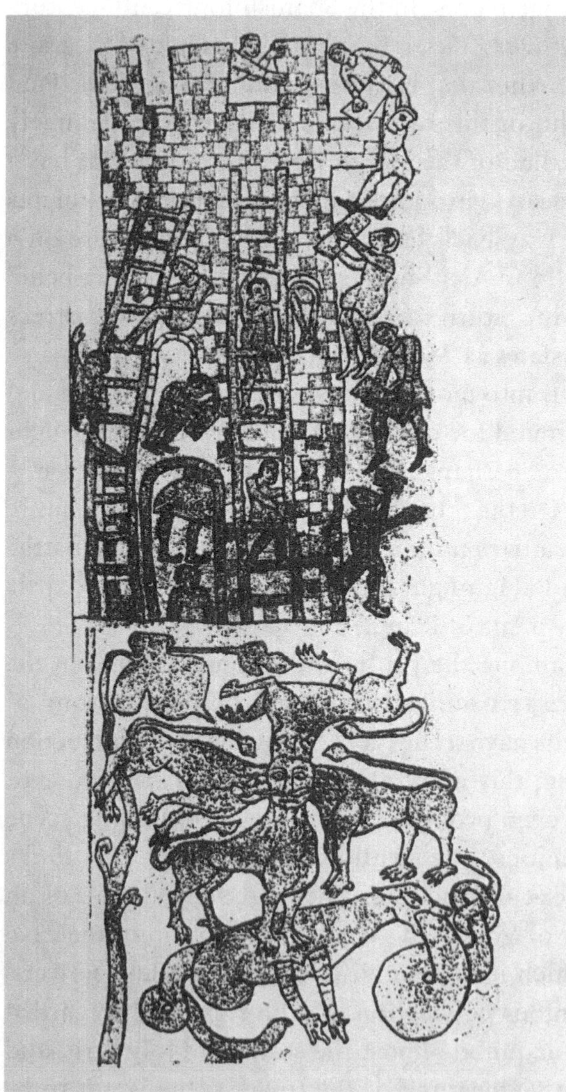

Fig. 2: The Tower of Babel or the Castle of Vortigern? At the bottom register the fighting Dragons and the Lion of Justice from Merlin's Prophecies? Floor mosaic in Otranto Cathedral, Italy, dated 1165.

Fig. 3: Boar Hunt, possibly the hunt of the boar Trwch Troynt, with Arthur's dog, Cabal. Floor mosaic in the apse of Otranto Cathedral, Italy.

As told in Nennius's 'mirabilia' (Wonders: chapter 73), there was

> ... a marvellous thing in the region which is called Buelt. There is at that place a pile of stones and one stone placed over and above this heap with the footprint of a dog on it. When he was hunting the boar Troynt, Cabal, who was the dog of Arthur the soldier, impressed his footprint on the stone, and Arthur afterwards gathered together a pile of stones under the one on which was the footprint of his dog, and it is called Carn Cabal. And men come and carry the stone away in their hands for the space of a day and a night, and on the next day it is found back on its pile.[9]

The dog Cabal does not play any role in later Arthurian romances; it is only in works by modern authors (Tennyson, Rosemary Sutcliff, Mary Stewart, Victor Canning) that he makes a re-appearance.

A dog's footprint is a highly unusual feature in European folklore; peculiar hollows or other markings on rocks are more likely to be interpreted as hoof prints of horses, such as the Rosstrappe in the Hartz Mountains, or the hoof prints attributed to the daring escape of a captive robber knight on the curtain wall of the citadel at Nürnberg. The name of Arthur's dog, *Cabal*, 'horse', might indicate that the print on the stone topping Cam Cabal was a horse's hoof print before it became called a dog's footprint. In 'Culhwch and Olwen' the boar is brought to bay by

Arthur's mare *Llamrei* ('Swiftpace'), though she is ridden not by Arthur, but by Cadw of Prydein.[10] The boar is then killed by 'Cafall, Arthur's own dog', though it had been prophesied that the kill should be done by other dogs. Interestingly, the three huntsmen, Bwlch, Cyfwlch and Syfwlch, sons of Cilydd Cyfwlch, grandsons of Cleddyf Difwlch, whose participation was an essential pre-condition for the hunting of the boar Trwch Troynt, had three dogs, Glas, Glesig and Gleisad, and three horses, named Call, Cuall and Cafall.

Strangely, Arthur did not ride his own horse, the mare Llamrei, in the boar hunt, though this was the one steed able to catch up with the hunted boar, but instead borrowed *Gwyn Dhu*, the horse of Gweddw, for the hunt.

The horned animal that is Arthur's mount in the Otranto mosaic has been the subject of much speculation. In most descriptions of the mosaic it is called a goat, though all authors have had to admit their inability to explain why Arthur was given such an unusual steed. The present shape of the pointed horns is due to a nineteenth-century restoration, when a large missing section of the mosaic containing the right arm and part of Arthur's head (his crown is also part of this restoration; originally he was not crowned) had to be recreated. It is possible that these horns were originally just the reins of the riding animal. Whether this creature was meant to be a horse (though admittedly very poorly drawn) is a debatable point. Possibly it was a horned horse, under the influence of the legends surrounding Alexander the Great, who is also represented in the Otranto mosaic, as mentioned earlier. Because of his name, *Bucephalos*, 'Bull-head', Alexander's famous war steed was credited with having horns in medieval legend.[11]

In a most intriguing study, *The Black Horsemen: English Inns and King Arthur* (1971), S. G. Wildman pointed out that the distribution of inns with the name 'The Black Horse' coincides with the border line between sixth-century Saxon and British areas of settlement.[12] (See Chapter 20.) Since the White Horse was a totem animal of the Saxons (it is still the coat-of-arms of Hanover and Lower Saxony, as well as Kent), Wildman suggests that the Black Horse was to be identified with the British fighting under Arthur.

It seems that the only one among modern authors who made any use of this interesting theory was Andre Norton in her *Merlin's Mirror* (1975), where Arthur's cavalry is called the Black Horsemen of the Border. In this context she even refers to the Saxon worship of the White Horse.

On the other hand, most modern retellings of the Arthurian legend insist on a regally white horse for their Arthurs. For instance, Rosemary Sutcliff in her landmark novel, *Sword at Sunset* (1963), has her Artos the Bear riding to battle on two white stallions, appropriately named Signus the Swan and Gray Falcon, though his very first steed, and the ancestor of his military stud farm, is The Black One. In Mary Stewart's *The Hollow Hills* (1973) Arthur repeatedly points out that his colour was white: white shield, white banner, and white horse.[13] Also, Victor Canning's Arturo/Arto the Bear, in *The Immortal Wound* (1978), rides The White One. The colour of Arthur's mare Llamrei in 'Culhwch and Olwen' is not mentioned, but the name of his borrowed steed, Gwyn Dhu, is usually translated as 'Dunmane' (or possibly Black Gwyn, Ed). The only other time that the name of Arthur's horse is mentioned in a medieval source seems to be in Chrétien de Troyes's *Erec et Enide* (*c.* 1170). There the horse's name is Aubagu. Chrétien pays great attention to horses, and particularly their colours, but he does not point out Aubagu's colour, though he mentions him alongside Guinevere's white Norwegian palfrey. However, since the name Aubagu is probably derived from the French word for 'dawn', *aube*, and the related term, *cheval aubere*, actually means 'a dun or a flea-bitten grey horse', the name itself would be indicative of the horse's colour. By contrast, in the English *Alliterative Morte Arthure* (*c.* 1360), Arthur's 'broun' or 'baye stede' is repeatedly mentioned, but not named.[14]

Among the major Arthurian heroes with famous horses of specific colours there is Gawain with his white Gringolet (significantly captured from a Saxon in some sources) as well as Lancelot with his 'snow-white steed' given to him by the Lady of the Lake, Parzival with his red horse as Red Knight, and of course Sir Bertilak de Hautdesert, the Green Knight, with his uncanny 'grene horse grete'.

Malory's *Morte d'Arthur* is surprisingly devoid of imaginary or mythical creatures. There are no dragons or unicorns, no griffins nor manticores; the only truly unreal monster in it is the Beste Glatissant or Questing Beast that appears in his 'Book of Sir Tristram of Lyonesse'. It is described as

> ... in shap lyke a serpentis hede and a body lyke a lybud (leopard), buttokked lyke a lyon and footed lyke a harte. And in hys body there was such a noyse as hit had bene twenty couple of houndys guestynge, and such noyse that beste made wheresomever he wente.

This strange animal is pursued first by King Pellinore, and then by Sir Palomydes, floating in and out of the course of events like a dream, stopping only once in a while to drink from a well in the forest. This also is the only time, when the 'questing' or baying in its belly would be stilled.[15]

Its name Questing Beast is a direct translation of the French *Bête glatissant* (from *glati*, 'to screech' and/or *glapir*, 'to yelp'), but by choosing the huntsman's term 'questing' for the baying of the pack of hounds in pursuit of their prey Malory skilfully creates a double meaning, also indicating the quest of the Beast's pursuers, King Pellinore and Sir Palomydes.

The Beast's composite nature is rather reminiscent of the description of 'The proprieties of a good Grehounde' in *The Book of Saint Albans*, by Dame Juliana Berners, and printed by Wynkyn de Worde, 1496: 'A grehounde sholde be heeded lyke a snake: and nekkyd lyke a drake: fotyd lyke a catte; tayllyd lyke a ratte; syded lyke a teme (an ox-yoke); and chynyd lyke a beme (a beam of timber).'

The Beast's origin is obscure. In Malory's Book I King Pellinore pursues it; in later books – after Pellinore's death – by Sir Palomydes. Palomydes/Palamede is its pursuer in French romances, while in Spanish and Italian stories Perceval hunts it. Perceval's connection with the Questing Beast might provide a clue as to the Beast's possible provenance. In the thirteenth-century Grail epic, *Der Jungere Titurel* by Albrecht von Scharfenberg, a continuation of Wolfram von Eschenbach's *Parzival*, there is mentioned a celebrated shirt of mail that had its rings tempered to the hardness of adamant in the blood of the animal *Tigris* (so named, because it escaped from Paradise and is the swiftest of animals, the same as the river Tigris that comes out of Paradise is the swiftest of rivers).[16] The animal Tigris is so swift that according to Albrecht only princes with the help of leopards can hunt it. This mail shirt was a gift to Parzival's father by the King of Baghdad/Babylon.

Interestingly, the Bête Glatissant was pursued by Perceval's father, Pellinore, King of Listenois. Was it the pun on 'listening to the noise' of the Questing Beast that proved irresistible to Malory, when he assigned Pellinore to the quest? In any case, in connection with the Questing Beast's possible ancestor, the animal Tigris, it could be significant that leopards were clan badges of Pellinore's family. They were borne as shield devices and crests by Pellinore's own brother, Lamorat, as well as by two of Pellinore's sons, Perceval's younger brothers, Agloval and Lamorat de

Galles, in fifteenth-century rolls of arms. Also, leopards were the crest and shield supporters in the arms of Sir Palomydes, who was the son of the King of Babylon.[17]

Notes

1. Roger S. Loomis and Laura H. Loomis *Arthurian Legends in Medieval Art*, London/New York, 1938; figs. 9, 9a; Walter Haug *Das Mosaik von Otranto*, Wiesbaden, 1977
2. Kenneth Hurlstone Jackson 'Arthur in Early Welsh Verse', in *Arthurian Literature in the Middle Ages*, Oxford, 1959; Chapter 2 p.14. E. K. Chambers *Arthur of Britain*, New York, 1967; p. 66: 'Worthy Kei went to Mona to destroy lions. His shield was small against Palug's Cat.' John Bollard 'Arthur in the Early Welsh Tradition', chapter II in the anthology *The Romance of Arthur*, New York, 1984; pp. 19-20: 'Cei the Pair went to Anglesey to destroy lions; his shield was small against the Clawing Cat.'
3. Malcolm Smith: *The Triads of Britain; compiled by Iolo Morganwg*, London, 1977; p. 65, no. 101. (see also *The Triodd Ynys Prydein* by Rachel Bromwich etc. Ed).
4. The detail of the Cat's claws being cut off, when stuck fast in Arthur's shield, parallels Gawain's fight with the Lion in Wolfram's *Parzival*.
5. W. Haug. *Das Mosaik von Otranto*; p. 31 ff.
6. Charles L. Nelson. *The Book of the Knight Zifar; A Translation of El Libro del Cavaliero Zifar*, Louisville, Univ. Press of Kentucky, 1983; series: Studies in Romance Languages: 27; chapter 105, p. 131
7. Edmund Gardner *The Arthurian Legend in Italian Literature*, London/New York, 1930; pp. 14-15
8. The tenth-century *Annales Cambriae*, in a prefixed computus, mention 'a discordia between Guitolinus and Ambrosius, which is Guoloppum, that is Cathguoloph'. Chambers, in *Arthur of Britain*, p. 16, is tempted to interpret this as a reference to a battle at Wallop in Hampshire. 'Cathguoloph' could also be easily transformed into 'Cath Palug' by scribal error.
9. John Morris. *Nennius: Arthurian Period Sources 8*, London, 1980: p. 42
10. Idris Llewellyn Foster. 'Culhwch and Olwen and Rhonabwy's Dream', Chapter 4 in *Arthurian Literature in the Middle Ages*, Oxford,

1959; p. 31 ff. Gwyn Jones and Thomas Jones, *The Mabinogion*, Rhonabwy's Dream BV, 1982; p. 115

11. The leaders of the first Saxons invited by Vortigern were Hengist ('Stallion') and Horsa. The Haestinga clan settling at Hastings probably derived their name from the Scandinavian haest = 'horse'.
12. S. G. Wildman, *The Black Horsemen: English Inns and King Arthur*, London, 1971; pp. 149, 154. Wildman admits that he knows only of one legend where the colours of the horses of Arthur's knights are mentioned, the Sleepers in Eildon Hill, reported by Sir Walter Scott, but there they are black.
13. David Nicolle, *Arthur and the Anglo-Saxon Wars*, London, 1987, series: Osprey Men-at-Arms, no. 154. The illustrations by Angus MacBride on the cover and on pl. C, a 'Romano-British cavalryman' are suggestive of Arthur himself, on a white horse, with a white shield, possibly inspired by this quote in the *Hollow Hills*.
14. Mary Hamel *Morte Arthure: A Critical Edition,* New York, 1984 pp. 134-135, v. 915, 918
15. Phyllis Ann Karr: *The King Arthur Companion*, Reston, VA, 1983, pp. 107-108. Reprinted by Chaosium Inc., 2019
16. Werner Wolff. *Albrecht von Scharfenberg: Der Jungere Titurel, Bern,* 1952; series: Altdeutsche Ubungstexte, 14; v. 1675-1686
17. Michel Pastoureau *Armorial des Chevaliers de la Table Ronde*, Paris, 1983; pp. 40, 81, 93

An earlier version of this essay was published under the title 'About Palug's Cat and the Mosaic of Otranto' in *Arthurian Interpretations* Vol 3., No. 2 (Spring, 1989) pp. 96-106. This version has been expanded and updated by the author.

15

Surviving Camlann

As is the case with practically all Arthurian 'facts' and sites, there is very little agreement about Arthur's last battle among the chroniclers and the poets dealing with the Matter of Britain. For the battle site, places as far apart as the river Camel in Cornwall and the Roman fort of Camboglanna on Hadrian's Wall have been suggested, and there is similar disagreement among Arthurian authors about who did survive the slaughter.

The first source that mentions the Battle of Camlann, the mid-tenth century *Annales Cambriae,* cryptically states that: 'Arthur and Medraut fell,' without explaining whether they were on the same side or were opponents, and nothing is said about any survivors (Brengle 7; Chambers 241).

Geoffrey of Monmouth in his *Historia Regum Britanniae* gives a more detailed account of the Battle at the River Camblam but lists only the most important casualties, 'with many thousands of the King's troops'. Constantine, the son of Cador Duke of Cornwall, to whom the mortally wounded Arthur hands his crown, was certainly alive to reign for four more years, but it is not clear at all whether he was actually fighting in the battle (Geoffrey xi.2).

On the final pages of his *Roman de Brut*, Master Wace says resignedly of the Battle at the Camel, over against the entrance to Cornwall, 'I neither know who lost, nor who gained that day. No man wists the name of overthrower or of overthrown. All alike are forgotten, the victor with him who died.' Though all of the knights of the Table Round perished, Arthur, 'wounded in his body to the death … caused him to be borne to Avalon for the searching of his hurts.' This could only mean that there were a few survivors, but 'all alike are forgotten' (Wace 113).

Layamon, in his *Brut,* is more specific; he tells us: 'There no more remained in the fight, of two hundred thousand men that there lay hewed in pieces, except Arthur the king alone, and two of his knights.' Arthur was 'wounded wondrously much' and was transported to Avalon 'to Argante the queen, an elf most fair' by a boat with two women, who took him aboard and departed with him. Before his departure he gives his kingdom to a lad of his kin, Constantine, Earl Cador of Cornwall's son. The two surviving knights remain nameless and are not mentioned again (Layamon 264).

According to Malory, at the end of the Battle of Salisbury Plain only the king himself, and two of his knights, Sir Bedivere and his brother, Lucan the Butler, were left alive on Arthur's side, while Mordred was standing all alone and 'lenyd vpon his swerde emong a grete hepe of deed men'. Against the advice of Sir Lucan, who himself was 'greuously wounded in many places', Arthur attacks and kills Mordred, but receives a mortal wound from his son's hand. Bedivere and Lucan manage to carry their lord from the battlefield to a nearby chapel 'not ferre from the seesyde', but when pillagers appear robbing the slain, Lucan suggests they move the king to safety in some town. In helping Bedivere to lift Arthur, one of Lucan's ignored wounds opens, and 'therwyth the noble knyghtes herte braste' (Malory 590).

There follows one of the best-known episodes of *Le Morte d'Arthur,* when Bedivere reluctantly throws Excalibur into the water, and Arthur is taken away to the Vale of Avalon in the barge of the three queens and the Lady of the Lake. The lone survivor Bedivere is left behind to cry out in anguish: 'A, my lord Arthur, what shal become of me, now ye goo from me and leue me here allone emong myn enemyes?' However, next morning he finds a hermit praying in a chapel with a 'tombe was newe grauen,' and is told that at midnight a group of ladies came with a dead man and asked him to bury the corpse. Bedivere now believes that this was king Arthur, and he becomes a hermit himself to care for tomb and chapel and to pray for King Arthur (Malory XXI, 5-6).

By contrast, in the *Vulgate Cycle* it is not Bedivere but Sir Griflet who is the last knight left alive at Arthur's side and who is the one to throw Excalibur into the lake *(Death* 223-24). Griflet le Fils de Do (sometimes transformed into Le Fise de Dieu) was a son of the Duke of Carduel, and in some sources is called a cousin of Lucan's (Pastoreau 71; no. 85), though his relationship to Bedivere is left open. According to Malory, Griflet came to the court at Carlion shortly after the king's reunion with his mother, Igraine. He was the squire of the good knight, Sir Mylis, who had been slain by Pellinore, the Knight of the Fountain.

Griflet asked to be dubbed knight in order to avenge his master's death. Arthur grants him his wish but makes him promise that he would joust only one course and, 'whether it falle ye be on foote or on horsbak, that ryght to ye shal come ageyne vnto me withoute makynge ony more debate.' Severely wounded, Griflet obediently returns and thus Arthur himself rides off to face the Knight of the Fountain. In this fight, Arthur's sword is broken and he himself rescued only by Merlin's 'enchauntement to the knyghte that he felle to the erthe in a gret hepe'. As a replacement for the broken sword, Merlin helps Arthur to get a new sword, called Excalibur, from the Lady of the Lake (Malory I, 21-25).

Strangely enough, though Griflet is the indirect reason for Arthur obtaining the Sword from the Lake, his role of returning it again to the waters is taken away from him by Malory and given to Bedivere, Arthur's oldest follower, who in other sources, for instance in Geoffrey of Monmouth's *History* (x.9), is slain much earlier in the Battle of Saussy during Arthur's campaign in Gaul. However, the second-to-last survivor in the *Vulgate Death of King Arthur* is Lucan the Butler, brother to Bedivere. The dying Arthur embraces Lucan in farewell and in a spasm of pain presses him so hard that his heart burst inside him.[1]

In the *Mabinogion,* in the roll call of Arthur's companions in *Culhwch and Olwen* (Jones and Jones 102), we encounter Morfran son of Tegid ('no man placed his weapon in him at Camlan, so exceedingly ugly was he; all thought he was a devil helping. There was hair on him like the hair of a stag'), and Sandde Angel-face ('no one placed his spear in him at Camlan, so exceedingly fair was he; all thought he was an angel helping'), and Cynwyl the Saint ('one of the three men that escaped from Camlan. He was the last to part from Arthur, on Hengroen his horse').

Morfran son of Tegid is likely to be *li Lez Hardiz* (le Laid Hardi, the Ugly Brave), who is listed as the sixth-worthiest of Arthur's knights in the roll call in Chrétien de Troyes' *Erec et Enide,* right after *li Biax Coarz* (le Beau Couard = the Handsome Coward), who seems to be identical with Sandde Angel-face *(Erec* 1684-85; Pastoreau, 50, 80). Neither of them, however, appears as a survivor of the last battle in the French tradition. As far as the third survivor, Cynwyl the Saint, is concerned, he might have left a faint trace in Malory's *Morte d'Arthur* transformed into the hermit (the former archbishop of Canterbury), who buried in his chapel a corpse believed by Bedivere to be Arthur's.

In spite of their high ranking in Chrétien's roll call, neither the Ugly Brave nor the Handsome Coward has been made the hero of an epic of his own, and no special deeds are attached to their intriguing *noms de guerre*. Not even the real name of the Ugly Brave is recorded, though he is called a nephew of Sir Kay *(Durmart le Galois* 8468-77), and a cousin of Erec. By contrast, the Handsome Coward's name, Henor, is mentioned on occasion.

In the fictitious Arthurian heraldry of the fifteenth century le Beau Couard's coat-of-arms is a white horse with golden horseshoes in a black shield (Pastoreau 50, no. 29). Though the connections between Welsh and French Arthurian traditions are not very clear at best, this shield emblem of a white horse together with the name Henor is rather suggestive of Cynwyl's horse Hengroen ('Old hide'). At a time when horses were an indispensable part of everyday life, everybody was well aware that white horses are born dark and change to white with age.

Similarly, the shield supporters in the full arms of le Laid Hardi were two *femmes sauvages,* wildwomen covered with shaggy fur—an interesting parallel to the description of Morfran as being covered with hair like a stag! (Pastoreau 80, no.109).

Most of the modern writers, from Lord Tennyson to Rosemary Sutcliff, Mary Stewart, Catherine Christian, Thomas Berger, and Stephen R. Lawhead, follow Malory's lead and make Bedivere/Bedwyr the last survivor of Camlann. Mark Twain even quotes Malory verbatim and has Bedivere and Lucan the Butler still alive at the end of the battle (Twain XLII).[2]

Parke Godwin adds to Bedwyr a figure of his own invention, Dafydd the archer, while Joan Wolf lets Cai and Gawain survive besides Bedwyr. David Drake, Gil Kane and John Jakes make Lancelot the last survivor, but Gillian Bradshaw takes her clue from the *Mabinogion* and lets Sandde be the last of Arthur's men.

In an entirely different twist Peter Hanratty lets Mordred escape the slaughter. Percevale, who as a newly made knight was detailed as a courier and therefore did not participate in the fighting, takes it upon himself to become Mordred's nemesis; after having brought the mortally wounded Arthur out of the battle, Bedivere and Lucan perish in a nuclear holocaust Mordred unleashed with the help of Druidical secret science.

T. H. White nimbly sidesteps the Battle of Camlann itself and, as is his wont of underhandedly planting hidden meanings into innocent looking contexts, smoothly introduces Arthur's pageboy, Tom of Newbold Revel near Warwick, to be sent off by the king before the battle to keep him alive to tell the tale of Arthur's realm to future generations. In a similar way, Andre Norton lets a boy, Artos, son of Marius, fight bravely in the last battle and survive together with Marius, Gawain and another Roman-Briton, Sextus, to lay King Arthur to rest.

Notes

1. The original butler of Arthur's court was Bedivere, according to Geoffrey. Lucan, his brother, seems to have been invented as a substitute, when Bedivere was made Arthur's Master of the Horse (connétable) in the French tradition. Bedivere's role as a court official was always rather colourless compared to the admittedly controversial Kay the Seneschal. It did not help either that Bedivere/Bedoier/Bedwyr's name became confused with that of Bedwini/Baldwin the Bishop. Significantly, in the fictitious Arthurian heraldry of the fifteenth century Bedivere/Bedoier's coat-of-arms is: *Or, a gonfanon gules*. The *gonfanon,* a battle flag with three lappets, was derived from the Roman cavalry *vexillum,* a square flag mounted on the crossbar of a T-shaped staff. By the fifteenth century the *gonfanon* had gone out of military use and had become an ecclesiastical processional banner.
2. The quote from Malory is used as Clarence's newspaper report of the battle. In the final confrontation, the Battle of the Sand-Belt, as the post-script by Clarence indicates, there were no survivors except The Boss in enchanted sleep and his fifty-three doomed technicians.

Select Bibliography

Berger, Thomas. *Arthur Rex*. New York: Delacorte Press, 1979.

Bradshaw, Gillian. *In Winter's Shadow.* New York: Signet Books, 1982.

Brengle, Richard L. *Arthur, King of Britain.* New York: Meredith Publishing Company, 1964; 'Annales Cambriae,' Year [537].

Chambers, E. K. *Arthur of Britain*. New York: October House, 1967 (first ed. 1927); Records: V. 'Annales Cambriae,' An' xciii.

Chrétien de Troyes: Erec and Enide. Ed. and trans. Carleton W. Carroll, vol. 25, series A; New York: Garland Library of Medieval Literature, 1987.

Christian, Catherine. *The Pendragon.* New York: Alfred A. Knopf, 1979.

The Death of King Arthur. Trans. James Cable. Harmondsworth: Penguin Books, 1971.

Drake, David. *The Dragon Lord.* New York: TOR Books, 1979.

Geoffrey of Monmouth: *The History of the Kings of Britain.* Transl. Lewis Thorpe. Harmondsworth: Penguin Classics, 1984 (first ed. 1966).

Godwin, Parke. *Firelord.* New York: Bantam Books, 1982 (first ed. Doubleday, 1980).

Hanratty, Peter. *The Last Knight of Albion.* New York: Bluejay Books, 1986.

Kane, Gil and John Jakes. *Excalibur.* New York: The Pendragon Press, 1980.

Lawhead, Stephen L. *Arthur,* Westchester: Crossways Books, 1989.

Layamon's Brut: *Arthurian Chronicles.* Transl. Eugene Mason. London/New York: Everyman's Library, 1970 (first ed. 1912).

The Mabinogion. Transl. Gwynn Jones and Thomas Jones. London/New York: Everyman's Library, 1973 (first ed. 1949); Dragon's Dream, 1982.

Caxton's Malory: Le Morte Darthur (2 vols). Ed. James W. Spisak. Berkeley and Los Angeles: U of California, 1983.

Norton, Andre. *Dragon Magic.* New York: Ace Books, 1972.

Pastoreau, Michel. *Armorial des chevaliers de la table ronde.* Paris: Le Leopard d'or, 1983.

Stewart, Mary. *The Wicked Day.* New York: William Morrow, 1983.

Sutcliff, Rosemary. *Sword at Sunset.* New York: TOR Books, 1987 (first printed 1963).

Lord Tennyson, Alfred. *Idylls of the King.* Garden City: Dolphin Books, n.d. (first publ. 1859-1885).

Twain, Mark. A *Connecticut Yankee in King Arthur's Court* New York: Bantam Books, 1983 (first publ. 1889).

Wace's Brut: *Arthurian Chronicles.* Transl. Eugene Mason. London/New York: Everyman's Library, 1970 (first ed. 1912).

Originally published in *Quondam et Futurus.* Vol 3., Number 1., Spring, 1993, pp. 32-37.

16

A Crown Found and A Grail Tournament Held at the 'Castle of The Maiden'

In 1955 during excavations in the bombed-out historical centre of the city of Magdeburg, the broken pieces of three identical gilt pewter strips, each with three figural scenes in silhouetted relief (see above), were found in a refuse pit containing pottery and other artifacts datable to the second half of the 13th century. The find attracted considerable attention right from the beginning (Schramm 64-66; Friese 104-05) and was thoroughly examined in two essays by Ernst Nickel – alas, no relation of mine – the director of the Historical Research Centre Magdeburg (E. Nickel 1956, 239-243; 1960, 40-42). Because of their motifs of chivalry – a knight fighting a winged monster, a *Minneszene [Minne,* courtly love] with an embracing couple, and a joust before a turreted castle – Nickel suggested a possible connection between these *Zinnfigurenstreifen* (strips of pewter figurines) and a celebrated Arthurian tournament that had taken place at Magdeburg, the town whose name means 'Castle of the Maiden'.

A detailed description of this famous event has been handed down to us in Magdeburg's *Schöppenchronik* (Appendix, pp. 41-42), a collection of historical local records commissioned by the city's magistrates and compiled by the *Schöppenschreiber* (secretary of the jury court), Heinrich von Lammspringe, between 1360 and 1372 (Jänicke 7, 168-69).[1]

Magdeburg was one of the most important and wealthiest towns of medieval Germany; positioned at the single bridge across the Elbe River, it was the gate to the newly colonized lands east of the Elbe. Out of civic pride, the *kunstabelen,* an exclusive club among the 'richest burgher's sons' used to hold chivalric entertainments at Whitsuntide, such as the Roland,[2] the *schildekenbom, tabelrunde* and other games. 'The 'Roland' was a quintain tilt, the *schildekenbom* (tree of shields) a tree hung with the shields of the *kunsabelen* as defenders for the tournament; by touching his lance to one of these shields a 'comer' would formally challenge its owner to a joust. The *tabelrunde (*Round Table) event should be self-explanatory for Arthurians.

Probably in 1279,[3] these *jeunesses dorées* asked 'a learned man' among them, Brun (with the tell-tale nickname Artus!) von Schonebeck (Schröder 4-5), to compose a *vreidlich spel* (merry pageant) for the enhancement of that year's tournament. As invitations Brun-Artus wrote courtly letters in rhymes, which he sent to the equivalents of chambers of commerce at Goslar, Hildesheim, Brunswick, Quedlinburg, Halberstadt and other cities up to 70 miles away.[4] The response was enthusiastic, and the participants outdid each other in the splendour of their outfits. Those of Goslar came with fully caparisoned horses, those of Brunswick had horse trappings and surcoats all of green,[5] and most of the other towns had their teams arrayed in their own coats of arms and livery colours.

On arrival, all comers were met by two of the *kunstabelen* for some ceremonial welcome jousts before the gates. In the meantime, Brun-Artus had 'made a gral' set up in a nearby meadow, near the *schildekenbom* with the shields of *kunstabels de in dem grale waren* (those who participated in the Grail) and where many tents and pavilions were pitched. This meadow was still known as the *Gralswerder* (*Werder,* grassy river island) in the 16th century and the adjacent section of the Long Bridge across the Elbe river was called *Gralsbrücke* (Bridge of the Grail).

The festival's main attraction, which also has been called 'one of the oddest tournament stories' (Barber and Baker 56), was *vrowe Feie* (Dame Fay, obviously Morgan le Fay), a local beauty remarkably free of bourgeois inhibitions, who had agreed to be the prize to be *geven den, der se vorwerfen konde met tuchten unde manheit* (given to whoever would win her by chivalry and prowess). Somewhat anti-climactically, the victorious champion was a middle-aged merchant from Goslar, who apparently was already married. As a good sport with praiseworthy family values, he gave Dame Fay a handsome dowry to enable her 'to give up her wild life' and to marry her true love (Loomis 1959, 555; E. Nickel 1960, 40-42; Sachs 249-59; Barber and Barker 56).

For his pageant Brun-Artus von Schönebeck could draw on a considerable amount of local Arthurian tradition. From the presence of the 'gral' it is clear that the *kunstabels de in dem grale waren* must have play-acted as Grail Knights from Wolfram von Eschenbach's *Parzival* (c. 1210). On the other hand, the first German version of the Tristram story was *Tristant* (c. 1180), by Eilhart von Oberge, a Saxon knight who took his name from a castle located between Brunswick and Hildesheim. The popularity of the Tristram story in the North of Germany is attested by the three famous *Tristan-Teppiche [Teppich,* tapestry] of c. 1300,1330, and 1370, embroidered by the nuns of Kloster Wienhausen, near Brunswick, and still preserved in the convent (Loomis 1937, pls. 76-79, 83-86, Wilhelm 7-25). Other tapestry fragments, related to the *Tristan-Teppich II,* of c. 1330, with scenes from the adventures of Gawain in Wolfram's *Parzival,* are in the Landesmuseum Brunswick (Loomis 1937, pls. 143-44). Gawain's son, Guingalin/Wigalois, had his own German romance, *Wigalois, der Ritter mit dem Rade* (The Knight of the Wheel) *c.* 1205. Its popularity is indicated by thirty-odd surviving manuscripts. Though it was composed by an East-Franconian, Wirnt von Grafenberg, its finest copy was written and illustrated in 1372 by Jan von Brunswick, a monk in the Cistercian abbey of Amelungsborn[6] near Hildesheim (Loomis 1937, pp. 367-74).

In examining the three *Zinnfigurenstreifen* newly found at Magdeburg, Ernst Nickel, in his first essay (1956, 243), thought that these might have been sold as souvenirs or as children's toys at fairs accompanying a tournament. The fact that all three strips were cast from the same mould led him to the conclusion that they were cheap 'serial ware'. Although not one survived unbroken, he estimated that their length was about 8 inches (20 cm) each. In piecing together the fragments he found that each strip was bent in a curve, and fastening devices at either end indicated that they were intended to be joined into a frieze. Going one step further, Rainer

Sachs suggested, in 1983, that these strips originally made up a circlet and, being gilded, they would be something better than toys or simple souvenirs (Sachs 251). It was perhaps their presumed 'serial production' that led Sachs to his further suggestion that all ladies participating at the tournament festivities of 1279 would have worn such identical 'crowns' as a sort of common badge (Sachs 252).

In 1955, even before Ernst Nickel's publication, Percy Ernst Schramm had wondered whether the *Zinnfigurenstreifen* would illustrate *eine bestimmte 'Geschichte'*, a specific 'story' (Schramm 64-66). In his second essay Ernst Nickel proposed that the scenes were direct illustrations of the grail festival pageant (E. Nickel 1960, 40). The joust before the turreted castle would be the encounter between a 'comer' and one of the *kunstabelen* at the gates of Magdeburg, and the embracing couple could be the champion receiving his prize, *vrowe Feie*. The tree with the round top composed of triangular, i.e. shield-shaped elements should then be the *schildekenbom* (E. Nickel 1960, 41). Unfortunately, in this interpretation the scene of the knight fighting the winged monster is left unexplained. The detailed report in the *Schöppenchronik* does not mention a fight with a monster, an unlikely omission had such a spectacle been part of the pageant. In summing up, the *Schöppenchronik* tells that Brun von Schönebeck had written a *ganz dudesch bok* (an entire book in German) about this tournament. Alas, this book, which possibly was one of the sources of the chronicle and which could have settled so many nagging questions, is lost.

Percy Ernst Schramm drew comparisons between the Magdeburg *Zinnfigurenstreifen* and the figural decoration on the Cross of the Crowns, in the treasury of Wawel Cathedral, Krakow (Schramm 64-66). Mounted on its traverse arms are eleven tile-shaped gold plaques, parts of a dismantled crown (Kovacs 231-38; Sachs 251-52). Tiny figures of falconers and of tilting knights cast from three basic moulds are integrated into the scrollwork of the plaques. Schramm sees them simply as chivalric motifs of jousting and hunting. Rainer Sachs, on the other hand, sees them as representing the Adventure of the Sparrowhawk in Chrétien's *Erec et Enide,* leading him to propose an Arthurian theme for the *Zinnfigurenstreifen*, too. Sachs suggested that the 1279 tournament at Magdeburg was a re-enactment of the Tournament of Kanvoleis in Wolfram von Eschenbach's *Parzival* (Sachs 251-52).

The Tournament at Kanvoleis was a highlight in the career of Parzival's father, Gahmuret, who at that time was a knight-errant in the service of the Baruc of Baldac (the Caliph of Baghdad). One of Gahmuret's jousting opponents was King Hardiess of Gascony, who bore as his device a demi-griffin. [7] Wolfram likes to call heroes by their heraldic devices as *noms de guerre*. Gahmuret, for instance, is often called 'the Anchor' after the device he bears in the Baruc's service (Parzival 37, 47, 51; H. Nickel 3, 4:11-12). Therefore, Rainer Sachs suggests that the winged monster as a *Vogel Greif* (*griffin*) would be a heraldic representation of King Hardiess in his joust against Gahmuret. The embracing couple would then be Gahmuret and Herzeloyde, the Queen of Waleis, who was 'the lofty prize, to wit, her lands and her royal person' (*Parzival* 46-47; Sachs 251), just as *vrowe Feie* was the prize at the Magdeburg tournament. The third scene of the *Zinnfigurenstreifen,* the joust at the castle, would represent the battle before Baghdad, in which Gahmuret lost his life. The detail that one jouster hits the helmet of his opponent with his lance is seen as proof of this interpretation, because Gahmuret was killed by a lance thrust that pierced his adamant helmet (Leckie 29-30).[8] It is strange, though, that a rather unimportant figure, King Hardiess, would be singled out to be represented by his oversized demi-griffin device, since the story's hero, Gahmuret 'the Anchor', is not identified in any way.

The crucial problem here is the zoological classification of the winged monster. Although it sports a huge beak, it does not have the four legs and lion's tail of a 'proper' griffin. Admittedly, a demi-griffin such as that of King Hardiess would have had only two feet, but it also should have a squared-off body and not the pointed reptilian tail of this monster. In spite of its beak, it is more likely that the creature is meant to be a dragon.

Strange to say, dragon fights – so beloved by Hollywood filmmakers, cartoonists, and authors of sword-and-sorcery tales – are relatively rare in medieval literature, the legend of St George and the Dragon and the saga of Siegfried the Dragonslayer notwithstanding.[9]

There are, however, two 'Geschichten' (both Arthurian) that not only contain episodes to fit all three scenes but would have been well known in thirteenth-century Magdeburg. The first of these stories is that of Tristan and Isolde. Two of the most popular episodes in German art were Tristan's duel with Morold/Marhaus, and his fighting the Dragon of Ireland, where Isolde's hand was to be the reward for the dragonslayer. Significantly, all three of the *Tristan-Teppiche* at Kloster Wienhausen depict these two combats, but only one tapestry shows any scenes from the love affair itself, such as the wedding night fraud, the discovery of the sleeping lovers in the forest, and the tryst under the tree at the well (Loomis 1938, pls. 76-79; Wilhelm 7-23).

The other story known to thirteenth-century Magdeburgers would be *Wigalois, der Ritter mit dem Rade.* One of the story's main episodes is Wigalois' fight with the Red Knight, who had robbed Queen Elamie of Tyre of her talking parrot in its golden cage (her prize at one of those beauty contests ubiquitous in chivalric romances). Another main event is Wigalois' slaying of the dragon Pfetan. By this deed he rescued a fellow knight, the husband of Lady Beleare. Like Tristram in his dragon fight, Wigalois is overcome by the dragon's poison and swoons after the kill. Fisherfolk find him lying unconscious and, seeing only a welcome case of booty, blithely strip him of his armour and clothes. Shortly after, Wigalois regains consciousness, Lady Beleare discovers him as she searches for the rescuer of her husband. She wraps him in her mantle to cover his nakedness.

The diminutive size of the figures did not lend itself to the representation of shield emblems or helmet crests – Gahmuret's anchor, Tristan's boar (after Gottfried von Strassburg)[10] or Wigalois' wheel – that would have made positive identification of the knights possible. On the other hand, the cloak so conspicuously draped between the two 'embracing' figures, could be a hint at Lady Beleare's rescue of Wigalois in distress.

The ambiguous iconography of the *Zinnfigurenstreifen* that permits more than one interpretation was possibly intentional, as was the 'one size fits all' large circlet. The fragile strips were presumably mounted on a *Schapel,* a pillbox-shaped headdress, like those on the statues of two margravesses of Meissen, Uta von Ballenstedt and her sister-in-law Reglindis, in the donors' choir of Naumburg Cathedral (*c.* 1250). Such a *Schapel* with the *Zinnfigurenstreifen* as its circlet would be a likely 'crown' for the lady chosen to preside over the tabelrunde tournaments at 'Maiden Castle'. Maybe it was the crown of *vrowe Feie* herself. Was there a deep dark Gothic secret that led to its being thrown into a refuse pit? Though it probably would be the very stuff for a Gothic novel, we will never know.

Die Magdeburger Schöppenchronik, Vol. 7, p. 168 F
In dussen tiden, weren hir noch kunstabelen, dat weren die rikesten borger kinder; de plegen dat spel vortostande in den pingsten, als den roland. den schildekenbom, tabelrunde unde ander spel, dat nu

de ratmannen sulven vorstand. In dem vorgeschreven stride was ein kunstabel. de heit Brun van Sconenbeke, dat was ein gelart man. Den beden sine gesellen de kunstabelen, dat he on dichte unde bedechte ein vreidlich spel. Des makede he einen gral unde dichte hovesche breve, de sande he to Gosler. to Hildesheim unde to Brunswik. Quedlingeborch, Halberstad unde to andeen steden. unde ladeden to sik alle koplude. de dar riddcrschop wolden oven, dat se quemen to Magdeborch; se hedden eine schone vruwen, de heir vrow Feie. de scholden men geven den de se vorwerfen konde mi tuchten unde manheit. Dar von worden bewegen alle junglichen in de steiden. De van Goslere kemen mit vordecketen rossen, de van Brunswick kemen alle mit gronem vordecket unde gecleidet, unde andere steden hadden ok or sunderlike wapene und varwe. Do se vor disse stad quemen, se wolden nicht inriden, men entpfeng se mit suste unde dustiren. Dat geschach. twe kunstabele togen ut unde bestunden de unde entpfengen se mit den spcren. De wile was dc grale bereit up dem mersche, unde vele telt unde pawelunge upgeslagen. Unde dar was ein bom gesat up der mersche, dar hangenden der kunstabelen schilde an, de in dem grale waren. Des anderen dages, do de geste missen hadden gehort unde gegeten, so togen vor den gral unde beschauweden den. Dar wart on vorlorovet. dat malk rorde einen schilt: welkes jungelinges de schild were, de queme her vor unde bestunde den rorer. Dat geschach och allen. To lesten vordeinde vrowen Feie ein olt kopman van Goslere: de vorde se mit sik unde gaf se to der e unde gaf or so vele mede, dat se ores wilden levendes nicht mer ovede. Hir van is ein ganz dudesch bok gemaket. De sulve Brun Sconenbeke makede sedder vele dudescher boke. als Cantica conticorum, dat Ave Maria unde vele gudes gedichtes.

At those times there were here *kunstabelen* that were the sons of the richest burghers; they used to stage games at Whitsuntide, such as the *Roland*, the *schildekenbom, tabelrunde* and other games that were presided over by the magistrates themselves. Involved in this competition was a *kunstable* whose name was Brun von Schonebeck, who was a learned man. His fellow *kunstabels* asked him that he should bethink himself and compose rhymes for a merry pageant. Thus he made a *gral* and composed in rhymes courtly letters that he sent to Goslar, to Hildesheim and to Brunswick, Quedlinburg, Halberstadt and to other towns, and invited all the merchants who wanted to act out chivalry that they should come to Magdeburg. There they had a beautiful damsel called Dame Fay, which was to be given to whoever could win her by chivalry and prowess. This made all the young gentleman in those towns really excited. Those from Goslar came with fully caparisoned horses, those from Brunswick came all in green trappings and clothes, and other towns had also special coats of arms and colour schemes.

When they arrived before the town, they did not want to enter unless they would be met with some jousts. This was done. Two *kunstabels* rode out and met them in a contest with lances. In the meantime the Grail was set up in the marsh, and many tents and pavilions pitched. And there was a tree erected in that marsh, on it were hung the shields of those *kunstabels* who took part in the Grail.

At the next day, after the guests had attended mass and breakfasted, they rode out to the Grail and admired it. There, announcement was made that when one touched a shield, the young gentleman whose shield it was would come forward and fight the toucher. This was done by all. At long last an elderly merchant from Goslar won Dame Fay; he took her along and gave her into marriage and gave her that much that she could abandon her wild life. About all this an entire book in German has been made. The same Brun Schonebeck has since made many books in German [i.e. translated, such as *cantica canticorum*, the *Ave Maria*, and many fine poems].

Acknowledgements

For valuable advice and assistance in preparing this essay it is my pleasure to express my gratitude to the late Ernst Nickel, as former director of Forschungsstelle Vor-und Frühgeschichte Magdeburg; to Gert Böttcher, Abteilungsleiter Geschichte, Museum der Stadt Magdeburg; to Rainer Sachs, of the Institut Historii Architektury, Wroclaw/Breslau; to Donald LaRocca, the Metropolitan Museum of Art, New York, and especially to Roger F. Gardiner, University of Western Ontario, London, Ontario.

Notes

1. *Schöppe* is a dialect form of *Schöffe* (juror). The legal code of the city of 1188, the *Magdeburger Stadtrecht,* with its insistence on trial by

juries of peers, became the model of many German city charters, and also of the much better known Magna Charta of 1215.

2. 'Roland' statues were symbols of civic liberty. Usually representing a knight in full armour with drawn sword, they were placed in market squares or in front of city halls of German towns. Within a radius of 50 miles from Magdeburg there were about twenty towns that had such a 'Roland'. Magdeburg's own 'Roland' statue was destroyed during the Thirty Years War, at the Sack of Magdeburg, 1631. Apart from these official 'Roland' statues there were 'Spielrolande' in popular use, quintain figures for jousting games; the 'Roland' of the Magdeburg *kunstabels* must have been such a temporarily set up 'Spielrolande' (Lejeune and Stiennon; Kottwitz).
3. The date 1279 is a conjecture by Rainer Sachs; the text of the *Schöppenchronik* says only 'in dussen tiden' (at those times), very much like Nennius' 'in illo tempore' (at that time) as the beginning of Arthur's battle list. Ernst Nickel proposes 'the 60s or 70s of the 13th century', Roger S. Loomis gives the date as 1281, and Richard Barber as 1281-82.
4. Distances from Magdeburg are: Halberstadt *c.* 25 miles, Quedlinburg 30 miles, Brunswick and Goslar 45 miles, Hildesheim 70 miles. Lammspringe is halfway between Goslar and Hildesheim, and Schönebeck is just ten miles to the south of Magdeburg.
5. Green was the colour of *minne* (courtly love) in medieval German lore.
6. The abbey Amelungsborn is located *c.* 10 miles south of Hildesheim, adjacent to Bodenwerder, where in the mid-1700s a special branch of adventure literature was founded by the redoubtable lord of Castle Bodenwerder, Hieronymus Baron von Münchhausen.
7. Wolfram, with his wry sense of humour, gives King Hardiess the forepart of a griffin as personal device, but to his retainers he allots *des grifen zagel*, the griffin's hind-quarters!
8. Gahmuret's helmet of adamant had been treacherously softened by an application of goat's blood.
9. The scenes on the *Zinnfigurenstreifen* do not correspond with either story. Although St George does rescue a maiden from the dragon, there is no joust in his legend. Siegfried, the German dragonslayer *par excellence*, fights his dragon, Fafner, on foot, and neither a woman nor a joust was involved. In the Arthurian cycle, Yvain fights a dragon, but with the help of a lion.

10. Gottfried von Strassburg gives his Tristan a black boar as shield device, on the Wienhausen *Tristan-Teppich I* his crest is a golden wing, but he has no shield at all. In *Tristan-Teppich II* he bears a halved star as shield emblem and crest, but in *Tristan-Teppich III* his device and crest is a lady's head with long blond hair. In armorials of the 15th century the arms of Tristram 'of Lyonesse' are 'canting': *Vert, a lion or* (H. Nickel 3, 3; 6, 20).

Select Bibliography

Barber, Richard and Barker, Juliet. *Tournaments: Jousts, Chivalry and Pageants in the Middle Ages,* New York: Weidenfeld and Nicholson, 1989.

Friese, Karl. *Reise in die Romanik*, Leipzig: Prisma-Verlag, 1967.

Janicke, K. [ed.] *Die Chroniken der deutschen Städte vom 14. bis ins 16. Jahrhundert:* vol. 7 'Die Magdeburger Schöppenchronik', Leipzig: C. Hegel, 1869.

Kottwitz, Eberhard. *Rolandder Ries*, Leipzig: VEB FA. Brockhaus, 1982.

Kovacs, Eva. 'Über einige Probleme des Krakauer Kronenkreuz.es', *Acta Historiae Artium Scientiarum Hungaricae* 17 (1971), Budapest: 231-68.

Leckie, R. William, Jr. 'Mutable Substance: The Diamond Helmet and the Death of Gahmuret in Wolfram's Parzival', *Arthurian Interpretations*, vol. 3, no. 2 (Spring 1989): 23-37.

Lejeune, Rita and Jacques Stiennon. *La légende de Roland dans l'art du moyen age*, (2 vols.), Brussels: 1967.

Loomis, Roger Sherman. 'Arthurian Influence on Sport and Spectacle', *Arthurian Literature in the Middle Ages: A Collaborative History*, Oxford: Clarendon Press.1959: 553

Loomis, Roger S. and Laura Hibbard Loomis. *Arthurian Legends in Medieval Art*, London: Oxford Univ. Press, 1938.

Nickel, Ernst. 'Ein mittelalterlicher Zinnfigurenstreifen aus Magdeburg', *Ausgrabungen und Funde* 1 (1956), Magdeburg: 239-43.

______ 'Zur Deutung des Magdeburger Zinnfigurenstreifens', *Ausgrabungen und Funde* 5 (1960): 40-42.

Nickel, Helmut. 'Notes on Arthurian Heraldry: The Retroactive System in the "Armagnac" Armorial', *Quondam et Futurus: A Journal of Arthurian Interpretations* 3, no. 3 (Autumn 1993): 1-23.

Sachs, Rainer. 'Die Magdeburger 'Zinnfigurenstreifen' und ihre Funktion', *Zeitschrift fur Archaologie* 17 (1983), Berlin: 249-68.

Schramm, Percy Ernst. 'Kaiser Friedrichs II Herrschaftszeichen', *Abhandlungen der Akademie der Wissenschaften in Gottingen: Philologtsch-Historische Klasse* III, 36 (1955)

Schroder, E. 'Bruno Artus von Magdeburg', *Korrespondenzblatt des Vereins fur niederdeutsche Sprachforschung*, Hamburg 1930 (1928-29), Heft 42: 4-5.

Wilhelm, Pia. *Die Bildteppiche* (serie Kloster Wienhausen III), Celle: n.d.

Wolfram von Eschenbach. Parzival, trans. A.T Hatto, New York: Penguin, 1980.

Originally published in *Arthuriana* 7 no. 3, Autumn 1997.

17

Who Was Eslit?

Chrétien de Troyes lists 'Eslit' as the eleventh best of Arthur's knights, but in spite of this Eslit does not play any significant role in any Arthurian epic. Although the Round Table was established to indicate the equality in valour of all its knights, there was nevertheless a sometimes fierce competition concerning who was the 'best of knights', and in the very first roll call, given in Chrétien de Troyes' *Erec et Enide* (*c.* 1170), the first ten 'best knights' are set apart from the rest.

In W. W. Comfort's prose translation of *Erec et Enide,* published 1913 in Everyman's Library (Vv. 1691-1750), Gawain is listed as the foremost of knights, Erec the son of Lac, as the second, and Lancelot of the Lake as the third. Gornemant of Gohort is the fourth and the fifth is the Handsome Coward. The Ugly Brave is sixth, Meliant de Liz seventh, Mauduit the Wise eighth, and Dodinel the Wild ninth. After having tallied Gandelu, 'a goodly man', as the tenth, Chrétien claims that numbering bothers him, and that he will mention the other knights from now on without order. Of the forty-one named knights that follow, the first is Eslit, listed together with Briien, and Yvain the son of Urien.[1]

In the verse edition by Carleton W. Carroll in Garland Library of Medieval Literature, 1987, the list is shortened to thirty-one names altogether. Gauvain is first, Erec *le fils* Lac is second and Lancelot del Lac third. The fourth is Gonemanz dc Goort, the fifth *li Biax Coarz* (the Handsome Coward) and the sixth *li Lez Hardiz* (the Ugly Brave). Melianz des Liz comes as the seventh, Mauduiz *le Sages* as eighth,

Dodines *li Sauvages* as ninth and Gaudeluz is tenth, '*car an lui at maintes bontez*' (for in him were many good qualities). However, Eslit and Briien are omitted, and it is Ywain the Valiant (*Yvains li preuz)* who leads the twenty-one unnumbered knights (II.1680-1714).[2]

Chrétien's German follower and adapter, Hartmann von Aue, in his 'Erec' (*c.* 1190) claims to list the full number of one hundred and forty knights of King Arthur's court, but his roll call amounts to only seventy-five. Although Hartmann adds some thirty new names to Chrétien's list, in general he follows it quite closely, in spite of some misunderstandings in translation. The first thirteen names of Hartmann's roll call are an exact parallel to those in *Erec et Enide* of the Everyman's Library edition; first comes Gawein, 'the brave knight', next *Eric fils de roi* Lac, and Lancelot of Arlac, then follow Gornemanz of Groharz, *li bels Coharz* (the Handsome Coward), *Lais hardiz* (the Ugly Brave), Meljanz of Liz, Maldwiz *li sadges,* wild Dodinel and good Gandelus. 'With them sat Esus, then the knight Brien and Iwein fil li roi Vrien.'[3]

Between 1210 and 1240 the Austrian poet Heinrich von dem Türlin wrote his Grail epic, *Diu Crône* ('The Crown'), which contains two tests for 'the best of knights and truest of ladies'. In the Test of the Tankard the names of sixty-three knights appear in a sequence that bears a strong resemblance to the list in Hartmann's *Erec.* It starts with Gawein, then follow Lanzelet of Arlac, Erec *fils du roi* Lac, Iwein, Kalocreant, Parzival the Welshman, Lenval, Lais of Lardis, Milianz de Lis, Maldis the Wise, Dinodes the Old, Gandaluz, Elies of Landuz, King Brien, Urien of Lof, Iwein of Canabus, and so on. For good measure Heinrich also adds 'Elis of Climon' in the forty-eighth place.[4]

From their positions in these lists, between Gandelu/ Gandeluz/ Gandaluz and Briien/ knight Brien/King Brien, it is clear that Eslit, Esus, and Elies of Landuz must be one and the same person, in spite of the difference in spelling the name. But the nagging question remains: Who is this elusive person, who evidently was counted among the most important – although not one of the ten best, at least the eleventh – knights of King Arthur's court, but who does not show up as an active figure in any Arthurian epic?

Phyllis Ann Karr, in her *The King Arthur Companion* (1983) does not mention Eslit at all, and in its enlarged form, *The Arthurian Companion* (1997), there is only the terse entry: 'ESLIT' followed by a dagger symbol. The dagger symbol after Eslit's name indicates that he does not appear in Sir Thomas Malory's *Le Morte d'Arthur,* and neither is Eslit found among the 178 knights of the Round Table with known – of course fictitious – coats-of-arms listed alphabetically in Michel Pastoureau's *Armorial des chevaliers de la Table Ronde* (1983).[5]

There is a common feature in the roll calls by Chrétien de Troyes, Hartmann von Aue and Heinrich von dem Türlin: they all three list Eslit/Esus/Elies, but conspicuous by his absence is Bors, who, after all, is a major character in the Grail stories.

In the mid-thirteenth century another roll call, quite independent from the pattern established by Chrétien, is found as preface to *L'Ystoire de Meliadus et de Gyron le Courtoys et du Bon Chevalier sans Paour.* The printed edition of *c.* 1501 under the title *Gyron le Courtoys* mentions Rusticiano de Pisa as its author, but the earlier manuscripts give author's credit to 'Helie de Borron' (Pickford, introductory note). Among its 169 knights Bors is mentioned in the third place, after King Arthur himself and Lancelot, but before Gauvain (Pickford, a ii).[6]

Interestingly, the seventh knight is Helyas le blanc, the son whom Bors begat in his single lapse from chastity with the daughter of King Brangoire. Helyas le blanc is not in the lists compiled by Chrétien, Hartmann, and Heinrich von dem Türlin. On the other hand, Malory mentions at the Tournament of Surluse a knight 'that hyghte Elys la Noyre' and was 'in the gouernaunce' of Duke Chaleyns of Claraunce. He 'encountered with' King Bagdemagus, who smote him 'that he made hym to auoyde his sadel'. Possibly he was invented as counterpart to Helyas le blanc. 'Elias la Noire' is mentioned only in passing by Phyllis Ann Karr, as a follower of Duke Chaleins; his mere cameo appearance at Surluse did not deserve an entry of his own.

In the *Armorial des chevaliers de la Table Ronde,* Michel Pastoureau lists 'Bohort' (Bors) as entry no. 34, and he mentions that *parfois* – sometimes – he was called *l'Essilie'* (the Exile) for difference to his father, 'Bohort *Roi di Gaunes.*'

Could it be possible that the enigmatic and elusive 'Eslit' of Chrétien's roll call, as *'l'Essilie'* became a surname attached to Bohort/Bors? In this guise 'Eslit' not only could maintain his rightful place among the foremost knights of King Arthur's court, but as Bohort he was even promoted to third best, while 'Helyas le blanc' was created as Bors' son and could also be safely placed among the ten best knights.

Notes

1. Erec & Enide' in *Chrétien de Troyes: Arthurian Romances,* ed. and trans. W. W. Comfort (London: Everyman, 1967), pp. 1-90.
2. *Chrétien de Troyes: Erec et Enide,* ed. and trans. Carleton W. Carroll (New York: Garland, 1987).
3. *Hartmann von Aue: Erec,* ed. and trans. Thomas I. Keller (New York: Garland, 1987).
4. *The Crown: A Tale of Sir Gawein and King Arthur's Court by Heinrich von dem Türlin,* ed. and trans. L.W. Thomas (Lincoln: University of Nebraska Press, 1989).
5. Phyllis Ann Karr, *The King Arthur Companion* (Reston.VA: Reston Publishing Company, 1983); *The Arthurian Companion* (Chaosium Publication, 1997; revised 2019), p.152; Michel Pastoureau, *Armorial des Chevaliers de la Table Ronde* (Paris: Le Léopard d'Or, 1983).
6. *Gyron le Courtoys,* fasc. of Anthoine Verard edition (Paris, c. 1501), ed. and trans. Cedric E. Pickford (London: Scolar Press, 1977, repr. 1979). Rusticiano de Pisa was Marco Polo's friend who wrote down and helped in editing the *Travels.*

Originally published in *Arthuriana* vol 14, no. 2., Summer 2004, pp. 64-6.

18

What Kind of Animal Was the Questing Beast?

Much like the elusive Unicorn, which in Arthurian stories has only cameo appearances in *le conte du papagaulx* and Spenser's *Faerie Quene,* the Questing Beast has so far escaped zoological identification.

Among the animals found in the Arthurian stories there are some remarkable specimens, such as the monstrous boar Trwch Troynt and the terrible cat Chapalu. On the positive side there are King Arthur's dog Cabal, his horses Aubagu, Dhu, and Llamrei, Gawain's steed Gringolet, and Yvain's faithful lion. The most enigmatic creature, however, is the Questing Beast, so called because from its belly emanated a noise 'like unto the questing of thirty couple houndes'.

This strange feature seems to be taken from the *Gesta Regum* of William of Malmesbury, who reports a haunting dream King Edgar had while sleeping under an apple tree.[1] He dreamed of a bitch whose whelps could be heard barking in her womb. This is explained by his pious mother as an omen of future attacks on the Church. In *Perlesvaus,* the 'questing' in the Beast's belly is seen as Christ being hounded by the twelve tribes of Israel, and in Gerbert of Montreuil's *Continuation de la Conte del Graal* the Beast is the Church 'worried by people who disturb the sacred service by talking and complaining of hunger'. In both these early sources the Beast is killed by its offspring. Interestingly, in a South Slavic tale, the Twelve Dreams of Schachi, there appears a bitch with yelping whelps in her body. This tale also has an Arabic variant, which is probably its ultimate source.[2]

King Arthur had encountered the Questing Beast at a well in the forest and found that the barking only stopped when the Beast drank.[3] However, the questing after the Questing Beast was done by King Pellinore and

Sir Palomydes the Saracen. Eventually, at the Tournament at Surluse, Sir Palomydes 'desguysed himself' by taking the 'questynge beeste' as the charge on his shield and horse trappings.[4] Since Sir Palomydes was the rival of Sir Tristram for the love of La Beale Isoud, his unending and unrequited love is mirrored by his unsuccessful and unending pursuit of the Questing Beast.

Though the Questing Beast's allegorical and spiritual significance has been variously scrutinized and interpreted, little attention has been paid so far to what kind of real animal (if any) did serve as the model for this strange and seemingly imaginary creature whose physical appearance was far from consistent.[5]

In *Perlesvaus* the beast is white as a fresh snow, bigger than a hare, but smaller than a fox, and it was pleasing to behold in its great beauty and its eyes that resembled two emeralds. By contrast, in Gerbert de Montreuil's *Continuation de la Conte del Graal,* the beast is called *grant a merveille*, 'wondrously big'. In the *Merlin* section of the Boron cycle, one version (ms. 112) gives a detailed description of the Beast's appearance:

> Head and neck of a serpent, bristly [maned?] and flexible, eyes of carbuncle glowing like torches, a maw of fire, ears upright like a greyhound's, body like a lion, legs like a stag's … a hide spotted in all the colours of the world … wings on its shoulders that flash like rays of the sun.

This last detail that makes the Beast look rather like a dragon was perhaps suggested by its serpent-like head and neck. Incidentally, 'live' dragons are rare in Arthurian literature, the helmet crests and battle standards of Uther Pendragon and Arthur himself notwithstanding.

In the *Prose Tristan,* the Beast is described as having the head and neck of a serpent, the body of a leopard, hindquarters and tail of a lion and feet of a stag. Here the wings and the maw of fire are omitted. The *Prose Tristan* description has become the standard for the Questing Beast's appearance. Interestingly, the description is practically the reverse of that of the most notorious monster of classical antiquity, the Chimaera, which according to Homer had a lion's head, a serpent's tail, and the body of a goat (which presumably included feet with cloven hoofs and perhaps also a many-coloured pelt). The Chimaera did not harbour any yelping whelps, but its breath came out in terrible blasts of burning flame.[6]

Malory's description of the Beste Glatysaunt follows the one given in the *Prose Tristan;* his Questing Beast has 'a hede like a serpents hede, and a body lyke a lybard, buttocks lyke a lion, and fote lyke an herte' (a head like a serpent's, the body of a leopard, the hind quarters of a lion and the feet of a hart). And, of course, there is the noise coming from its belly 'like unto the questing of thirty couple houndes'.[7] The detailed description of the Beast's body from the *Prose Tristan* is also taken up by the author of the *Roman de Palamedes* with the addition that the neck is like that of an animal called '*Douce* in his [Palamedes') language'. In *Perceforest,* it is said that the Beast's 'strange neck' resembles that of an animal that the Saracens call *Dagglor,* and it has 'all the colours of the world'.

From this description we can deduce that the Beast was an exotic animal, most likely from Saracen lands. Indeed, the name *Douce* 'in his (Palamedes') language' might give a clue to the Beast's identity. The French *doux* (fern, *douce)* means 'sweet, charming, pleasant' and it is generally thought that an Arabic word *zrf, zurafa* meaning 'graceful, nice, sweet' would be the root of 'giraffe'. However, Arabic scholars insist that this is a false etymology and 'giraffe' is more likely derived from *zrf-zaraffa,* which the Arabic-English Lexicon lists as 'camelopard or giraffe, a certain beast of beautiful make, the fore legs are longer than its hind legs; said to be called by a name signifying it has the form of an assemblage of animals, i.e. camel-ox-leopard, because it has resemblances to the camel and the ox and the leopard.'[8] It seems that with the name *Douce* the author of the *Roman de Palamedes* picked the wrong *zrf,* although he was on the right track. The long swaying neck of a giraffe can be word-pictured as that of a serpent – more flattering than that of a camel – the body with its pattern of irregular spots reminds of the spotted pelt of the leopard, while its narrow hind quarters and tufted tail are comparable to those of a lion that look even more narrow against its imposingly maned shoulders. Feet 'like a stag's' or 'like those of an ox' obviously means that there were cloven hoofs. Unfortunately, the Arabic-English Lexicon does not yield any explanation about the animal *Dagglor.*

In support of the notion that the Questing Beast might be based upon a description of a giraffe, there is from the other end of the world a report about an animal from foreign lands that was brought to the court of the Ming Emperor at Beijing in 1418. On its arrival it was expected to be the wonderful Ki-lin, the mysterious Unicorn of Chinese lore and harbinger of Golden Ages to come. In one of those amazing examples of record-keeping in the Middle Empire, it was soon realized that this marvel of a creature matched the description of an exotic beast duly reported almost two hundred years earlier, in 1225, by a customs official at the seaport of Quanzhou. Although it seems that this official had his information only second-hand, probably from some far-travelled sea captain, the description is quite remarkably accurate in painting a word-picture of a giraffe, as an animal called *zula* (probably a Chinese transliteration *of zurafa),* 'with a leopard's hide, a cow's hoofs, a ten-foot-tall body, and a nine-foot neck'.[9]

It has been suggested that the Cat Chapalu might have been a leopard, perhaps a surviving escapee from a former Roman zoo. An escapee giraffe would have had less chance of surviving in Arthur's Britain, even in an enchanted forest. Perhaps the description of the Questing Beast was styled after a tale about the private *menagerie* of Emperor Frederick II (1194-1250), who liked to amaze his Italian and German subjects by taking his exotic pets, such as elephants, camels, lions, leopards and giraffes – presents from the sultan – along on his travels through his realm.[10]

Notes

For kind help in securing hard-to-find sources it is my pleasure to thank my friends and colleagues at the Metropolitan Museum, Joan Mertens, Curator, Dept. of Greek and Roman Art; Marilyn Jenkins-Madina, Research Curator, Dept. of Islamic Art, and Stuart W. Pyhrr, Arthur Ochs Sulzberger Curator of Arms and Armor.

1. Lynette Ross Muir, 'The Questing Beast: Its Origins and Development', *Orpheus* 4 (1957): 24-32; and William Albert Nitze, 'The Beste Glatissante in Arthurian Romance', *Zeitschrift für Romanische Philologie* 56 (1936): 409-18.
2. Nitze, 'Beste Glatissante,' 415.
3. *Caxton's Malory: A New Edition of Sir Thomas Malory's* Le Morte d'Arthur *based on the Pierpont Morgan Copy of William Caxton's Edition of 1485,* ed. James W. Spisak and William Matthews (Berkeley: University of California Press, 1983) 1: 19.
4. Spisak and Matthews, *Caxton's Malory,* p. X, 41.
5. Antonio L. Furtado, 'The Questing Beast as Emblem of the Ruin of Logres in the Post-Vulgate,' *Arthuriana* 9.3 (1999): 7-51; Muir 'Questing Beast', 24-32; Nitze, 'Beste Glatissante,' 409-18

6. Homer: *The Iliad,* trans. E.V. Rieu (New York: Penguin, 1950), p. 122.
7. Spisak and Matthews, p. IX, 12.
8. William Edward Lane, *Arabic-English Lexicon* (London: Williams and Norgate, 1867), pp. 1226-27.
9. Samuel M. Wilson, *The Emperor's Giraffe and Other Stories of Cultures in Contact* (Boulder: Westview Press, 1999), pp. 122-24.
10. Willy Ley, *Dawn of Zoology* (Englewood Cliffs: Prentiss-Hall, 1968), p. 86, ill.

Originally published in *Arthuriana* vol. 14, no. 2., Summer 2004, pp. 66-69.

'How King Arthur saw the Questing Beast', one of Aubrey Beardsley's 1893 illustrations for *Le Morte D'Arthur*. (Public domain)

19

Who Was Trebuchet, the Smith who Forged Perceval's Sword?

In Chretien's *Perceval* (v. 3130-3180) at Perceval's visit to the Fisher King's castle a squire arrives with a precious sword, a gift from the Fisher King's 'lovely blonde niece'. The Fisher King, noting the fine steel, is told by the squire that the master who forged it made only three in his lifetime, and 'no sword will be quite like this sword.' However, 'it would not break / save with its bearer's life at stake / on one occasion, one alone, / a peril that was only known / to him who forged and tempered it.' The Fisher King right away presents the sword to Perceval, who accepts it in spite of the squire's dire warning and carries it in addition to the sword he took from Ither the Red Knight whom he had slain earlier.

The next day, in the forest, Perceval meets a maiden seated under an oak, who is holding her slain lover in her lap. The maiden turns out to be his cousin, who, in spite of her own distress, is enough concerned about her naive relative to tell him: 'Do not trust this sword you wear. It will betray you without fail.' In answer to Perceval's worried inquiry, 'If the sword breaks, do you know how / and whether it can be repaired?' the maiden informs him that the only man who could 'rehammer, temper and remake' it would be its maker, the smith Trebuchet, who made only three swords in his lifetime. This master smith dwells at Cotoatre (3652-3684), which has been interpreted as a phonetic approximation to 'Scottewatre', meaning the Firth of Forth.[1]

Chretien's *Perceval* remained a fragment and therefore we do not know what Chretien envisioned as the sword's further fate, especially when and why it will break. On the other hand, in Wolfram von Eschenbach's *Parzival,* as the earliest complete Grail story, the breaking of the sword is a crucial moment in Parzival's fight with his yet unknown half-brother Feirefiz. Although Wolfram solemnly declares that he does not follow Chretien, who in his opinion got the entire story wrong, the events that occurred after Parzival acquired the sword at the Grail castle (as his second sword) are with only minor variations practically identical to those experienced by Perceval. In the forest Parzival encounters his weeping cousin seated at a linden tree with the embalmed body of her slain lover in her arms (I, 5 249-254). While Perceval's cousin is left nameless by Chretien, Wolfram has a name, Sigune, for her and also one, Schionatulander, for the dead knight. Sigune tells Parzival not only the sword's secret that it would break at a second stroke, but she also tells him the smith's name, Trebuchet. The broken sword could be healed by exactly fitting the pieces together and dipping it before sunrise into the magic spring, Lac, near Karnant. According to Wolfram, this can be done without the help of the smith.[2]

The smith's name, Trebuchet, has been puzzled over without much result. Its similarity to that of the site of the tenth battle in Nennius' list of Arthur's victories, 'in litore fluminis quod vocatur Tribruit', has been duly noticed. In search for Celtic origins a possible connection with Turbe, the father of the Irish divine smith, Goibhniu, has been suggested,[3] but Goibhniu's weapons carried the guarantee of never failing or missing in a cast and that no one wounded by them would survive.[4] A linguistic claim has been made that names starting with 'Tre-' would be of Cornish origin,[5] but it is more tempting to look for a French source – after all, Chretien wrote in French.

In my French dictionary I find a verb *trebucher,* 'to stumble, to slip; to trip, to err'. Thus, Trebuchet would indicate a person challenged in walking, and indeed, the smiths of medieval legends were lame, such as the dwarves Brock and Sindri of the Edda, Regin, who healed the sword of the Volsungs for Sigurd, and Wayland the Smith himself, as well as his ancestral prototypes, Vulcan and Hephaistos, of classical myth.

The name Trebuchet seems to have been invented by Chretien. Perhaps Chretien created it not only in order to hint at the lameness that characterizes smiths of legend, but also using the secondary meaning of *trebucher*, 'to err' as a wry comment on Trebuchet's flawed masterpiece.

Appendix

One of the crucial stages in the making of a sword blade is its steeling by quenching in water. Therefore, all smiths of legend and myth are somehow connected with water: Trebuchet, according to Chretien, was living at Cotoatre, i.e. the Firth of Forth, Wolfram lets the broken sword be healed by the magic spring Lac, Wayland/ Wieland was the son of a water fey and worked at the banks of the Rhine, with a swan maiden as his mate, the very name of Brock meant bog iron, Hephaistos was saved by the sea goddess Thetys, when Zeus threw him as a child out of the heavens, causing his lameness. Even in recent German folk lore there are artful dwarf smiths who are limping because of their having duck feet(!).

The earliest representation of the encounter with the maiden under the tree with a dead or sleeping warrior resting his head in her lap is on a pair of gold scabbard mountings, Altai/Sauromatian, *c.* 400 BC (Si 1727,1/161), in the so-called Siberian Treasure of Peter the Great, in the State Hermitage Museum, St Petersburg. Typically, the mirrorwise doubled mountings are for a pair of swords, and thus the episode is an integral part of the motif complex of the Knight with Two Swords.

Notes

1. Chretien de Troyes, *Perceval or, The Story of the Grail,* transl. Ruth Harwood Cline, Pergamon Press, New York, 1983
2. Wolfram von Eschenbach, *Parzival,* ed. Karl Lachmann, transl. Wolfgang Spiewok, ReclamUniversal-BibliothekNr.3681, Stuttgart, 1981
3. Ronan Coghlan, *The Encyclopaedia of Arthurian Legends,* Element Books Ltd., Shaftesbury, Dorset/Rockport, Massachusetts, 1991; Mike Dixon-Kennedy, *Arthurian Myth & Legend: An A-Z of People and Places,* Blandford, London, 1995
4. Proinsias Mac Cana, *Celtic Mythology,* Hamlyn, New York, 1970
5. Phyllis Ann Karr, *The Arthurian Companion,* A Chaosium Book, 1997

Previously unpublished.

20

Black against White

What Colour Was King Arthur's Horse?

Among the various theories about the cavalry aspect of King Arthur's Knights of the Round Table, ranging from R. G. Collingwood's blunt statement, 'King Arthur's knights are myths' to Robert Graves's vision of' 'mounted commandos' led by a 'heroic British cavalry general named Arturius', one of the most intriguing and original is presented by S. G. Wildman in his book *The Black Horsemen: English Inns and King Arthur.*[1]

S. G. Wildman found that among English inn signs with animal names the most popular are 'The White Hart' and 'The White Horse', but there are also more than two hundred named 'The Black Horse'. While 'The White Hart' (as the badge of King Richard II) and 'The White Horse' (as the badge of the Hanoverian dynasty) could be heraldic in origin, this does not apply to 'The Black Horse'. On the other hand, 'The Black Horse' is not necessarily simply a counterpart to a local inn named 'The White Horse', but is found distributed over the map of England in a most peculiar pattern,

Of the various explanations tried, such as whether 'The Black Horse' could have been code-names for safe houses for Catholics during the persecutions of the seventeenth century, or named so by Jacobites in defiance of 'The White Horse,' which was seen as the badge of the Hanoverian kings, none turned out satisfactorily. Finally, by looking at the map of England, Wildman found 'The Black Horse' inns mainly in seven areas that correspond to the 'frontier' of the fights between Britons and Saxons in the sixth century, in short, to the presumed sites of King Arthur's battles (with minor adjustments).

Although he had to admit that he could not find any medieval literature mentioning the colour of King Arthur's horse, Wildman came to the conclusion that the cavalry horses of the *dux bellorum* Arthur were of a breed black in colour. Therefore, the area controlled by Arthur's cavalry would have been Black Horse country, to be feared and avoided by the Saxons whose totem animal was the White Horse. These cavalry horses were thought by Wildman to have been of Frisian stock, which is black, and with a possible admixture of Fell ponies, also black. This theory must have inspired Anne McCaffrey's book *Black Horses for the King*. However, Anne McCaffrey's black horses were imported Libyan stock, acquired from an Egyptian trader at the horse fair of Narbo Martius in Septimania, in the South of Gaul.[2]

Earlier, the horse fair of Narbo Martius was the supply source for Arthur's cavalry mounts in Rosemary Sutcliff's *Sword at Sunset*. The prize stud stallion that Arthur acquired at Narbo Martius was the Black One, but despite that Rosemary Sutcliff's Arthur 'always rode a white horse in battle' – first Arain, then Signus, and Grey Falcon – not because he found them better than horses of any other colour, but because 'a white horse marks out the leader clearly for his men to follow.' Consequently, the cover illustration of the Crest Book paperback edition (1964) shows Arthur on his white steed holding aloft his sword like a cross.[3]

In *Erec et Enide* by Chrétien de Troyes (*c.* 1170) King Arthur's horse is named Aubagu, which seems to mean 'White Points', suggesting a dark overall colour.[4] The Alliterative *Morte Arthur* (*c.* 1360) mentions Arthur's 'broun' or 'baye' steed.[5] For the hunt of the boar Trwch Trwyth, in the Mabinogion's *Culhwch and Olwen,* King Arthur was to obtain Dun-mane, the steed of Gweddw, but he also owned a mare, Llamrei (Fastpace). Llamrei's colour is not mentioned. Gwyn, son of Nudd, for the same hunt had to borrow the horse of Moro Oerfeddawg, named Du (Black). Nevertheless, there are white horses in King Arthur's cavalry, too. In the third of the three romances in the Mabinogion, *Gereint, son of Erbin,* Gereint rides bare-legged a willow-grey steed, and in the *Tale of Geraint,* the hero fights in the Battle at Llongborth along with Arthur or Arthur's men: 'Before Geraint, the enemy's scourge, I saw white horses, tensed, red,' and 'Swiftly there ran under Geraint's thigh long-shanked (horses fed on) grass of wheat, roans (with the) onrush of speckled eagles.' The best known of Arthurian horses is perhaps Gawain's white Gringolet 'of the red ears', an epithet that sounds very much like the prized 'medicine hat' of the Plains Indians.

The White Horse as the badge of the Hanoverian kings goes back to the tribal totem of pre-Christian Saxony. If the Saxon war leaders of the Adventus, with their tell-tale names, Hengist (Stallion) and Horsa, bore any device on their shields, it presumably would have been a white horse, as it is still the charge in the arms of Kent, their first foothold in Britain. A white horse was the favoured sacrifice to Woden (see appendix). The sacrificed horse was then ritually eaten, a practice that Charlemagne had made punishable by death as a relapse to heathen cults after he finally succeeded in his thirty-year-long struggle to convert to Christianity the pagan Saxons. This is one reason why even today horsemeat is not eaten in Germany. On the other hand, since no sacred meal of horseflesh was known in pre-Christian France, no ban was needed, and French charcutiers happily specialize in selling horsemeat as a delicacy.

In the *Dream of Rhonabwy* appear several troops of warriors on colour-coordinated horses: those of the troop of Rhwawn Bebyr are red as blood, those of Addaon, son of Teliesin, from the front saddlebow white as the water lily, but downwards black as jet, those of the men of Llychlyn pale white with the forelegs black, and those of the men of Denmark with Edern son of Nudd black with forelegs pure white.

Colour-coordination within military units is of course highly desirable and a mark of sophistication. The Kings of France had two elite guards, 'les Mousquetaires gris' and 'les noirs', called after the colour of their horses (Dumas' d'Artagnan became captain of les noirs). The steppe nomads of the dawn of history were often divided into colour moieties, such as the black Coumans and the white, the white Kalpaks and the Kara (black) Kalpaks. In 201 BC, the Han emperor, Kao, in person led a campaign against the Hung-no, presumed ancestors of the Huns of history. As mentioned in Chapter 11, Far Eastern cosmology assigns colours to the five directions of the world: red for South, black for North, white for West, blue for East, and yellow for the centre. The army of the Hung-no was arranged accordingly, those warriors on red (brown) horses formed the vanguard, those on blacks the rear, those on whites were the right wing, and those on greys (the closest to blue) the left. The wily Hung-no leader, Mo-tun, succeeded in trapping and surrounding the Chinese army according to this cosmic colour code and, as the finishing touch, had in the centre of the trap the hapless Chinese emperor, whose sacred colour was the Imperial yellow.[6]

By the second century AD various steppe nomad tribes, Sarmatians and Alani, had drifted far enough westward to become a serious threat to Roman provinces along the Danube. In order to tender this threat more or less harmless, in 175 AD Emperor Marcus Aurelius took 8,000 Sarmatian tribesmen from Pannonia, today's Hungary, into the Roman army as auxiliaries. Sarmatian warriors were heavy cavalry; in fact, they were the prototype of the fully armoured cataphracts of the Late Roman and Byzantine armies. Of the 8,000 Sarmatians, 5,500 were sent to North Britain to fight Picts as cavalry attachments to the *Legio VI Victrix*, whose praefectus was a certain Lucius Artorius Castus.[7] At Newstead, the former Roman fort of Trimontium, pieces of Sarmatian horse armour were discovered together with nine horse skeletons.[8] In the thirteenth chapter of her *Sword at Sunset,* Rosemary Sutcliff makes use of this extraordinary find. These horse skeletons have been identified as similar to still existing Turkmenian breeds, such as the Kabardin.

It seems that Western steppe nomads, too, practised colour coordination of their horses. For instance, in Dacia, today's Bulgaria, the Roxolani (White Alani), cousins of the Sarmatians, were famous for their 'hoarfrost-coloured' steeds. We do not know the colour of the horses of Trimontium, but the Kabardin breed is black.[9]

Appendix

Woden was also the leader of the Wild Hunt that haunts the skies in the Twelve Nights after Christmas. These ghost riders, the souls of dead heroes fallen in battle, are following Woden on his eight-legged grey horse (the storm cloud). In the intricate use of kennings, metaphors, and code words in Germanic poetry, 'riding on the eight-legged horse' was a kenning for the dead hero on his bier carried by four men. Another leader of the Wild Hunt is Dietrich von Bern, who as Theodoric, King of the Ostrogoths (r. 471-526), was not only a historical contemporary of King Arthur but also his equivalent in German and Scandinavian mythology. Dietrich's steed, Schwarzer Falke, is black; it was a present from the legendary horse breeder Studa in the Black Forest, the eponymous hero of Stuttgart (the civic arms of Stuttgart, well known as the logo of Porsche, are a black horse in gold). About fifteen miles east of Dresden (my home town), there is a large forest district called Masseney, which when I was a boy was (and probably still is) a favourite hunting ground of 'Bandittrich', i.e. Dietrich von Bern and his Wild Hunt. In the middle of this forest is a country inn, 'Zum Schwarzen Ross' ('The Black Horsemen').

Notes

1. R. G. Collingwood, 'Arthur's Battles', *Antiquity* 3 (1929): 292-98; Robert Graves, Introduction to *Le Morte d'Arthur*, ed. Keith Baines (New York: Bramhall House, 1962), p. xii; S. G. Wildman, *The Black Horsemen: English Inns and King Arthur* (London: John Baker, 1971).
2. Anne McCaffrey, *Black Horses for the King* (San Diego: Harcourt Brace & Co., 1996).
3. Rosemary Sutcliff, *Sword at Sunset* (New York: Crest, 1964).
4. 'Erec and Enide' in *Chrétien de Troyes: Arthurian Romances*, ed. and trans. W. W. Comfort (London: Everyman, 1967), p. 54.
5. *Morte Arthure: A Critical Edition*, ed. Mary Hamel (New York/ London: Garland Medieval Texts, no. 9,1984) p. 134, lines 915, 918.
6. L. P. Potapov, 'Uber den Pferdekult bei den turksprachigen Volkern des Sajan-Altai-Gebirges', *Abhandlungen und Berichte des Staatlichen Museums fur Volkerkunde Dresden* 34 (1975) 46; Helmut Nickel, 'And Behold a White Horse...' Observations on the Colors of the Horses of the Four Horsemen of the Apocalypse,' *Metropolitan Museum Journal* 12 (1977): 179-83.
7. Helmut Nickel, 'Wer waren Konig Artus' Ritter? Uber die geschichtliche Grundlage der Artussagen', *Waffen-und Kostumkunde* 17.1 (1975): 1-28, note 67; and Nickel's 'Cavalry, Arthurian' entry in *The New Arthurian Encyclopaedia,* ed. Norris J. Lacy (New York: Garland, 1991), pp. 74-76.
8. James Curie, *A Roman Frontier Post and its People: The Fort of Newstead* (Glasgow, 1911) pp. 153ff, pi. XXXI.
9. Sir Richard Glyn, *The World's Finest Horses and Ponies* (Garden City, NJ: Doubleday, 1971), p. 109, pl. 117.

Originally published in *Arthuriana* vol. 14, No. 2 (Summer, 2004) pp. 69-72.

21

Arthurian Armings for War and for Love

Armour was the distinguishing mark of a knight, and therefore arming scenes play an important role in the chivalric literature composed for audiences of the knightly class by authors who were often knights themselves. Although these arming scenes were woven into tales of *faerie,* it was essential that they should not stray too far from known reality, either contemporary or as remembered from bygone days. Also, and significantly, care was taken to include in them one other important aspect of chivalry, the veneration of women, spiritual and secular, which gave the rough men's world of hard-bitten fighters its saving grace.

Arming a Christian Champion Going to War

The first arming scene to be discussed here is in Geoffrey of Monmouth's *Historia Regum Britanniae* (ix, 4), describing how King Arthur readies himself for battle. After exhortations by the saintly Dubricius, Archbishop of the City of Legions, Arthur and his men arm themselves:

> Ipse uero arturus lorica tantu rege digna indutus. auream galeum simulacro draconis insculptam. capiti adaptat. Humeris quoque suis clipeum uocabulo pridwen. in quo imago sancte marie dei genetricis inpicta ipsum in memoriam ipsius sepissime reuocabat. Accinctus ergo caliburno gladio optimo. & in insula auallonis fabricato. lancca dextram suam decorat. que nomine ron uocabatur. Haec ardua erat. lataque lancea. cladibus apta. (Griscom 438; Wright I 103-04)

> Arthur himself has put on leather armour [*lorica*, from *loreus*, leathern] truly worthy of such a great king. A golden helmet sculpted with the likeness of a dragon he fits on his head, also, on his shoulders [i.e. hanging from its neck strap] the shield named Pridwen.[1] whereon was the painted Image of Saint Mary, mother of God; thus he called her ever so often [i.e. as often as he looked at her image] back into his memory Furthermore he was girded with Caliburn, a sword of best quality, and forged on the island of Avalon. A spear called by the name Ron graced his right hand, tall and broad-bladed and well-suited to wreak havoc.[2]

However, this description is not at all that of armour of Geoffrey's own time, the first half of the twelfth century, when knights wore mail shirts, helmets without any crests, and 'Norman' shields of elongated almond-shape (Blair 19-36; Edge and Paddock 38-65; Norman, *History* 29-34; Norman, *Soldier* 196-205). Life imitates art, though, and the earliest documented English helmet crest, on the seal of Roger de Quincey, Earl of Winchester (d. 1264), is a dragon (Fox-Davies 334, fig. 615).

It is intriguing that the three elements of dragon-crested golden helmet, decorated leather *lorica*, and circular shield, have piece-for-piece their exact counterparts in actual objects found in 1939 at Sutton Hoo in the barrow of a seventh-century Anglo-Saxon king (Fig. 1). Circumstantial and stylistic evidence shows that these excavated armour elements must have been heirlooms from a considerably earlier period, probably *c.* AD 500, insofar as they are 'barbarized' versions of the equipment for high-ranking officers of the late Roman army (Gamber 208-16; Nickel, *Arms* 19-21; Nicolle 8-16, pls. A-C). Geoffrey's word-picture of objects he could not possibly have seen with his own eyes gives credibility to his assertion that he had 'an ancient book' as his source.[3] The interesting fact that the last line of the arming scene, '*Haec erat ardua lataque lancea, cladibus apta*', is an internally rhymed hexameter (Wright 1104), makes the possibility of a literary source – perhaps a praise poem – even more likely.

The most intriguing detail of Geoffrey's arming of Arthur is the icon of the Virgin Mary on Arthur's shield. It is first mentioned in Nennius's list of Arthur's battles, which is thought to be a translation of a lost Welsh poem of praise:

> Octavum fuit bellum in castello Guinnion, in quo Arthur portavit imaginem sanctae Mariae perperuae virginis super humeros suos, et

Fig. 1: King Arthur, according to Geoffrey of Monmouth, in sixth-century armour 'Sutton Hoo' style.

> pagani versi sunt in fugam in illo die, et caedes magna fuit super illos per virtutem Domini nostri Jesu Christi et per virtutem sanctae Mariae virginis genitricis ejus. (Morris, 76)
>
> The eighth battle was at the castellum Guinnion. where Arthur wore the image of Blessed Mary Ever Virgin on his shoulders, and the heathens were put to flight on that day and great slaughter was done to them by the grace of Our Lord Jesus Christ and that of His mother, the Blessed Virgin Mary.

It is generally accepted that the image of the Virgin Mary was worn not on Arthur's shoulders (*super humeros suos*), but on his shield. The Welsh word for shoulder, *ysquid*, is deceptively close to *ysquit*, 'shield'.[4] As I pointed out above, a shield would be hanging by its strap draped around the shoulders.

Geoffrey's rendering, *in quo ... inpicta,* has been translated in two different ways: One sees (Thorpe 217) the icon as a shield emblem; the other (Brengle 63) as a protective charm on the inside of the shield, where Arthur could have this revered image always before his eyes to give him strength in battle. Indeed, on the second day of the hard-fought battle Arthur piously invokes the name of the Blessed Virgin Mary, and thus succeeds in killing single-handedly, *solo caliburno gladio,* 470 of the enemy.

The first interpretation of the icon, as a shield emblem, is strongly suggested by the variant:

> ... clipeum quoque nomine Priduen
> Fert humeris, in quo Christi genetricis ymago
> Fulget
>
> (Wright V184)

'Also he carries the shield named Priduen on his shoulders, whereon the image of the Mother of Christ flashes like lightning.'

Similar images of female Victory deities on shields are documented in the illustrated muster roll of Late Roman army units, the *Notitia Dignitatum* of AD 428 (Nickel, 'Artus' Ritter' 10; Berger pls. 4, 6, 17, 50, 51, 130, 131). A secular example is the medallion with the portraits of Emperor Theodosius I and his empress on the shield of Stilicho, commander-in-chief of the Roman army (390-408), in his ivory diptych at Monza (Nickel, 'Artus' Ritter' 20; Berger pl. 103). The alternative interpretation of the Blessed Virgin's icon as an amulet on the inside of

Arthur's shield is found in the Welsh manuscript No. LXI of Jesus College, Oxford. Though the slightly garbled text docs not expressly mention any shield, the name 'prydwenn' clearly indicates that it is Arthur's shield that is described here:

> And then Arthyr put on a breast-plate worthy of a King; and on his head was a golden helmet with the likeness of a dragon of fire on it, and another image called prydwenn [blessed form), and on its inner side was carved the likeness of Mary. And this Arthyr bore with him when he went into battle-peril. [Griscom and Jones 438]

Arming a Knight to Serve his Lady in Courtly Love

Whereas in the *Historia Regnum Britanniae* armour is depicted in terms of bygone days, in contrast, the arming scene in Chrétien's *Erec et Enide* (*c.* 1170), describes in detail how a knight of Chrétien's own time is armed. In order to enter the Contest for the Sparrow Hawk, Erec has to borrow armour from his host, Enide's father. Armour is difficult to put on without assistance (Ascherl 276-77), and Enide herself helps Erec to arm:

> la pucele meismes l'arme;
> [ ]
> Lace li les chauces de fer
> et queust a corroie de cer;
> hauberc li vest de boene maille
> et se li lace la vantaille;
> le hiaume brun li met el chief:
> molt l'arme bien de chief an chief
> Au costé l'espee li ceint.
> Puis comande qu'an li amaint
> son cheval, et l'an li amainne;
> sus est sailliz de terre plainne
> La pucele aporte l'escu
> et la lance qui roide fu:
> I'escu li baille, et il le prant;
> par la guige a son col le pant
> La lance li ra el poing mise;
> cil l'a devers I'arestuel prise. [709, 711-26]

'The maiden herself arms him
[ ]
Ties on the iron *chauces*
and lutes them up with deer hide (thongs);
dresses him in the *hauberc* of good mail
and laces fast the *aventail*
She puts the burnished helmet on his head,
so he was well armed head to toe.
To his side she belts his sword.
Then she orders his horse to be brought,
and when it is led to him,
he leaps on it from the plain ground.
The maiden fetches the shield
and the sturdy lance.
She hands him the shield, and he takes it,
he hangs it around his neck by the *guige.*
She gives the lance into his fist;
he grasps it at the *arrestuel* and sets it in position.'

This description follows step by step the actual stages of a knight's arming, which has to be done from the feet up. The *chauces* are mail leggings, wrapped around the leg and laced up in back; they are tied to an interior belt to keep them in position, very much like stockings to a modern garter belt. The leathern lacings and tie straps were of tough deer hide. Next came the mail shirt or *hauberc* (from German *Halsberge,* 'neck cover'); it was slipped on over the head, like a sweater. It had an attached hood, the *coif,* with a triangular flap, the *aventail,* that could be pulled up and laced in position across the lower part of the face. Finally, the helmet *(heaume)* was set on the knight's head, and his sword belted on. The swordbelt also took up part of the drag of the sagging mail shirt (Fig. 2).[5]

A mail shirt weighed about twenty-five pounds,[6] the *chauces* five or six pounds each, the helmet up to five pounds, and the sword with scabbard and belt again not more than about five pounds. Therefore, Erec's jumping into his saddle directly from the ground (*de terre plainne*), without using a mounting block, was a sign of his prowess, but not at all an impossible feat. In fact, it would have been part of a knight's basic training. In order to survive in battle, a knight whose horse was killed had to be able to scramble onto the next riderless steed when there was no time to fumble for the stirrups.[7]

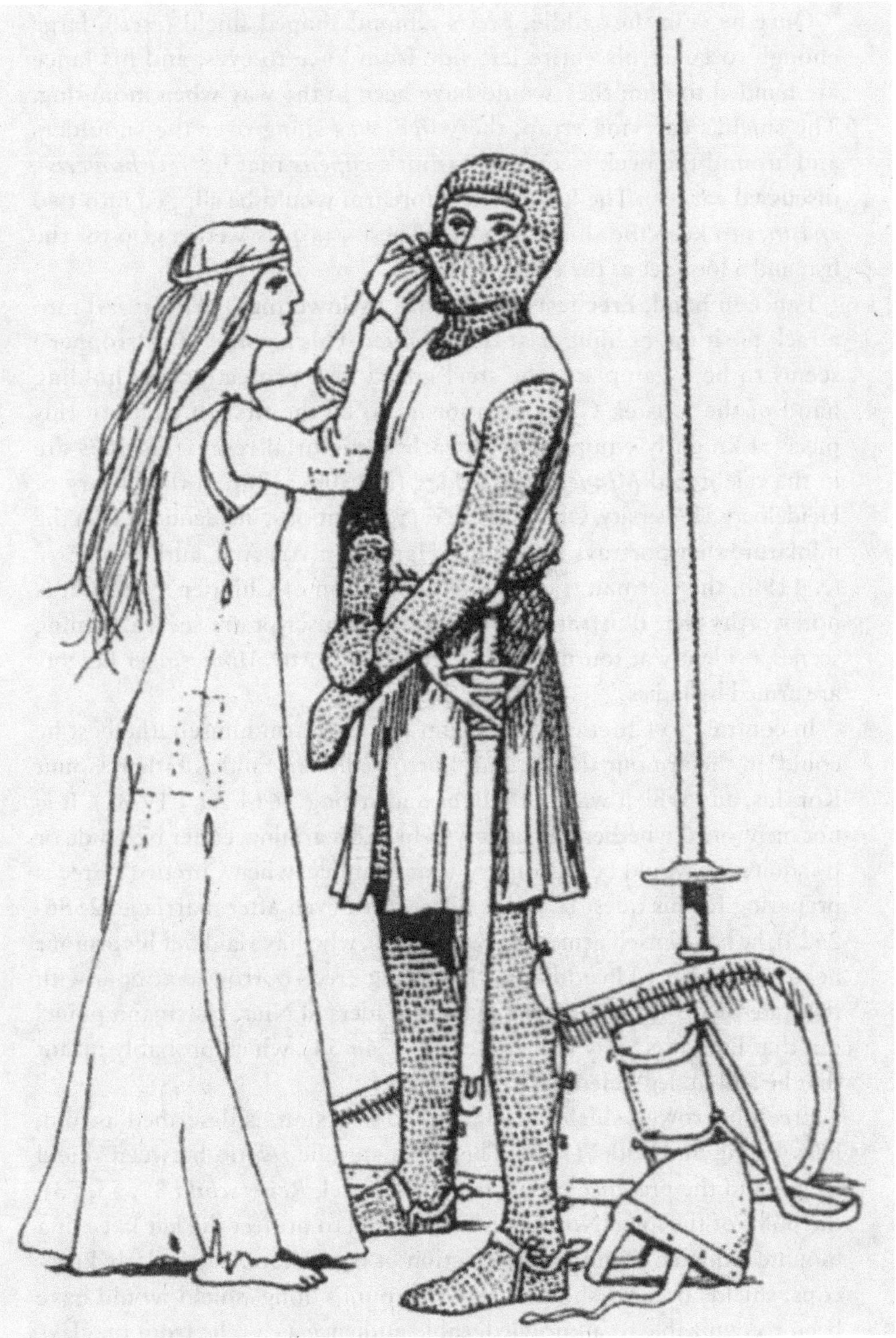

Fig. 2: Erec and Enid

Once he is in the saddle, Erec's almond-shaped shield (*escu*), large enough to cover his entire left side from knee to eyes, and his lance are handed to him; they would have been in the way when mounting. The shield's carrying strap, the *guige*, was slung over the shoulders and around the neck (see King Arthur's *clipeus* that he '*fert humeris*', discussed earlier). The knight's left forearm would be slipped into two *enarmes* to keep the shield 'braced'. These *enarmes* were a grip for the fist, and a loop set at the elbow.

Lance in hand, Erec tests its balance by lowering it (*l'a devers*) into attack position, holding it at the *arestuel*. This *arestuel* (the 'stopper') seems to be a vamplate, the steel guard disk protecting the holding hand of the jouster. Chrétien appears to be the first to mention this piece of knightly equipment. Its earliest pictorial representations are in the celebrated *Minnesinger Codex* (*c.* 1300-1320), in the library of Heidelberg University. One of these representations, incidentally, is in the miniature that portrays the knight Hartmann von Aue, author of *Erec* (*c.* 1190), the German translation/ adaptation of Chrétien's work. It is noteworthy that illustrated in the same manuscript are several arming scenes, evidently at tournaments, where the courtly *Minnesinger* knights are armed by ladies.[8]

In contrast to Chrétien, Hartmann lets Erec arm himself 'the best he could' in the armour that he had borrowed from Enide's father, Count Koralus, and which was both 'light and strong' (614-20, 714-31). It is not mentioned whether he had any help in his arming, either by Enide or by squires as would be customary. (For example, when Chrétien's Erec is preparing for his quest to prove his renown even after marriage (2586-2623), he has himself armed by two squires, who have laid out his armour neatly on a carpet.) In addition, comparing Erec's borrowed armour with the state-of-the-art equipment of his foe, Iders fil Niut, Hartmann points out that Erec was 'only half protected' (746-54), which probably meant that he had no leg-defences.

Erec's borrowed shield, in Hartmann's version, is described as 'old, heavy, long and wide' (746). There is a specific *relatio* between shield length and the presence of leg-armour (Nickel, *Reiterschild* 39, 55, 73); the point of the long 'Norman' shield served to protect the left knee of a mounted knight. With the introduction of leg-armour, particularly knee-cops, shields became shorter. The old count's 'long' shield would have been recognizable to a knowledgeable audience as a relic from the days before the introduction of *chauces*. (Notice that there are no leg-defences mentioned in Geoffrey's arming of King Arthur!) By leaving out leg-defences from Erec's armour, Hartmann possibly wanted to avoid any indelicacy that might be seen in Chrétien's arming scene, where Enide fastens Erec's *chauces.*

On the other hand, Hartmann goes farther than Chrétien in describing the poor state of Enide's clothes. Chrétien says that Enide's white dress over her linen chemise was so old and threadbare that it had holes in its sides, but Hartmann adds that both Enide's green[9] dress and her chemise were so worn and ragged that 'her body shone through as white as a swan ... like a lily that blossoms white among black thorns' (336-38). Erec insists that she should accompany him to the beauty contest of the sparrow hawk in these her poor clothes, because 'one should recognize whether a woman is worthy of praise by her person and not by her clothing' (646-50). It sheds an interesting light on the concept of chivalry that an impoverished nobleman keeps his expensive armour as status symbol, while his daughter's only dress is in tatters that literally barely cover her.

Later, when as an extended celebration of Erec's and Enide's wedding at King Arthur's court a tournament was to be held, Erec took special care to outfit himself properly. He had three shields and three horse trappings made, all matching though of different colours (2285ff.): one of silver, one red, and one golden. They all share the same *wâfen* [heraldic charge], a *mouwe* (lady's sleeve): the silver shield has a *mouwe* of gold; the red one has a silver *mouwe;* and the golden one a *mouwe zobelin,* i.e. *sable,* the heraldic term for black. In addition, there is a silver shield boss and radiating mountings, evidently of the kind that was to be called an *escarbuncle.* The inside was gilded, and '*Inerhalp ein vrouwe An den vordern orte: Der schiltrieme ein borte Von quotem gesteine.*' (2311-13) 'On the inside a lady in the dexter corner: the *guige* an ornamental ribbon with fine gems' (Schultz 83; Nickel, *Reiterschild* 91).

Though Alwin Schultz once suggested that the *mouwe* was a protective cover, it is now generally understood that Erec had a lady's sleeve as an heraldic charge (*wâfen*) on his three shields (*Erec* 162 n59), but the gold sleeve on silver violates the rule of heraldic tinctures.[10] This and the strange arrangement of a shield boss (*buckel*) with radiating metal mountings (*ris*) placed over the sleeve charge arc explained away by still loose rules during the developmental stages of heraldry.

As we have already noted, a lady's sleeve, torn off and leaving her arm deliciously bare, was one of the sexier 'favours' in the game of courtly love (see *Parzival,* 193). Such a 'favour' would be worn attached to the knight's shield, his helmet, or to other elements of his armour (Gravett 19; Nickel, 'Ladies' Favors' 31-34), but in this case it is neither a heraldic device nor a 'favour'. Alas, the *mouwe* (Fr. *manche*) is a mistranslation of *emmanché* (meaning 'with handles') from a French source other than Chrétien, who does not have the detail of the three shields. The term *emmanché* would apply to elaborate *enarmes* and perhaps padding (of sable pelt) on the gilded backs of the shields, complementing the jewelled *guige.*

However, the most interesting detail is the lady's image on the shield's inside and at the dexter corner, directly in front of Erec's face when the shield was 'braced' in fighting position: 'Innerhalp ein vrouwe An den vordern orte (2311-12). Presumably it was a portrait of Enide as a secular 'icon' of Erec's love, to give him strength when he looked at it. One of the few knightly shields surviving, the shield of Landgrave Konrad of Thuringia (d. 1241), in the University Museum Marburg, bears on its gilded (!) inner side, traces of a painted Minne scene. A knight with the arms of Thuringia on his surcoat, but without a helmet, is kneeling before an unfortunately only fragmentary preserved lady. Presumably she would have completed his arming by putting the helmet on his head (Warnecke no. 1; Nickel, *Reiterschild* 29-31).

Arming for a Quest under Spiritual Guidance

The most famous of Arthurian arming scenes is, of course, the arming of Sir Gawain in *Sir Gawain and the Green Knight* (*c.* 1370). (For more details, see Chapter 10.) Like Chrétien's Erec before his quest, Sir Gawain orders his squires to lay out his armour on a carpet for his inspection:

> [He] Askez erly hys armez, and alle were þay brozt.
> Fyrst a tulé tapit $ty_0$1 oucr þe flet,
> And miche watz pc gyld gerc J)at gleni peralofte.
> J'e stif mon steppez peron and pe nd hondeldez. (567-70)

> [Early in the morning] he calls for his arms, and they all were brought. At first a red carpet was spread on the floor, and there was much gilt gear that gleamed piled on it. The bold man steps on it and takes the steel in hand.

The actual arming is meticulously described. First he puts on a padded jerkin (dublet) and shoulder hood (capados) to prevent chafing, and then is armed, beginning at the feet:

Dubbed in a dublet of a dere tars
And sithen a crafty capados, closed aloft,
That with a bryght blaunner was bounden withinne.
Then set thay the sabatouns upon the segge fotes,
His legges lapped in stele with lovely greves,
With polaynes piched therto polysed ful clene,
Aboute his knes knaged with knottes of gold;
Queme quyssewes then that quayntly closed,
His thik throwen thyghes with thwonges to tached;
And sithen the brayden bruny of bryghte stele rynges
Umbeweved that wye upon wlonk stuffe,
And wel burnyst brace upon his both armes,
With good cowters and gay and gloves of plate,
And all the goodly gere that him gayn schulde
That tyde;
With rich cote-armure,
His golde spures spend with pryde,
Gurde with a bronde ful sure
With silk saynt umbe his side
When he was hasped in amies, his harnays was ryche:
He lest lachet oper loupe lemed of golde. (571-91)[10]

He was arrayed in a doublet of rich fabric of Tarsia, and then a well-made capados, fitted close, that was lined with light-coloured fur. Then they set the *sabatons* on the man's feet. His legs were enclosed in steel by elegant greaves with attached *poleyns*. Brightly polished [they] were fastened around his knees with golden buckles. Then came the *cuisses* that snugly enclosed his brawny thighs, attached by means of straps. And afterward the *byrnie*, wrought of bright steel rings enveloped the rich fabric [of the doublet]. And [they set] well-burnished *vambraces* [arm defences] upon both his arms, with good and shiny *cowters,* and *gauntlets* of plate. And all the fine equipment that he needed this time; with splendid *cote-armure,* his golden spurs proudly fastened on, girt with a trusty sword [brand] with a silken belt [sayn] to his side. When he was fully armoured, his harness was rich, the least buckle and clasp gleamed of gold.

Sabatons are articulated steel shoes, while *greaves* are leg-defences of steel plates (front and back) moulded to fit the lower leg snugly. *Poleyns* are knee defences, and *cuisses* cover the thighs (for a comfortable seat in the saddle they are buckled on only to the outer side). After the leg-armour is in place, the mail shirt, *burnie*, is put on next, and then the arm defences,

Fig. 3: The Arming of Sir Gawain.

braces, with *cowters* (elbow defences) and steel gloves (*gauntlets*). Over the mail *burnie* is put *cote-armure*, a fitted body armour of fabric reinforced with interior steel plates; it was often embroidered with heraldic devices (the original 'coat-of-arms'). As the last items, Sir Gawain's golden spurs (a privilege of knighthood) are buckled on over his *sabatons*, and his sword girded on with a silken belt over his *cote-armure* (Fig. 3).

Sir Gawain's armour is of the type some scholars call the 'transition' period, between mail armour and full plate armour. The *Gawain*-Poet makes it a point that, when Gawain comes to the Castle Hautdesert after his arduous winter journey, his thoughtful host, who has a well-trained staff at hand, orders 'both his paunce and his plates' (2017) to be sent to the armoury for cleaning and polishing. *Paunces* (cf. German 'Panzer') is mail armour that could not be cleaned by hand, and therefore was 'rokked' (2018) in a tumbling barrel half filled with sawdust for the absorption of rust and grime. (See Chapter 10, Note 3.) Armour maintenance posed a serious problem. Knights errant and free lances, who could not or would not pay a well-trained squire to keep their armour properly polished, had theirs painted; these are the black knights we encounter in the romances, who travelled alone. To be kept in good working order, small but important elements, such as buckles, *lachets* and *loupes,* had to be rustproofed. This was done by gilding, if the knight could afford it (fortunately Sir Gawain could); lesser folk had to make do with a tinwash.[11]

When Sir Gawain is mounted, his squires hand him helmet, shield, and lance:

Ienne hemes he be *helmr* and hastily hit kysses,
Iat wan stapled stifly, and stoffed wythinne.
Hit watz hyge on his hede, hasped bihynde,
Wyth a lyjjtly *vrysoun* ouer pe *auentayle,*
Enbrawden and bounden wyth pe best gemmez
On brode sylkyn borde, and bryddez on semez,
As papiayez paynted periling birwene,
Tortors and trulofez entayled so pyk
As mony burde fieraboute had ben seuen wyntcr
In toune.
I'e ecrele watz more o prys
hat vmbeclypped hys croun,
Of diamaumez a *deuys*
hat bopc wer bryy and broun. (605-18)

Then he takes the helmet in hand and kisses it quickly; it was stoutly riveted and lined with padding. It sat high on his head, enclasped in back with a lightweight *uryson* over the *aventail* embroidered and studded with finest jewels on its broad silken border, and birds depicted along the seams, such as popinjays among periwinkles and turtledoves and love knots entangled so thickly and so many a maiden had been busy with it for seven winters at court. The circlet that encircled the helmet bowl was even more precious. (It bore) a *devys* picked out in diamonds, both clear and black ones.

This well-padded helmet is of the bascinet type, with a curtain of mail, the *camail* or *aventail,* attached that covers neck and shoulders. The effigy of the Black Prince, Edward Plantagenet (d. 1376), in Canterbury Cathedral, is the best-known example of this type of armour, *cote-armure,* arm -and leg-defences of plate, [12] and bascinet with circlet and *camail (Cole* 212-15; Norman, *History* 89; Sedgwick 284). Sir Gawain's helmet is of special splendour, with a colourfully embroidered and jewelled fabric cover (*uryson*) over the mail of the *aventail,* and a diamond-studded circlet around the helmet bowl. These diamonds are set to form '*a devys*'.[13] This could be his war cry or motto (Fr. *devise): ORCANIE, ORCANIE* (Nickel, 'Lace' 22; Pastoureau 70), or more likely his badge, the pentangle that he bears on his shield as is mentioned a few lines further on. This shield he hangs around his neck by its shield strap, the baldric (*bauderyk*):

> ... ay schewed hym þe schelde, þat was of schyr goulez
> Wyth þe pentangel depaynt of pure golde hwcz.
> He braydez hit by the *bauderyk,* aboute [e hals kestes. (619-21)

> ... they showed him the shield, which was bright red with the pentangle depicted in pure golden hues. He grasps it by the *bauderyk,* and casts it around his neck.

The golden pentangle, 'Salamon's seal' or the 'endeles knot,' is explained by the *Gawain*-Poet himself as symbolizing not only that Gawain 'watz for gode knawen, and as golde pured' (633), but also his five, five-fold virtues as the 'gentylest knygt of lote'[14] (639): his faultless five senses, the dexterity of his five fingers, his devotion to the five wounds of Christ on the Cross, his five virtues of *fraunchyse, felawship, clannes, cortaysye,* and *pité*, and – most significantly – his fortitude received by virtue of 'þe fyue joyez / that he hende Heuen-quene had of hir chylde' (646-47). The poet explains: 'At þis cause þe knyjt comlyche hade / In þe inore half of his schelde hir ymage depayntcd, / þat quen he blusched þerto his belde neuer payred' (648-50). 'For this reason the noble knight had in the inner side of his shield her image painted that whenever he looked at it his courage would not fail.'[15]

The pentangle that Gawain bore on his shield and his *cote-armure* (637) was a badge, not his family coat-of-arms. These latter were either: *Argent, a canton gules*; or: *Purpure, a double-headed eagle Or, armed axure,* depending on which romance source one would choose to believe (Brault 39-43; Pastoureau no. 83, pp. 69-70, and no. 118, p. 84; Scott-Giles 338-39). By the middle of the fourteenth century, it had become the custom, especially in England, to adopt freely chosen personal badges – the best-known example is the three ostrich feathers of the Black Prince. It also became customary for a knight to have a 'garniture' of two shields, 'for War' and 'for Peace' (and matching *cote-armure* and horse-trappings). The triangular 'War' shield bore the family arms, to be carried in battle; the 'shield for Peace' was a squarish *targe* designed for tournament use, and it displayed the badge. Since he does not go to war. Sir Gawain quite correctly takes his 'shield for Peace' on his quest.

As was the case with King Arthur's shield and the tournament shields of Hartman's *Erec,* the most intriguing detail of Gawain's shield is that it also had an image, this time again the Queen of Heaven, painted on its inside.[11] Like King Arthur's icon in Geoffrey's *Historia,* it gave him spiritual strength and enduring boldness (cf. Morris 76), and, in an extended way, it saved him from the temptress, the Lady of Hautdesert, when 'Gret perile birwene hem stod, / Nif Maré of hir knyzt mynne' (1768-69). 'Great peril would have closed in on them, if Mary had taken less care of her knight.'

Spiritual Standards in Arming; and Indulging in Caricatures of Courtly Love

A century after the *Gawain*-Poet, the Catalan knight, Sir Joanot Martorell (*c.* 1414-1468), wrote *Tirant lo Blanc* (published 1490), judged to be 'the best book of its kind in the world' by no less an authority on romances of chivalry than the village priest in *Don Quixote* (Cervantes Ch. 6). Though not strictly an Arthurian romance, *Tirant* has an Arthurian interlude (Chs 190-202). Its hero, Tirant, is a starry-eyed youth being instructed by a hermit (a retired knight, of course) about the meaning and the rules of the 'lofty order' of knighthood, similar to those offered in manuals of chivalry, such as the anonymous French *Ordene de chevalerie* (before 1250) and Ramon Llull's (*c.* 1235-1316) *Libre del ordre de cavayleria*:

> I shall now tell you the significance of a Christian warrior's armour. It symbolizes the Church, which should be guarded and armoured by the knights who protect it. Just as the helmet shields the loftiest part of the body, so should a knight's spirit be lofty, that he may shield the people from wrongdoing by kings or anybody else. The vambraces [forearm defences] and gauntlets symbolize his duty to champion those in distress, sending no one in his stead to defend the Church and its flock but punishing the wicked with his own arms and hands. The rerebraces [upper arm defences] mean that no knight should permit murderers or sorcerers to befoul a house of worship. The cuisses and greaves mean that if a knight learns that infidels or anyone else seeks to destroy Christianity, he should quickly defend his religion on horseback or foot if necessary. [Ch. 34; p. 45]

Strangely, the hermit lists these elements in reverse to the order they would be put on. He also mentions neither the knight's body armour, mail shirt and/ or breastplate, nor his shield, whose triangular shape was commonly seen as a symbol of the Holy Trinity. Despite the loftiness of the chivalric ideal proclaimed here, we also find in *Tirant lo Blanc* examples of excess and even frivolity in pursuit of this ideal. Quite understandably, the relationship between a knight and his lady is not a point stressed by the hermit, but again and again this motif turns up in bizarre and sometimes slapstick fashion.

Smitten with the beauty of Princess Carmesina, the daughter of the Greek emperor, Tirant asks her for 'that tunic you wear next to your skin' as a lady's favour to be worn over his armour – and begs to be allowed to remove it with his own hands! To his disappointment, she retires into an adjacent room to change; however, he gets his 'favour' (Ch. 132; 217). On another occasion, (Ch. 189; 327), the day before a great Arthurian tournament[16] is to be held, Tirant succeeds at sneaking into his adored Carmesina's bed chamber while she is combing her golden hair, and there he attempts what to us today looks suspiciously like date-rape. He is prevented by her damsels from doing more than slipping his right leg between Carmesina's thighs but manages to abscond with her ivory comb. Overnight he has his lucky right stocking embroidered with gold thread and gemstones 'to the value of more than twenty thousand ducats'. Therefore, at the tournament he shows up with only his left leg armoured, and with the embroidered stocking on his right.

The correct procedure for jousters was to meet left side to left side, where they would be best protected by shield or targe; therefore, a jouster's right side was less exposed, and he could indulge in a risky fancy such as leaving his right leg unarmoured. The design on Tirant's stocking was probably his badge of sheaves of millet *(mill)*, with his motto: '*Una val mil e mill no valen una*', 'One is worth a thousand and all the millet in the world is not worth the one,' which at an earlier event (Ch. 119; 193) he wore embroidered in pearls on his hood and stockings. As his helmet crest he displays a replica of the Holy Grail,[17] containing Carmesina's comb! (189; 327.)

In the same chapter, a knighting ceremony occurs at the court of the Greek Emperor, where ladies, among them the empress and Princess Carmesina, are arming a new knight. The empress presents him with gold spurs to be affixed by her damsels, but the emperor forbids it, 'for those who wish to be knighted by ladies must wear half gold and half silver.' Knighthood was supposed to be conferred only by another dubbed knight; thus, this particular procedure seems to have been considered highly irregular and was therefore severely criticized by the emperor. In spite (or perhaps because) of that it became the model for the farce of Don Quixote's knighting assisted by the inn wenches La Tolosa and La Molinera (Cervantes Ch. 3, 73).

Emphasizing the internationality of the knightly class, as earlier exemplified by Wolfram's Gahmuret and Feirefiz, by Chaucer's 'gentyl parfyt knyght,' and by Sir John Mandeville, Joanot Martorell in *Tirant* lets even the infidels obey the rules of chivalry and demands of ladies' service (Ch. 153, 268). Therefore, in response to Tirant's challenge concerning how to recognize him in battle, the king of Egypt answers: 'I shall wear a scarlet jubbah that belonged to my virtuous lady. Her portrait will be painted on a little pennant atop my helmet,' mirroring Tirant's wearing of Carmesina's tunic over his armour, but the Egyptian king's pennant with the portrait of his lady (in violation of the Islamic prohibition against images) surpasses even Tirant's own banner (Ch. 125; 204) with his badge of the padlock *(Cadenat* in Catalan), whose first letter is Carmesina's initial, and its last letter is Tirant's.

The ultimate turnabout in arming for War *and* Love is found in chapter 155 (2-75), when Princess Carmesina, egged on by her friend and confidante Stephanie, decides to join Tirant and his squire Diaphebus (Stephanie's lover) on their campaign in Macedonia. Blithely ignoring the objections of her father, the emperor, who tells her, 'It is neither decent nor customary for damsels to visit battlefields,' the princess proceeds:

> The princess ordered a coat of mail, vambraces, and gauntlets of gold and silver She wore the gold on her right side and the silver on her left. She also ordered a small silver helmet, on which she could place her crown, [Ch. 155.275]

At least, in her use of half gold and half silver, she paid some token attention to her father's rulings about armour and ladies. Since neither *cuisses* nor *greaves* are mentioned, it seems to be understood that she was riding in skirts, as befitting a lady, however high-spirited. She was to be accompanied by sixty of the most gallant and beautiful damsels of the imperial court, with Stephanie as her grand constable. One damsel, Pleasure-of-my-life, bore their standard, emblazoned with a flower called love-in-a-mist and the princess's enigmatic motto: 'But not to me'.

Summary

The above examples of arming scenes in Arthurian literature were selected not only for the different approaches taken by different authors at different times, but also to point out the interesting details of female images painted on the inside of shields and feminine tokens displayed on arms that illustrate chivalric attitudes toward women. Geoffrey of Monmouth, who claims to write history, quite pointedly portrays King Arthur in armour of days long past, and thus displays his antiquarian knowledge. He emphasizes the mission of King Arthur as the supreme Christian champion against Britain's heathen foes by putting the icon of the Blessed Virgin on Arthur's shield.

On the other hand, Chrétien, who was possibly a herald, and Hartmann, who was a knight, matter-of-factly describe arms and armour of their own time. Hartmann takes care to include elements, such as horse trappings, that had been only recently introduced. He also adds the charming touch that Erec, as behoves a champion of courtly love, as soon as he was in a position to order a new shield for himself, had a picture of his lady painted on its inside, obviously as an inspiration and a protective (though secular) talisman.

The *Gawain*-Poet wrote at a time when armour had become much more complex. His description of the arming of Gawain is the most instructive in all chivalric literature, although his *paunces* and plates will be of no avail in his Quest to uphold the honour of the Round Table at the Green Chapel. His real protection is spiritual, represented by his targe that outwardly bears the mystical pentangle, and inwardly the image of the Queen of Heaven, his shield against temptations and perils.

Chivalric prowess and Love are the themes expounded to enormous lengths in *Tirant to Blanc*. In contrast to the *Gawain*-Poet, about whom virtually nothing is known, we are quite well informed about *Tirant's* author, Joanot Martorell. Sad to say, although he was not lacking in the knightly virtue of courage, his chequered career was short of *felawship* and *cortayse*. Knighthood was for him a sacred institution, but, in his writing, this did not stop him from indulging with gusto in the (for us) zanier follies, such as jousting with parts of armour discarded,[18] in order to make a point to impress a lady.

Acknowledgements

For good advice and valuable help in procuring source material, I would like to thank my friends and colleagues Ann Willard and Donald LaRocca, The Metropolitan Museum of Art, New York, and Roger F. Gardiner, University of Western Ontario, London, Canada.

Notes

1. Pridwen is also the name of Arthur's ship in *The Spoils of Annwn;* there is possibly a confused memory of a magic shield that could be enlarged to serve as a ship (*cf.* the knife of Osla Bigknife that could serve as a bridge). In the *Edda* the ship *Skidbladnir* could be folded up and stored in a satchel.
2. All translations in this essay are my own unless otherwise specified.

3. A parallel would be the boar-tusk helmet of Odysseus in the *Iliad,* a type that was unknown in Homer's time, but was excavated at Mycenae by Schliemann.
4. In the *Annales Cambriae* (mid-10th century) the battle is that of Mount Badon, and the emblem is the Cross of our Lord Jesus Christ.
5. In order to emphasize the intricacies of arming a knight correctly (and for comic relief after the tension of a combat scene), both Chrétien and Wolfram von Eschenbach use Perceval/Parzival's inexperience with things chivalric for some rather macabre clowning, when he tries in vain to pull off the armour of the Red Knight he just killed (by a javelin throw into the eye slit of the helmet). He has to be aided in this endeavour by the well-trained squire Yvonet, who had followed him out of curiosity, hoping to bear tidings of the unequal duel back to Arthur's court. Yvonet then helps him in donning the vanquished Red Knight's armour as his prize *(Perceval* 1119-91; *Parzival* 88-89).
6. Enide's father points out the quality of his hauberk as 'qui antre cinc cenz fu esliz' ('one chosen from five hundred'), and that it and the *chauces* are 'boenes et fresches et legieres' ('good and new and light') 616-18.
7. A knight's sword was worn on the left hip, and therefore he could mount his horse only from the left side, as is still the custom today.
8. Miniatures with ladies arming their knights (Herr Winli, Schenk von Limburg, Herr Otto von Thurme) are in the *Minnesinger* or *Manesse Codex* (named after its compiler, the knight Rüdiger Manesse of Zurich, d. 1304). The classical English example is in the fourteenth-century *Luttrell Psalter,* BL Add. MS 42130, fol. 202v, where Sir Geoffrey Luttrell is armed by his wife and daughter-in-law.
9. Green was the colour *of minne* (courtly love) in medieval Germany. The surcoat of Iders fil Niut, as champion of his ladylove, is green, and Erec, for the tournament at his wedding, wears a green surcoat, although the colours of his shields and horse trappings are silver, red, and gold. Hartmann's mentioning of an angel (symbol for Enide?) as Erec's helmet crest (2354) seems to be the first time such an heraldic device appears in Arthurian literature, except for Geoffrey's antiquarian dragon on King Arthur's helmet.

10. The rules of heraldry demand that a 'metal' (gold or silver) be placed on 'colour' (red, blue, black, green, or purple), or vice versa. This contrasting of light-hued 'metals' against darker 'colours' was to ensure that a shield charge could be clearly recognized from a distance. There is a German figure of speech '*Ich weiss nicht, was er im Schilde fuhrt*' (I don't know what he bears on his shield) for not knowing what someone is up to, which perfectly illustrates the dilemma of two knights errant meeting in the dark forest.
11. Chaucer's persiflaging arming scene in *Sir Thopas* starts with the knight's underwear, but is correct in all details, such as the helmet 'of latten bright'. An overlay of *laton* (a brass-like alloy) was another rust-proofing technique.
12. The gauntlets of the Black Prince are still preserved at Canterbury.
13. Circlets on bascinets are relatively rare, because they would interfere with the attachment of a visor. In most cases where circlets are present they make a statement. The Black Prince wears his crown circlet as a sign of his rank on his open-faced bascinet. Sir John Marmion (d. 1386) in his tomb effigy at West Tanfield, Yorkshire, bears a visorless bascinet with a circlet studded with heraldic roses (Blair 67), evidently because the Marmion crest was a rose (Fairbairn 320, pi. 105). The actual bascinet of George Castriota Skanderbeg, Prince of Albania and claimant to the throne of Byzantium (1403-1466), is preserved in the Hofjagd-und Rüstkammer, Vienna; it is without a visor or aventail. but bears a circlet engraved: in 'pe * ra * to * re * bt, the pairs of letters interspaced with rosettes.
14. Gawain as 'gentylest knyght of lote' is perhaps a pun about his being the best of the five sons of King Lot.
15. There are shields preserved, such as the tournament targe, ace. no. 25.62.1, in The Metropolitan Museum of Art, New York, that have St Christopher icons on the inside. To look at a St Christopher image saved one from hurtful danger for that day. It seems that no shields with icons of Our Lady on the inside have survived, although there are numerous examples of her image on breastplates (MMA, 14.25.716. 33.164).
16. The tournament was held for the 'ladies who had loved most truly': Queen Guinevere and Isolde among them.

17. Joanot Martorell was a native of Valencia, and the main relic of the cathedral of Valencia is a Late Roman agate cup, venerated as the *Sangreal.*
18. Similar feats of bravado were done in real life with dangerously skimpy tournament armour, such as in German lands the helmetless courses, *Wulstrennen* and *Pfannenrennen,* the latter with a steel square not more than twelve inches wide as sole armour *(Triumph* 53, 56), both undertaken with sharp lances!

Select Bibliography

Ascherl, Rosemary 'The Technology of Chivalry, *The Study of Chivalry.* Ed. Howell Chickering, and Thomas H. Seiler. Kalamazoo: Western Michigan University, 1988. 263-311.

Berger, Pamela C. *The Insignia of the Notitia Dignitatum.* New York: Garland, 1981.

Blair, Claude. *European Armour* London: Batsford, 1958.

Brault, Gerard J. *Early Blazon: Heraldic Terminology in the Twelfth and Thirteenth Centuries with Special Reference to Arthurian Literature.* London: Oxford UP, 1972.

Brengle, Richard L. *Arthur King of Britain: History, Chronicle, Romance & Criticism.* New York: Appleton-Century-Crofts, 1964.

Brooke-Little, J. P. *An Heraldic Alphabet* New York: Arco Publishing Co., 1973.

Burrow, J. A. Ed. Sir *Gawain and the* Green *Knight,* Baltimore: Penguin Books, 1972, 1l.568-589.

Cervantes Saavedra, Miguel de. *Don Quixote of La Mancha* Trans. Walter Starkie. New York: Signet Classic, 1957.

Chrétien de Troyes. *Erec et Enide.* Ed. and trans. Carleton W. Carroll. New York: Garland, 1987.

______ *Perceval, The Story of the Grail.* Trans Ruth Harwood Cline. New York: Pergamon P, 1983.

Cole, Huber. *The Black Prince.* London: Hart-Davis, MacGibbon, 1976.

Dennys, Rodney. *Heraldry and the Heralds.* London: Cape, 1981.

Edge, David, and John Miles Paddock *Arms and Armor of the Medieval Knight: An Illustrated History of Weaponry in the Middle Ages.* Greenwich, CT: Bison Books, 1988.

Fairbairn, James. *Fairbairn's Crests of the Families of Great Britain and Ireland.* Chatham, Kent: Dorset P, 1992

Fox-Davies, Arthur Charles. *A Complete Guide to Heraldry.* New York: Dodge Pub Co., 1909; repr. New York: Bonanza Books, 1978.

Gamber. Ortwin. 'Some Notes on the Sutton Hoo Military Equipment', *Journal of the Arms and Armour Society* 10 (December 1982): 208-16.

Geoffrey of Monmouth, *The Historia Regum Britanniae of Geoffrey of Monmouth* Ed. and trans. Acton Griscom. Together with Welsh MS No. LXI, Jesus College, Oxford. Trans. Robert Ellis Jones. London: Longmans, Green 8c Co., 1929

______ *The Historia Regum Britannie of Geoffrey of Monmouth.* Ed. Neil Wright. 1 (Bern, MS. 568); II (First Variant Version); V (Gesta Regum Britannie). Cambridge, Eng.: D. S. Brewer, 1991.

______ *The History of the Kings of Britain. Trans.* Lewis Thorpe. New York: Penguin Books, 1966.

Gravett, Christopher. *Knights at Tournament.* London: Osprey Elite Series 17, 1988.

Hartmann von Aue. *Erec.* Ed. and trans. Thomas L. Keller. New York: Garland,1987.

Martorell, Joanot, and Marti Joan de Galba. *Tirant lo Blanc.* Trans. David H. Rosenthal. New York: Schocken Books, 1984.

Nennius, British History and The Welsh Annals. Ed. and trans. John Morris. London: Phillimore & Co., 1980.

Nickel, Helmut. 'About Lace and Knot in *Sir Gawayne and the Green Knight' Quondam et Futurus* 1.1 (Spring 1991): 15-24. *Der mittelalterliche Reiterschild des Abendlandes.* Diss. phil. Freie Universitat, Berlin, 1958. 'Wer waren König Artus' Ritter?: Über die geschichtliche Grundlage der Artussagen.' *Waffen-und Kostumkunde* 1975, 1, pp. 1-28, ill.

Nicolle, David. *Arthur and the Anglo-Saxon Wars.* London: Osprey Men-at-Arms Series 154, 1984

Norman, A. V. B. *A History of War and Weapons: 440 to 1660.* New York: Thomas Y. Crowell Co., 1966.

______ *The Medieval Soldier.* New York: Crowell, 1971.

Pastoureau, Michel. *Armorial des chevaliers de la Table Ronde* Paris: Le Léopard d'Or, 1983.

Schultz, Alwin. *Zur Waffenkunde des älteren deutschen Mittelalters.* Quedlinburg and Leipzig, 1867.

Scott-Giles, C. W. 'Some Arthurian Coats of Arms.' *The Coat of Arms 8* (Oct. 1965) 332-39, and 9 (Jan. 1966): 30-35.

Sedgwick, Henry Dwight. *The Life of Edward the Black Prince: 1330-1376*. Indianapolis: Bobbs-Merrill Co., 1932.

The Triumph of Maximilian I: 137 Woodcuts by Hans Burgkmair and Others. Ed. And trans. Stanley Applebaum. New York: Dover, 1964.

Warnecke, Friedrich. *Die mittelalterlichen heraldischen Kampfschilde in der St. Elisabethkirche zu Marburg*. Berlin, 1884.

Wolfram von Eschenbach. *Parzival*. Trans. A. T Hatto. Harmondsworth. Middlesex: Penguin Classics, 1980.

Woodcock, Thomas, and John Martin Robinson. *The Oxford Guide to Heraldry*. Oxford: Oxford UP, 1988.

Originally published in *Arthuriana* vol. 5, no. 4 (Winter 1995) pp. 3-21.

22

The Fight About King Arthur's Beard and for the Cloak of Kings' Beards

Among the marvels and courtly adventures to be found in Malory's *Le Morte d'Arthur* there are two episodes of a jarringly gruesome nature. In the first (Book 1,26), the young King Arthur receives a message from King Royns (also 'Ryence', 'Ryens', 'Ryons') of North Wales, all Ireland, and the Isles, informing him that Royns has discomfited and overcome eleven kings so far, and that each of them has done him homage. As a token of submission

> ... they gaff theire beardes clene flayne off... For kynge Royns had purfilde a mantell with kyngis berdis, and there lacked one place of the mantell; wherefore he sente for hys bearde, othir ellis he wolde entir into his londis and brenne and sle, and nevir leve tylle he hathe the hede and the bearde bothe.

Though Arthur is still hard pressed to assert his authority against the resistance of the dissident kings of Britain, he rejects this 'most orgulus and lewdiste ... moste shamefullyste message' and promises instead that it will be King Royns who will do him 'omage on bothe his knees, othere ellis he shall lese his hede'.

In the war that follows, King Royns is caught in an ambush and defeated in single combat by Balin, the Knight with the Two Swords, who takes him to Arthur as a prisoner.[1]

A similar cloak is mentioned in the grisly story about the Giant of St Michael's Mount in *The Noble Tale of King Arthur and the Emperor Lucius* (Book V, 75v-78v).[2] Arthur, on the eve of his invasion of France, takes time off to hurry to the rescue of the 'duchesse de Bretayne' who has been abducted by the terrible giant. On the mountainside Arthur finds 'a carefull wydow wryngande hir handys, syttande on a grave that was new marked', who tells him that he is too late, but warns him that the giant

> ... hath vanquysshed xv kynges and hath maade hym a cote ful of precious stones embrowdred with theyre berdes whiche they sente hym to haue his loue for sauacion of theyr peple at this Crystemasse.

The fifteen kings' supreme sacrifice for this unusual Christmas gift was in vain, though. The unappreciative giant continued harassing the surrounding countryside, and Arthur finds him

> ... at his soupere alone gnawyng on a lymme of a large man, and there he beekys his brode lendys by the bryghte fyre... And three damesels turned three brochis, and thereon was twelve chyldir but late borne, and they were broched in maner lyke byrdis.[3]

King Arthur defeats the giant in a gruelling fight, and to his two companions, Kay and Bedivere, he states afterwards:

> This was a freysh gyaunte and mykyll of strength, for I mette nat with suche one this fyftene wyntir sauff onys in the mounte of Arrabé I mette with suche another, but this was ferser.

On Arthur's command, Bedivere cuts off the giant's head as a victory token to show to Sir Howell, the aggrieved husband of the abducted and so foully murdered duchesse de Bretayne, in order to 'bydde him be mery, for his enemy is destroyed. And aftir in Barflete lette brace hit on a barbican, that all the comyns of this contrey may hit beholde.'

This somewhat awkward duplication of the motif of a cloak trimmed with kings' beards results from Malory's attempt to reconcile two divergent traditions about Arthur's fights with giants and about cloaks decorated with flayed beards.

In Geoffrey of Monmouth's *History of the Kings of Britain* (1135)[4] Arthur, having just landed in Gaul for his campaign against

Lucius Hiberius, goes to the rescue of Helena, the niece of his ally Duke Hoel of Brittany, who has been abducted by the Giant of St Michael's Mount. Arthur, Kay, and Bedivere come too late to save the unfortunate girl, but they surprise the giant at his evening meal of whole roast pigs. After a fierce fight, Arthur kills the giant; he then orders Bedivere to cut off the monster's head and show it to his army.

Arthur reminisces to his two knights that he has not come across anybody quite so strong since he slew the giant Retho on Mount Arvaius. This Retho had himself made a fur cloak from the beards of kings he had slain, and he wanted Arthur's beard too. Because he considered Arthur to be more distinguished than any of the other kings, Retho promised him the honour of having his beard sewn higher up on the cloak than the others. He offered Arthur the chance to rip off his beard himself and send it to him for his cloak, but if he refused, Retho would challenge him to a duel: whoever proved to be the stronger should have the cloak as a trophy and the beard of the loser. Thus, after having won the fight, Arthur took the cloak and the giant's beard too.

Wace in his *Roman de Brut* (1155)[5] tells the same two stories, linked together in the same way, but here the name of the giant with the cloak of beards is Riton, and the battle takes place upon 'Mount Aravius, in the far East'. Wace also supplies a name, Dinabuc, for the Giant of Mont-Saint-Michel.

By contrast, in the *Alliterative Morte Arthure (c.* 1360), the model for Malory's *Tale of King Arthur and the Emperor Lucius,* it is the Giant of Mont-Saint-Michel who is the collector of kings' beards and who would appreciate King Arthur's beard in his collection more than if someone gave him either Burgundy or Brittany.[6]

Thus, of the two battles that Arthur fights with giants, the one against the owner of the cloak trimmed with kings' beards (Retho, Riton) is originally just a flashback linked to the fight on St Michael's Mount, as told by Geoffrey and his follower Wace. Malory divides the two linked stories into separate tales and leaves one beard-trimmed cloak with King Royns, who now, though no more a giant, is in his proper chronological sequence,[7] and gives the other 'mantell' to the Giant of St Michael's Mount, who always was a fiendish rapist/cannibal, but became connected with the cloak of beards only in the *Alliterative Morte Arthure*. Malory also changes the story so far that King Royns is not killed by Arthur but overcome by Balin, the Knight of the Two Swords. It is interesting to notice that in the *Chevallier aux Deux Espies* (first half of the 13th century) there appears a King Ris, who challenges Arthur for his beard, and Meliadeus, 'Li Chevaliers as Deus Espees', vanquishes him in Arthur's stead and sends him as prisoner to the court.[8]

It is generally taken for granted that motifs found in Arthurian stories are of Celtic origin, and there is indeed the strange motif of the shaving of the beard of Yspaddaden Penkawr (Chief Giant) in *Culhwch and Olwen* (*c.* 1100) immediately preceding the beheading of the giant on a mound at the end of the tale.[9] However, this shaving is one of the conditions the giant himself sets for suitors of his daughter Olwen to perform; and though it is done in a most cruel way, skin and flesh cut through to the bone and the ears taken too, the beard is not treated as a trophy. The Celts, for sure, were great collectors of trophy heads, but there is no evidence of scalp hunting among them.[10]

In *Culhwch and Olwen* there is also the episode of the obtaining of the beard of Dillus the Bearded, to be braided into a magic dog leash for the chase of the two supernatural boars, one of the tasks set by Yspaddaden Penkawr. Here Cai and Bedwyr surprise Dillus while he is roasting a whole pig and pull out his beard with wooden tweezers before cutting off his head. This is, of course, a toned-down version of the evil giant story, but exactly because it is now in a thoroughly Celtic context, the original alien motif of the flayed trophy beard and the trimming of the cloak of beards have become eliminated.

Scalp collecting is first reported of the Scythians in the fifth century B.C. Herodotus, in describing the customs of these nomadic barbarians of the steppes to the north of the Black Sea, practically at the edge of the known world, gives detailed information: how the scalp is to be stripped off the skull by an encircling cut above the ears, how it is scraped clean with the rib of an ox and, finally, how it is massaged by hand to make it supple. These trophy scalps were hung on horses' bridles, but 'many Scythians sew a number of scalps together and make cloaks of them.'[11]

In the frozen tombs of Pazyryk in the Siberian Altai region (Kurgan II), the body of a richly tattooed warrior had been preserved; killed in battle, he was scalped, and a false scalp was sewn onto his skull with horsehair for burial.[12] Though these Scythian trophies were head scalps and not beards, there is a documented instance of beard scalping in medieval Eastern Europe. After the Battle of Tannenberg (1410), in which an alliance of Christian Poles, newly converted Lithuanians and still pagan Tartars defeated the Teutonic Knights, the victorious Poles flayed the beards off the slain Grand Master of the Order and his knights, who were wearing full beards according to Templar Rule. These trophies were sent to Cracow for display in the Cathedral of St Stanislas, together with the banners captured in the battle.[13]

This seemingly bizarre practice had its roots in tradition handed down from antiquity. The Polish nobility, if not the entire Polish nation, considers itself – though now thoroughly Slavicized – to be of Sarmatian descent. The Sarmatians were a group of Iranian-speaking horse nomads from the steppes between the Black Sea and the Caspian; according to Herodotus, the Sauromatae (Sarmatians) were the offspring of a liaison between adventurous Scythian youths and the Amazons.[14]

Steadily drifting westward, Sarmatians were in contact with the Roman world in the Danube area from the second century A.D. onward. In 175, Emperor Marcus Aurelius, who afterwards accepted the surname 'Sarmaticus', hired 8000 Iazyges of the westernmost tribe of Sarmatians, as auxiliary cavalry into the Roman army. Most of these, 5,500 in all, were sent to northern Britain to fight the Picts.[15]

These Sarmatians were the first heavy armoured cavalry seen in Western Europe. They carried as battle standard a windsock-like dragon on a pole, and they worshipped their tribal god of war in the shape of a naked sword thrust into the ground or set on a platform.[16]

The last remaining speakers of a Sarmatian language are the Ossetians in the Caucasus. They preserve a rich tradition of sagas and heroic epics (as is typical of nomads, who cannot carry many material possessions in their saddle bags, but who can sing their heroes' deeds at their campfires) which are centred on the Narts, a tribe of legendary heroes who lived larger than life in days long past. One of these heroes, Sosryko, was miraculously born from a rock and possessed a body of steel. Thus, he was not only the 'sword in the stone' personified, but also the prototype for the nom de guerre of another Caucasian, Jozef Dzugashvili, who called himself *Stalin,* 'the man of steel', as mentioned in Chapter 12. In a series of adventures Sosryko collects, by force as well as by dicing for high stakes, a number of scalps and beards, which he has sewn into a fur cloak by the maidens of the Nan village.[17]

The Iazygan cavalrymen in Britain never returned to their homeland, Pannonia, after their 20-year term of service had expired. Pannonia (today's Hungary) had slipped behind the Roman equivalent of the Iron Curtain in the meantime, and it seemed definitely unwise to send several thousand Roman-trained warriors to the other side. Instead of being repatriated, they were put in military settlements, very much like Czarist

Cossack villages or Israeli kibbutzim, to raise horses for the Roman cavalry and also to guard the coasts against Pictish and Irish pirate raids. One of their settlements, *cuneus veteranorum Sarmatorum* (the Troop of Sarmatian Veterans) at *Bremetennacum* (today's Ribchester in Lancashire), was still documented in 428 A.D., which makes it likely that it still existed in the days of the 'historical Arthur'.[18]

The fact that these veterans were, after more than 250 years in Britain, still known as Sarmatians would indicate that they had preserved a sizable part of their tribal traditions. Possibly one or the other enterprising Sarmatian had established himself somewhere either as an outlaw 'giant' or as a local 'king,' keeping alive the old Sarmatian custom of collecting scalps and beards to make himself a fur cloak.

In any case, the motif of the cloak of beards is another proof that Geoffrey of Monmouth did not invent his stories altogether, but that he made good use of traditions he found preserved over centuries, perhaps even in a 'very ancient book'.

Notes

1. Eugene Vinaver, ed., *The Works of Sir Thomas Malory*. 3 vols. (Oxford: Clarendon Press, 1967). I. 54 (Bk.I,26); I, 74 (Bk.II,9).
2. Vinaver, *Malory*, I, 200-05.
3. In the Winchester MS the giant sups on 'syx knave chyldirne'. The 'carefull widow' bemoans the fate that is in store for the three fayre rnaydens who are forced to turn the spits, 'for they shall be dede within four oures or the fylth is fulfylled that his fleyshe askys.' The poor 'douches' was killed, when the giant 'forced hir by fylth of hymself, and so aftir slytte hir unto the navyill.'
4. Geoffrey of Monmouth, *The History of the Kings of Britain*, trans. Lewis Thorpe (Baltimore: Penguin, 1966), pp. 237-40 (x, 3).
5. Wace and Layamon, *Arthurian Chronicles*, trans. Eugene Mason (London: Everyman. 1962), pp. 81-85. Here the giant broiled a whole hog on a spit.
6. Vinaver, *Malory*, III, 1378; commentary to p. 201.
7. Though Malory has made the challenge by King Royns and his defeat two separate episodes, he still uses the flashback technique when he recalls the fight on Mount Arrabe after the battle against the Giant of St Michael's Mount.

8. Robert Thedens, ed., *Li Chevaliers as Deus Espées* (Göttingen, 1908), pp. 93-94.
9. 'Culhwch and Olwen', *The Mabinogion,* trans. Gwyn Jones and Thomas Jones (New York: Everyman, 1972), pp. 95-136.
10. E. K. Chambers. *Arthur of Britain* (New York: October House, 1967), pp. 70-72. Gerhard Heim. *Die Kelten: das Volk, das aus dem Dunkel kam* (Düsseldorf: Econ Verlag, 1975), pp. 91-93.
11. Herodotus, *The Histories,* trans. Aubrey de Sélincourt (Baltimore: Penguin. 1954), p. 291 (65).
12. Karl Jettmar, *Art of the Steppes* (New York: Crown Publishers, 1964), pp. 27-8, 103, 105, 131. E. D. Phillips, *The Royal Hordes: Nomad Peoples of the Steppes* (New York: McGraw-Hill, 1965), p. 82.
13. Sven Ekdahl, *Die 'Banderia Prutenorum' des Jan Dlugosz: eine Quelle zur Schlacht von Tannenberg 1410,* Abhandlungen der Akademie der Wissenschaften in Göttingen, Philologisch-Historische Klasse, 3, F/104 (Göttingen, 1976), pp. 76-77.
14. Herodotus, *Histories,* p. 278 (21); pp. 306-09.
15. Dio Cassius Cocceianus, *Roman History,* trans. Earnest Gary Foster, 9 vols. (London: Loeb Classical Library, 1914-27), LXXII, 22.3.
16. *Ammianus Marcellinus,* trans. John C. Rolfe (Cambridge: Harvard University Press, 1935-39), XXXI, 2.23. Tadeusz Sulimirski, 'The Forgotten Sarmatians', *Vanished Civilizations of the Ancient World* (New York: McGraw-Hill, 1963), ch. 12. Tadeusz Sulimirski, *The Sarmatians* (New York: Praeger, 1970), pp. 31-32, 81, 120, 127, 150-51, 167. Ortwin Gamber, 'Dakische und sarmatische Waffen auf den Reliefs der Trajanssäule', *Jahrbuch der Kunsthistorischen Sammlungen, Wien,* 62 (1964), 74 ff. Ortwin Gamber, 'Kataphrakten, Clibanarier, Normannenreiter,' *Jahrbuch der Kunsthistorischen Sammlungen, Wien,* 64 (1968), 7 ff. E. D. Phillips, *The Royal Hordes: Nomad Peoples of the Steppes (*New York: McGraw-Hill. 1965), pp. 94 ff. J. W. Eadie, 'The Development of Roman Mailed Cavalry.' *Journal of Roman Studies,* 57 (1967), 161-73. Helmut Nickel, 'Wer waren König Artus Ritter? Über die geschichtliche Grundlage der Artussagen,' *Waffen-und Kostümkunde* (Munich; Berlin, 1975) pp. 1-28. David Nicolle and Angus McBride, *Arthur and the Anglo-Saxon Wars,* Osprey / Men-at-Arms (London. 1984).

17. H. Hübschmann, 'Sage und Glaube der Osseten,' *Zeitschrift der Morgentandischen Gesellschaft.* 41 (1887), 528.
18. Otto Seeck, ed. *Notitia Dignitatum* (Berlin, 1876), p. 212 (Oc. XL, 54). I. A. Richmond. 'The Sarmatae, Bremetennacum Veteranorum and the Regio Bremetennaciensis', *Journal of Roman Studies,* XXXV (1945), 16-29. Helmut Nickel, 'The Dawn of Chivalry,' *From the Lands of the Scythians, The Metropolitan Museum of Art Bulletin* (Special Issue), XXXII, no. 5 (1975) pp. 150-52.

Originally published in *Interpretations: A Journal of Idea, Analysis, and Criticism*, vol. 16, Number 1, Autumn, 1985, pp. 1-7.

23

About Divers Precious Stones

Of Colours and Their Virtues

In his note 'Variation in Names of Heraldic Colours' (vol. XI, no. 4, p. 26) Colin J. Parry drew our attention to two intriguing alternatives in blazoning, the use of planet names and/or precious stones for the tinctures of heraldry, quoting 17th-century examples for this practice.

The use of precious stones as equivalents of the heraldic colours appears already in the very first printed treaty about heraldry, in *The Book of St. Albans,* I486.[1] It informs us

> ... how longe cote armures were begonne afore the Jncarnacon of our lorde Jhesu Cryste ... And after two thousand yere & eyghtene before the Jncarnacon of Cryste / cote armures was made & fyguryd at the siege of Troye: wherein gestys troianonu it tellyth. y the fyrste begynnynge of the lawe of armys was the whiche was effygured & begon byfore any lawe of the worlde: but the lawe of nature, and before the x. comaundementes of god.
>
> And this lawe of armys was groundyd vppon the ix. orders of angellys in heuen encrownyd wyth ix. dyuerse precyous stonys of colours and of vertues dyuerss. Also of theym are fyguryd the ix. colours in armys. as in nombre to begyn the fyrste stone is callyd Topasion ... sygnyfyenge golde in armys.

This stone Topasion is a semy stone: and golde it is callyd in armys. The vertue therof is: that the gentylman the whiche this stone in his cote armure beryth a sure messager in his kyngis batayll shal be. The whyche stone is reserued in the angels crowne that was a true messager & a sure in his kyngis batayll of heuen whan they faughte wyth Lucifer.

The other stones and colours are:

> Smaragdus a grauely stone: sygnyfyenge vert in armys... Ametisce a dusketly stone brusk it is calde in armys... Margarete a clowdy stone Plumby it is calde in armys... A Loys. a sanguein stone or synamer it is called in armes... Ruby a redly stone, gowlys it is callyd in armis... Saphyre a blewe stone Asure it is callyd in armys... Dymond: a blacke stone/Sable it is callyd in armys... Carbuncle a shynynge stone. syluer it is callyd in armys.

Their 'vertues' are:

> 'Kene & hardy' (Smaragdus), 'fortunable of wictory' (Ametisce). 'grete gouernaunce of chiualrie' (Margarete), 'myghtyfull of powr (A Loys), 'hote and full of courage' (Ruby),'wyse & vertuous in theyr werkyng' (Saphyre), 'durable and vnfaynt' (Dyamond), and 'fuH doughty gloryous & shynynge' (Carbuncle) in 'kyngis batayll'.

The use of precious stones as the equivalents of heraldic colours appears already in the first half of the 15th century. In the group of French manuscripts known as *Clement Prinsault's Treatise*[2] there are already several possibilities suggested for circumscribing the tinctures of heraldry – 'en vertues, en pierrerie, des planetes, des jours':

metailles	en virtues	en pierrerie	des planètes	des jours
Or	Noblesse	La topaze	Le soleil	Le Dimanche
Argent	Richesse	La perle	La lune	Le lundi
Gueules	Prouesse	Le rubis	Saturne	Le samedi
Azur	Loyaulte	Le saphir	Vénus	Le vendredi
Sable	Humblesse	Le diamant	Mars	Le mardi
Sinople	Honneur	L'émeraude	Mercure	Le mercredi
Poupure	Largesse	Le balay	Jupiter	Le jeudi

It is immediately evident that these two lists not only differ from the 17th-century sources and examples given by Mr Parry, but they differ from each other. This confusion is made worse when in the so-called *Augmented Version of Prinsault's Treatise* still another version of this list is being offered.

Heraldic Colour	Virtues	Precious Stones	Planets	Days
Or: gold	Nobility Good will Comfort Majesty	Carbuncle	Sun	Sunday
Argent: silver	Humility Loyalty Purity Chastity Innocence	Pearl	Moon	Monday
Gules: red	Courage Audacity	Ruby	Saturn	Saturday
Azure: blue	Loyalty Beauty Majesty	Sapphire	Venus	Friday
Sable: black	Mourning Richness	Diamond	Mars	Tuesday
Sinople: green	Love Honour Courtesy	Emerald	Mercury	Wednesday
Pourpure: purple	Generosity Abundance Wisdom	Amethyst	Jupiter	Thursday

In addition to these equivalents the *Augmented Version* has four other terms, though these apply only to some of the tinctures:

Heraldic	Complexions	12 Signs	Elements	Metals
Argent: silver	Phlegmatic	Cancer Scorpio Pisces	Water	
Gules: red	Choleric	Ares Leo Sagittarius	Fire	Latton = molten copper mixed with calamine, which makes a red face

Heraldic	Complexions	12 Signs	Elements	Metals
Azure: blue	Sanguine	Gemini Libra Aquarius	Air	Fine Silver which makes blue
Sable: black	Melancholic	Taurus Virgo Capricorn	Earth	Iron, which makes black
Sinople: green				Quicksilver, which makes green
Pourpure: purple			The Heavens	Tin

The planets as connected with heraldic colours seem to appear first in *Bellifortis* by Konrad Kyeser of Eichstatt, 1402. In the introduction of this technical handbook Kyeser portrays the planets as horsemen in fashionable contemporary costume, and he describes their '*vexilla*': Saturnus – black, Jupiter – green, Mars – red, Sol – gold, Venus – blue, Mercurius – brown, Luna – white.[3]

The latest list of this kind was composed by Ottfried Neubecker in his *Heraldry, Sources, Symbols and Meaning,* 1976,[4] as follows:

Heraldic Colour	Precious Stones	Planets	Symbols of
Or: gold	topaz	Sun	Understanding Respect Virtue Majesty
Argent: silver	pearls	Moon	Cleanliness Wisdom Innocence Chastity Joy
Gules: red	ruby	Mars	Eagerness to serve one's country
Azure: blue	sapphire	Jupiter	Fidelity Steadfastness
Sable: black	diamond	Saturn	Mourning

Heraldic Colour	Precious Stones	Planets	Symbols of
Vert: green	emerald	Venus	Freedom Beauty Joy Health Hope
Purpure: purple	amethyst	Mercury	Majesty

Though there are considerable differences between all of these systems, which must have made a herald's life quite miserable if he had to figure out what 'carbuncle' or 'Saturn' was supposed to mean, they at least all agreed in leaving out the furs.

Notes

1. *The Book of St. Albans,* first ed. 1486; second ed. by Wynkyn de Worde, 1496. Facsimile edition, Abercrombie & Fitch. New York, 1906.
2. L.C. Douet d'Arcq, 'Un Traite du blason du XV siècle' in *Revue Archéologique,* 1st series, vol XV (1858), pp. 322-324.
3. *Bellifortis* by Konrad Kyeser aus Eichstatt, ed. Gotz Quarg; VDI-Verlag Dusseldorf, 1967, 2 vols; I. fol. 6-11; II, pp. 10-15
4. Ottfried Neubecker *Heraldry; Sources, Symbols and Meaning* with contributions by J.P. Brooke-Little, Richmond Herald of Arms, McGraw-Hill, New York, 1976, p. 86.

Originally published in *Heraldry in Canada* XIV 3, September, 1980, pp. 18-21.

24

The Naked and The Best
Tests, Temptations, and Triumphal Rescues

Despite the proclaimed symbolism of the Round Table as a representation of the equal worthiness of all its members, there were ongoing competitions for the title of 'the Best Knight in the World'. Presented here is a loosely compiled collection of tests to gain this coveted title, and, to give the ladies their due, also that of 'the Truest Lady'. However, diverse as they are, these episodes have one obvious feature in common, namely that one or the other of the acting persons is found to be naked. The motivation for these examples of nudity – from heroic and lofty to titillating and frankly pornographic – varies not only from case to case, but also as can be expected from author to author.

In the catalogue of the special exhibition *Die Ritter,* held at Burg Gussing, Austria, May-October 1990, is an illustration of a nineteenth-century redrawing of a miniature from an unidentified illuminated manuscript (*Ritter* 240, cat. no. V.4). It shows a knight in armour of the early fourteenth century laying hands on the rim of a tub from which a rather woebegone damsel emerges. The damsel, as is quite natural for a bathing scene, is naked except for an elaborate netted headdress (Fig. 1). In its caption this illustration is named *Erotische Szene,* and it is accompanied by an explanatory text stating that in surprising a lady in her bath this knight would be committing a grave offence against the code of chivalrous conduct: 'Although a certain amount of frivolity had its legitimate place in Minnesinger poetry and in Ladies' Service, nudity in front of others was considered unseemly.'[1]

This evaluation of nakedness as unseemly is of course at first found in the situation immediately after the first failed test in mankind's history, the Temptation and Fall of Adam and Eve. On the other hand, the author of this so quaintly Victorian sounding interpretative entry, with its undertones of contemporary sexual harassment, gives as his source a work by H. P. Duerr with the tell-tale title: *Nacktheit und Scham: Der Mythos vom Zivilisationsprozess* (Nudity and Ashamedness: The Myth of Civilization's Progress), Frankfurt/Main, 1988. This picture, however, far from condemning a lack of values in the attitude of the knight towards the lady in her bath, quite to the contrary represents a test for the Best of Knights.

A practically identical scene is depicted on the dust cover *of Arthurian Literature in the Middle Ages: A Collaborative History*, edited by Roger Sherman Loomis, where a knight on a fully caparisoned horse riding through a summer landscape encounters a naked damsel in a tub placed incongruously at the wayside. The background of this late fifteenth-century miniature, with a multi-arched bridge leading into the gate of a

Fig. 1: Drawing of Lancelot and the dolorous lady in the boiling bath. After *Die Ritter.*

walled city, identifies the scene as Lancelot at the Pont de Corbenic. In the beginning of Book Eleven of the *Morte d'Arthur*, *The Birth of Galahad*, Malory describes how, when Sir Lancelot passed over the Pounte of Corbyn, he saw the fairest tower and thereunder the fairest town full of people, who welcomed him as the Flower of Knighthood who would help them out of danger. Upon his inquiry, Sir Lancelot is told that in the tower is 'a dolourous lady', who suffers for many winters under enchantment to boil in a bath of scalding water. The townspeople also volunteer the information that recently Sir Gawayne had been there and could not help her. Quite reasonably, Sir Lancelot answers that in this case there might not be much that he could do either and he would have to leave the dolorous lady in her painful and embarrassing situation just as Sir Gawayne did.

Two sorceresses, Morgan Le Fay and the Queen of North Galys, had plunged this dolorous lady into that hot bath five years ago out of envy because she was called the fairest lady in the country, and they had put a spell on her so that she could be only delivered when the best knight in the world took her by the hand. At long last, yielding to the voluble entreaties of the crowd, Lancelot does agree to help after all.

When Lancelot was guided into the tower, the iron doors of the chamber where the lady was held unlocked and unbolted by themselves, and he entered the bath chamber that was 'as hote as ony stewe'. Lancelot then and there 'toke the fayrest lady by the hand that euer he sawe, and she was naked as a nedel' (Caxton's Malory 400). As soon as she had some clothes on, the lady asked Lancelot to accompany her to a nearby chapel to give thanks to God. This done, all the people, 'both lerned and lewde', also gave thanks unto God and to Lancelot and asked him, since he had succeeded in delivering this lady, would he also deliver them from a dragon that dwelt in a nearby tomb. Ever happy to oblige, Lancelot slays this fire-spitting dragon.

These episodes, the welcoming by the townspeople, the damsel delivered from the boiling bath and the fight with the dragon from the tomb are neatly put together in a charming woodcut from the first printed *Lancelot* (1488), that is illustrated in *The New Arthurian Encyclopaedia*, p. 522, fig. 91 (Fig. 2).

After the damsel is delivered and the dragon vanquished, the lord of Corbenic, King Pelles, invites Lancelot to his castle as a ruse so that he will get his daughter Elaine with child, Galahad – who was prophetically forecast to be an even better knight than his sire. Nothing more is said about the damsel of the boiling bath, in spite of the fact that as soon as she was dressed, 'Syre Launcelot thoughte she was the fayrest lady of the world, but yf it were Quene Gueneuer.[2]

When bedtime comes, an enchantment is laid on Lancelot by another resident enchantress, Lady Brysen, to ensure that he will sleep with Elaine, believing that he is making love to Guinevere. In the sober light of the morning the spell wears off, and Lancelot is enraged enough to draw his sword to kill Elaine, whom he sees as a 'fals traitresse'. But 'fayr Elayne skypped oute of her bedde al naked' and kneeled down before Sir Lancelot. When she identified herself as King Pelles' daughter, who had only obeyed her father's prophecy, Lancelot took his leave 'myldely at that yonge Lady Elayne.[3] But, after he has been rebuked by Guenevere for his indiscretion, Lancelot runs raving into the woods to live there as a naked madman.

Fig. 2: Woodcut of Lancelot's adventures at Pont de Corbenic (Courtesy Newberry Library).

Even though all the elements of a damsel-dragon-rescue are present in the happenings at Corbenic, Malory keeps them separate from each other; the episode of the dolorous lady in the boiling bath is not causally connected with the dragon fight. The combination of naked damsel in distress, dragon, and pre-ordained best of champions that has become a stock set of motives in modern swords-and-sorcery stories turns up first – and there twice for good measure – in Ariosto's *Orlando Furioso* (1519) as the rescues of Angelica and of Olympia by Ruggiero and Orlando respectively (10: 100, 104; 11: 37), and it became imprinted on the reading public's mind by Doré's glorious illustrations, published in

Fig. 3: Gustave Doré: 'Ruggiero rescuing Angelica', woodcut illustration from Ariosto's *Orlando Furioso*, Canto 10:104. (Wikimedia Commons)

1879 (Dore 30, 35, 37). There we find Angelica chained naked to a rocky cliff as prey for the sea monster that is duly slain by Ruggiero, who is coming to her aid mounted on the hippogryph (Fig. 3).

This airborne rescue is of course a remake of the story of Perseus and Andromeda, though it should be pointed out that in representations of this classical myth before the sixteenth century, Andromeda is always more or less fully clothed, and it is Perseus who by contrast, at least in antiquity, is portrayed in heroic nudity. In the legend of St George as the Christian derivative of the Perseus-and-Andromeda story, there is of course no question that the virginal princess about to be sacrificed to the Dragon is chastely clothed.

The standard image of a knight rescuing a naked damsel in distress was coined in 1870 by the Sir John Everett Millais painting, *The Knight Errant* (Fig. 4). Although the knight, in order to avoid eye contact, has to reach awkwardly around the bole in his attempt to cut the ropes that tie the hapless victim to the tree, and though the head of the blushing maiden was altered and 'modestly turned away' (originally she was looking at the viewer), *The Knight Errant* was considered pornographic in Victorian days (Girouard XVII, 159). Probably for this very reason

Fig. 4: 'The Knight Errant' by Sir John Everett Millais. (Wikimedia Commons)

it became the seminal work for the myriads of ankle-clingers that are writhing on the covers of today's sword-and-sorcery paperbacks.

Among the tests independent from rescues, the classical Test-who-is-the-Best done in the nude is the Judgment of Paris. Here are three goddesses undressing before the eyes of a mortal competing for the coveted title of 'the Fairest'. The piquanterie involved in this test offered a welcome subject to legions of illustrators and painters,[4] and its disastrous result, the Trojan War, provided literary material for more than two millennia. This Matter of Greece, through its spinoff, the Story of Aeneas and Brutus, became deftly woven into the Matter of Britain by the skilled hand of Geoffrey of Monmouth.

Among the three tests of virtue that King Arthur and his court have to face in the early German Grail epic, *Diu Crône* [*The Crown*] by Heinrich von dem Türlin, *c.* 1230, there is one that is particularly titillating, and reminiscent of the Judgment of Paris, because it, too, was intended to spoil a wedding festival. During the celebration of the wedding of Gawein's sister, a damsel arrived at King Arthur's court at Caridol in the usual way of an 'adventure' and presented a pair of gloves having the magic property to make their wearer invisible, though there were demanding and potentially embarrassing test conditions to be faced. Each glove, when put on, had the power to make one half of the wearer's body disappear, but

> ... any man or woman whose heart has been corrupted by inconsistency and whose life has been dishonoured in some measure by the mark of shame, so that it is not in every respect as true as steel, will be betrayed on attempting to wear the glove... With both maidens and women, it can disclose peculiar failings – of speech and thought with maidens, of thought and deed with women.

In a most remarkable addition, it is stated that 'if she can be faithful and sincerely care for him, a woman may have a secret lover whom her heart has chosen and praises in silent joy, even if she is married.' Whoever passes the test of the right glove, will receive the left one too, as reward for her or his virtue (*Crown* 259-60). In more than one thousand lines, Heinrich gives a blow-by-blow account of the effects of the glove, lingering on the more embarrassing details with obvious relish.

Of course, as can be expected in a male-dominated society, no matter how chivalrous, it was the ladies' lot to be tested first, and not even

Queen Ginover (who in German Arthurian epics is usually blameless of adultery) succeeds completely; her red lips are still to be seen, when all of her right side disappears.[5] Most of the other ladies fare far worse. The glove's magic works on a layered principle; it makes clothing disappear from sight and bares bodies, sometimes in part and often in toto. For instance, of all of Lady Laudine's dress only a bit of cloth on her right shoulder remained, Lady Enite's entire right side disappeared with exception of her foot and bare hip, and her neighbour, who was unhappily in love with Sir Parzival, similarly had her right side vanish except for her leg 'which stretched forward and could be seen from foot to navel'. When Lady Parkie donned the glove, it 'performed as usual: it concealed her right side but was a little malicious. Although not entirely unkind, it still let the back part of her be seen.' Lady Flursensephin, whose favour Gawein had won with feats of valour, but then let her go to marry his friend, Quoikos, was in for even more embarrassment, when almost all of the right half of her body disappeared, with exception of 'the true creator', as Heinrich put it. For each of these ongoing tests Keii the Seneschal provides biting comments in his usual inimitable style. When it is the turn of his own ladylove, Dame Galaida, her clothing disappears, but of her body only her eye vanishes, 'everything else was bare for all to see.' Keii coolly explains this away by claiming that she does not open her eye out of excessive modesty!

The knights, on the other hand, get away much more easily. King Arthur shows his blamelessness by passing the disappearance test completely, Gawein (who is the *Crown's* Grail Knight)[6] and Lanzelet have the right halves of their bodies vanish with exception of their faces, and by others only a hand, a foot or a bare back remain to be seen. Even Parzival (Wolfram's Grail Knight) leaves a strip two fingers wide of his bare body in sight.

Right at the beginning of the test, Keii had tried to snatch the glove, but it had itself wrapped around his hand in a most painful manner and did not release him until he had asked forgiveness for the verbal offences he so often committed. After everyone had tested the glove, it should have been Keii's turn to try it, too, but he refused. The damsel messenger is said to have been surprised at his words, though Heinrich's audience presumably was not (*Crown* 259-77). The pair of gloves was finally left with King Arthur, who after all was the clear winner of the test (*Crown* 279), but, strangely, he makes no further use of them.

Gawain's reputation as the great lover leads him on two significant occasions into situations where his code of honour and his integrity are severely tested by naked – or almost naked – seductresses. In *Le Chevalier à l'Espée* he is hospitably received at a castle with a strange custom, where the host insists that Gawain has to spend the night with the host's beautiful daughter, 'nu a nu, en son lit', but without taking advantage of the situation (Johnston and Owen 37, Chevalier 277-84).

As soon as Gawain was in bed, the damsel, naked, slipped into his arms: 'Si s'est lez lui cochiée nue...' 'If she laid down naked next to him...' (Chevalier 516.) Among kisses and embraces, however, the damsel warns Gawain before things go too far:

> 'Sire, merci!
> Il ne puet pas aler issi;
> Je ne sui pas o vos sanz garde.' (Chevalier 523-25)

> 'Sire, have mercy!
> It cannot go on beyond this;
> I am not without a guard to keep you away.'

She points out to him that above the bed a sword is hanging from a silver thread around its golden pommel. Installed by her loving parent as her safeguard, it would fall and skewer a would-be violator, as has happened already to more than twenty other knights. Gawain is caught in a dilemma. On one hand, he has an obligation to uphold his reputation as an intrepid lover, who should not be frightened off by a mere mechanical device. On the other hand, there is his perception that the damsel seems not to be a fully willing participant in the custom of the castle. Therefore, Gawain makes a token approach. Promptly the sword descends, but it only nicks his shoulder. In the morning, when to everybody's surprise, he is found alive, he is hailed as the Best of Knights, and is given the hand of the damsel in marriage.

The most famous Arthurian temptation episode is of course in *Sir Gawain and the Green Knight*. Here, the temptress comes to Gawain's bed clothed (it is mid-winter after all), but at her third and most crucial visit she wears under her fur-lined cloak only her kirtle, a skimpy undergarment[7] cut low:

> ... hir throte throwen al naked,
> Hir brest bare bifore, & bihinde eke. (*GGK*, 1740-1741)

... her shapely throat all naked,
Her breast bare in front and the same in the back.

In spite of this alluring undress, Gawain remains steadfast in rejecting her thrice offered favours, though he finally weakens so far that he accepts the magic green girdle. His rejection of the advances made by Sir Bertilak's lady is a matter of principle, because – as even his denigrators have to admit – no matter how generously he partakes of freely offered favours of unattached damsels, he never uses his irresistible charm to seduce a married woman.

A convoluted and quite cruel innocence test involving ever diminishing clothing is found in Chrétien's *Perceval* and in Wolfram's *Parzival.* The unfortunate maiden in the tent beside the fountain, whom the innocent fool, Perceval, had kissed against her will and relieved of her emerald ring, was unjustly punished by her lover, the Proud Knight of the Moor:

'...You will not put
new clothes on till I have his head.
You'll follow me on foot,' he said,

... and naked; I will not consent
to any other punishment.'
(*Perceval* 828-33)

Months later Perceval, now in the role of the Red Knight, meets the damsel again, riding her miserable palfrey:

So dreadful was her wretchedness
that not a handful of her dress
was of whole cloth. Her nipples showed
through her torn bodice which she sewed
with clumsy stitches here and there,
or tied a knot to close a tear
and try to keep the cloth attached. (*Perceval* 3719-25)

Wolfram, in his *Parzival,* also gives a detailed description of the sorry state of Jeschute's (his name for Chrétien's unnamed damsel) attire that was barely a net of knotted bits of rags. In his love for puns and wordplays Wolfram points out that it would be wrong to call this 'naked duchess' Jeschute a vilân (villain) because she did not have 'vil an' (much on); her lover, by contrast, is guilty of dastardly unchivalrous villainy. Like Chrétien, Wolfram pays special attention to the wretched lady's high, white breasts, 'round as if turned on a lathe', which she has to cover with her hands from the gaze of doughty Parzival (*Parzival,*136).

Of course, Perceval, challenged by the Proud Knight of the Moor, defeats him, as does Parzival with Orilus von Laland (Wolfram's rendering of l'Orgueilleux de la Lande). By these feats of prowess, the ladies' honours are restored, proof of their innocence delivered in knightly fashion at sword point in a trial by combat[8] (*Perceval* 3917-49; *Parzival* 138-140).

Knights too, and among them in particular the Best of Knights, such as Yvain, Lancelot, Tristram, Orlando, and Don Quixote, undergo naked test periods of roaming in the wilderness, usually having been driven mad when rebuked by their adored ladies for fancied or real offences against their steadfastness in love. These episodes of madness in combination with nakedness are thought to harken back to early Celtic traditions of champions, such as the Gaesatae ('spearmen') mentioned by Polybius and Diodorus Siculus, who went into battle naked (Wilcox 10, 24, 26, 33; Newark 37, 46,54). This was done even though armour was widely in use, and mail armour specifically seems to have been a Celtic invention of the Late Iron Age. Presumably these Celtic champions – and presumably exactly those, who qualified for the 'Champion's portion' at the king's banquet – rushed into the fray naked not only in a show of bravado, but were believing themselves fey, magically protected through possession by supernatural forces. As a vestigial remnant of this tradition, the 'wild Irish' were known to remove their breeches before battle as late as the sixteenth century (Fig. 5). The courtly knights of Arthur's Round Table were fighting men, too, and would have known everything about battle frenzy; although they were unlikely to know of the naked Gaesatae champions of one thousand years earlier, it seems to be significant that precisely the Best Knight had spells of violent madness roaming naked in the woods, only refined as the result of ill-starred love.

In dealing with Yvain's madness, Chrétien permits himself a little Gallic tongue-in-cheek, when he describes how a lady with her two servant girls finds Yvain, naked and mad, asleep in the forest. In her nearby castle the

Fig. 5: Engaving by Abraham de Bruyn, 'Four soldiers'. To the far left an Irish kern; the others are Scottish, French, and Italian. *(*Antwerp, 1588.)

lady keeps a magic ointment, given to her by Morgan le Fay that has the power to cure 'fever in the brain'. She sends one of her maids back to the forest with the precious salve and stern warnings to use it very sparingly, just on temples and brow. The girl had only very reluctantly followed her mistress back to the castle, because she could barely tear her gaze away from Yvain's splendid physique. Now, on her joyful return to the forest, she yields to temptation and rubs the ointment all over Yvain's body, head to toe, using up the entire box and 'would not have stopped if she had five times more'. (*Yvain* 2887-3010)

Yvain, thus restored to his status as one of the Best Knights in the World, comes eventually to the Castle of Infinite Misfortune, where three hundred maidens are held captive in the medieval equivalent of a sweatshop.[9] Though they were sewing and embroidering in silk and gold thread, they were dressed so poorly and scantily that many did not even wear a sash, and those lucky enough to own shifts or dresses had them 'torn at the breast and out at the elbows' (*Yvain* 5194-5202, 5298-5310). These poor maidens were ransom tribute, thirty to be sent every year, from the King of the Isle of Virgins to the lords of the castle. With the help of his faithful lion, Yvain then slays the two devilish champions upholding this evil custom and frees the maidens.

In the above instances the naked or almost naked women were victims of circumstances beyond their control, even both of Gawain's temptresses had been forced into their roles. Most of these unfortunate damsels had to suffer passively until they were delivered from their miseries by the hero, preferably by a predestined 'best knight in the world' who succeeded where others had failed.

The one shining example of a naked heroine saving her knight in an Arthurian epic is found in the *Livre de Caradoc,* part of the *First Continuation of Chrétien's Perceval* (Thompson 212-14; Brodman 38, 39; Furtado 48). Here the good knight Caradoc of Vannes has been afflicted by his wicked mother, Ysave, and her magician-paramour, Eliavres, with a serpent attached to his arm. This evil reptile is agonizingly sapping away his life-force and he will die within two years. Fortunately, Guignier, the sister of Caradoc's friend, Cador of Cornwall, is in love (roman-oblige, as Marian Masiuk Brodman puts it) with Caradoc, and is willing to make a desperate attempt to save him.

For the disenchantment she immerses herself in a vat of milk, letting her right breast hang temptingly over the rim, while Caradoc has to soak up to his chin in a tub of vinegar next to the maiden's milk vat. Cador is standing by with drawn sword, and when the serpent, disgusted with the vinegar, leaps for the offered sweeter source of nourishment, Cador chops off its head in mid-air, though he could not avoid slicing off his sister's nipple, which later has to be replaced (in gold) by 'good' magic. Eventually, in one of the adventurous tests that periodically happen at King Arthur's court, the test of the drinking horn, Caradoc is the only one to pass, thanks to Guignier's immaculate fidelity.

Most of the Best Knights had their reputations gloriously established and fiercely upheld on the tournament field, but there were also more subtle tests to gain this coveted title. The standard test adventure was either the rescue of a damsel in distress, a test at court, such as the Test of the Glove or the Test of the Drinking Horn, or – morally even more uplifting – a successful resistance to the temptations of the flesh. In these tests, the element of nakedness was introduced for various reasons, some lofty and others less so.[10] In temptation episodes it is obvious that her nudity is the most potent weapon an actively seductive temptress can bring to bear against a Best Knight. On the other hand, in rescue situations a damsel in distress found her status as a hapless victim greatly enhanced if she could be portrayed as pitifully bereft even of her clothes – and if an author had to ingeniously stage a bathing scene, as in the case of the dolorous lady in the tower at Pont de Corbenic. By contrast, the Test of the Glove in *Diu Crône* is a sly 'soft porn' burlesque used quite unabashedly to titillate the audience.

The true Best, however, are the self-sacrificing heroines, such as Guignier and especially Elaine, whose supreme sacrifice to Lancelot, Best Knight in the World, will lead to the birth of Galahad, the Best of All.

Notes

1. 'Frivolität hat in der Minnedichtung und damit im Minnedienst einen gewissen Stellenwert, andererseits galt Nacktheit vor anderen als unschicklich. So ist auch diese Szene zu interpretieren, in der ein Ritter offensichtlich eine Frau beim Bad überrascht, was als Verstoss gegen die ritterlichen Tugenden gewertet werden kann.'(*Die Ritter*, exh. cat. 1990; cat.no. V.4.)

   'Although a certain amount of frivolity had its legitimate place in Minnesinger poetry and in Ladies' Service, nudity in front of others was considered unseemly. Therefore, this scene, in which a knight obviously has surprised a lady in her bath, has to be interpreted as representing a grave offence against the virtues of chivalry.'
2. Another episode involving a bath and a dragon fight is in the Tristram story. Sent to Ireland to ask for Isolt as a bride for his uncle, King Mark, Tristram finds that Isolt's father has promised her hand to whoever succeeds in killing a land-devastating dragon. Tristram slays the dragon but is overcome by its poison. In the process of being nursed back to consciousness and health by Isolt he is put into a healing bath. While Tristram is in the bath, Isolt discovers that his sword has a notch that fits the steel shard she had retrieved from the skull of her uncle, the Morholt, whom Tristram had killed on an earlier occasion. Sorely tempted to take revenge on the helpless Tristram, she has second thoughts on considering that there is also a false claim about the dragon slaying by a suitor she likes even less than the killer of her uncle (Newstead 123). The bath episode was a favourite motif in illustrations of the Tristram story (Loomis 68, 70, 78, 79, 80, 82, 85).
3. In spite of this double infidelity of Lancelot sleeping with the fair Elaine, while lusting for Guinevere, he remains the Best Knight in

the World for Malory. Significantly, Gawain is mentioned to have failed in this test. This is in keeping with the tradition of denigrating Gawain, who used to be the Best Knight, in order to further Lancelot (Matthews). A charming recent representation of the episode is the illustration by Victor Ambrus (Riordan 75).

4. In fifteenth- and sixteenth-century representations of the Judgment of Paris, most notably in paintings by Lukas Cranach (1472-1553), Paris, though he is supposed to be herding his father's flocks, is shown as a knight wearing full armour (Nickel 117-29).
5. In the attempted rape of Ginover by Gasozein de Dragoz, she permits herself to become partially disrobed in a vain attempt to appease her abductor; in the nick of time she is rescued by Gawein (*Crown* 130-132).
6. In Heinrich von dem Türlin's *Diu Crône* Gawein encounters several adventures involving naked maidens and women, though not as tests (*Crown* 161, 320). In one such episode an ugly hag riding a triple-homed beast, green as grass, whips along a bound and naked moor (*Crown* 161-62). With the hindsight of 'Jurassic Park' this beast looks uncannily like a triceratops. Though dinosaurs have become common knowledge only less than one hundred and fifty years ago, it should be mentioned that a triceratops skull found near Klagenfurt, the capital of the Austrian province of Carinthia, was fondly identified as that of a dragon in a local medieval legend. The city arms of Klagenfurt, at least since the fourteenth century, are: *Azure, a tower argent, a dragon vert over all.* Heinrich von dem Türlin is thought to have hailed from Carinthia.
7. Medieval underwear is rarely, if ever, shown in art. An actual kirtle (probably fourteenth century) was found in 1867 in the Castle Rahnis, Thuringia. It is of linen, barely knee-length, with narrow shoulder-straps allowing for a deep décolletage (Kohler 177, Mutzel 159).
8. The delicate motif of a maiden 'toute nue' in enchanted sleep, and suffering what would today be called date rape, is found in the Troilus and Zellandine episode in the *Roman de Perceforest* (Roussineau 30-45).
9. The hard-worked girls tell Yvain that they are paid only four pennies a day, 'and that's not enough to feed us or put clothes on our backs ... and the ones we work for are rich because of what we produce'

(*Yvain* 5309-10, 5318-19). Hartmann von Aue is even more specific; the spokeswoman of the sweatshop tells Iwein:

'Man gît uns von dem pfunde
niuwân vier pfennige.
Der lôn ist alze ringe
Vür speise und vür cleider'

'For every pound, they give us
Only four pennies.
Our wages are much too meagre
To buy food or clothing.' *(Iwein*, 6398-6401)

10. Outside the Arthurian complex the universally known example of the naked heroine would be Lady Godiva and her ride through Coventry.

Select Bibliography

Brodman, Marian Masiuk. 'Terra Mater-Luxuria Iconography and the Caradoc Serpent Episode', *Quondam et Futurus,* vol. 2, no. 3 (Autumn 1992).

Caxton's Malory: A New Edition of Sir Thomas Malory's Le Morte Darthur based on the Pierpont Morgan Copy of William Caxton's Edition of 1482 (2 vols.), ed. William W. Spisak, William Matthews, and Bert Dillon. Berkeley & Los Angeles: University of California Press, 1983.

Chrétien de Troyes. *Perceval, or The Story of the Grail,* trans. Ruth Harwood Cline. New York: Pergamon Press, 1983.

______ *Yvain, The Knight of the Lion,* trans. Burton Raffel. New Haven & London: Yale University Press, 1987.

Die Ritter, exh. cat. Burgenländische Landesausstellung, Burg Gussing, May-October, 1990, Eisenstadt, 1990.

Doré's Illustrations for Ariosto's Orlando Furioso. New York: Dover Publications, 1980.

Furtado, Antonio L. 'A Source in Babylon', *Quondam et Futurus,* vol. 3, no. 1 (Spring, 1993)

Girouard, Mark. *The Return to Camelot: Chivalry and the English Gentleman.* New Haven & London: Yale Univ. Press, 1981.

Gollancz, Sir Israel, ed. *Sir Gawain and The Green Knight.* London: Early English Text Society, 1940.

Grigsby, John L. 'Caradoc, Livre (or Roman) de,' entry in *The New Arthurian Encyclopaedia.* New York & London: Garland Publishing, 1991.

Hartmann von Aue. *Iwein*, ed. & trans. Patrick M. McConeghy vol. 19, series A, Garland Library of Medieval Literature, New York & London, 1984.

Heinrich von dem Türlin. *The Crown: A Tale of Sir Gawein and King Arthurs Court,* trans. J. W. Thomas. Lincoln & London: University of Nebraska Press, 1989.

Johnston, R. C. and D. D. R. Owen. *Two Old French Gauvain Romances.* New York: Barnes & Noble, 1973.

Karr, Phyllis Ann. *The King Arthur Companion.* Reston, VA: Chaosium, Reston Publishing Company, 1983. Reprinted by Chaosium Inc., 2019.

Köhler, Carl. *A History of Costume.* New York: Dover Publications, first published 1928.

Loomis, Roger Sherman, ed. *Arthurian Literature in the Middle Ages: A Collaborative History.* Oxford: Clarendon Press, 1959.

Loomis, Roger Sherman and Laura Hibbard Loomis. *Arthurian Legends in Medieval Art.* London & New York: Oxford Univ. Press, 1937.

Malcor, Linda and John Matthews, *Artorius: The Real King Arthur.* Stroud, Amberley 2023

Matthews, John. *Gawain: Knight of the Goddess, restoring an Archetype.* London: The Aquarian Press, 1990.

Mützel, Hans. *Von Lendenschurz zur Modetracht.* Berlin: Widder-Verlag, 1925.

The New Arthurian Encyclopaedia, ed. Norris J. Lacy. New York & London: Garland Publishing, 1991.

Newark, Tim. *Celtic Warriors: 400 BC-AD 1600.* New York: Blandford Press, 1986.

Newstead, Helaine. 'The Origin and Growth of the Tristan Legend', *Arthurian Literature in the Middle Ages.* ed. R. S. Loomis, Oxford: Clarendon Press, 1959.

Nickel, Helmut. '*The Judgment of Paris* by Lukas Cranach the Elder: Nature, Allegory, and Alchemy.' *Metropolitan Museum Journal* 16 (1981).

Riordan, James. *Tales of King Arthur,* illustrated by Victor Ambrus. Chicago, New York & San Francisco: Rand McNally, 1982.

Roussineau, Gilles. 'Tradition Litteraire et Culture Populaire dans L'Histoire de Troilus et de Zellandine (Perceforest, Troisième partie), Version Ancienne du Conte de la Belle au Bois Dormant', *Arthuriana,* 4.1 (Spring 1994)

Thompson, Albert Wilder. 'The Additions to Chrétien's Perceval' in *Arthurian Literature in the Middle Ages.* London: Oxford University Press, 1959.

Wilcox, Peter. *Rome's Enemies (2): Gallic and British Celts.* London: Osprey, Men-at-Arms Series 158, 1985.

Wolfram von Eschenbach, *Parzival,* trans. A. T Hatto, Harmondsworth, Middlesex: Penguin Books, 1980.

Originally published in *Arthuriana* 9 no. 3 (Autumn, 1999) pp. 81-96.

'My strength is as the strength of ten,/ Because my heart is pure.' Illustration to Tennyson's 'Sir Galahad' by W. E. F. Britten, 1901. (Public domain)

25

A Pictorial Source for The Grail Maiden?

> The Grail is, in one of its aspects, a historical and literary puzzle, and there is an insatiable appetite for solutions to such mysteries and puzzles. (Richard Barber)

For more than eight hundred years the search for the Grail has been going on. As shown by the bestseller-phenomenon of *The Da Vinci Code,* tinkering with the Grail in its many and varied forms and meanings, whether Celtic Cauldron of Plenty, Christian dish, chalice of the Last Supper or the holy blood line, has become almost a cottage industry. It seems presumptuous to add yet one more piece to the puzzle, but in spite of this and in all humility, I would like to do just that. Although in dealing with the Grail it is inevitable to get sidetracked, I will focus on the image of the Grail bearer and put some stray thoughts on the nature of the Grail into the notes.

In his comprehensive *The Holy Grail: Imagination and Belief*, Richard Barber states that in 1180 nobody knew anything about the Grail.[1] Its first appearance in literature is in about 1190, in Chrétien's description of the procession in the Grail castle as witnessed by Perceval (v. 3192-239), where a squire came carrying a white lance.[2] From its tip a drop of blood would drip and run along the shaft down to the squire's hand, followed by another drop. Two more squires entered, each held a golden candelabrum, blazing with at least ten lighted candles, and then

Un graal entre ses deus mains
Une demoisele tenoit
Qui avec les vallés venoit,
Bele et gente et bien acesmee.

Fig 1: The Damsel of the Sanct Grael by Dante Gabriel Rossetti, 1857. (Public domain)

A grail between her two hands
a damsel held
who with the squires came,
lovely, gentle and well attired.

When the damsel bearing the grail entered (it was of finest gold and enamelled, set with the rarest and most precious gems to be found on land or sea), it cast such a brilliant light that the candles seemed to pale, as the stars do at the rise of the sun or the moon. The grail bearer was followed by another damsel carrying a silver platter.[3]

More than three thousand lines later, Chrétien tells of Perceval's visit to the hermit (v. 6415-3429), who is the Grail king's brother, and Perceval's own uncle on his mother's side. Here, Perceval is told that the Grail sustains the ailing king's life by bringing him a single mass wafer, instead of more worldly food, though it is large enough to hold a pike, lamprey or salmon (v. 6421: '*lus ne lamproie ne salmon*') and 'was such a holy thing'.[4]

The enigmatic motif of the Grail maiden bearing the Grail that contains a communion wafer is sometimes accepted without further comment; on the other hand, it has evoked wildly differing and esoteric explanations ranging from it being the remnant of a pagan fertility cult, a suspected Cathar ritual, and a part of the Jewish Passover seder (order or procedure – the conduct of the meal, all the dishes, the blessings, the prayers and the songs written in the Haggadah, which determines the order of Passover and tells the story of the Exodus from Egypt), to it representing the Sovereignty of Ireland.[5] However, 'a picture says more than a thousand words' and there is indeed a sacred picture that corresponds to Chrétien's description of the Grail maiden. In the Apollon monastery at Bawît in Egypt there is a Coptic mural of the Virgin, thought to have been painted before AD 600 (Fig. 2). Its iconography is based on the Late Roman motif of Victoria holding in her hands an oval shield (*clipeus*) with the portrait of the Emperor or a consul. The Madonna of Bawît is, as my friend the late Heinz Stafski has pointed out, the crucial step in the motif's development from Late Roman secular pageantry into a Christian sacred icon.[6]

In his fundamental *The Iconography of the Mother of God,* N. P. Kondakov stated:

The characteristic type of the Mother of God, which was formed in the Coptic icons of the V-VII centuries, was the majestic image of the

Fig. 2: Mural of the Madonna, St Apollon monastery, Bawît, Egypt. Coptic, before AD 600. Courtesy Heinz Stafski.

> Mother of God enthroned, holding in both her hands an oval shield or medallion with the representation of the Saviour Christ Emmanuel. The oldest and possibly the basic type of such an image is the large fresco in the altar niche of a chapel at Bawît in Egypt... [It] represents the Mother of God between two archangels in a Paradise-landscape (with orange trees)... This Greco-Eastern type has been taken over, with a few changes, into the Byzantine iconography, and has also been preserved in the oldest monuments of the West.[7]

In the Bawît mural, the Virgin is holding in her hands what at first glance appears to be a mandorla surrounding the full figure of the Christ child. Since, however, the Madonna's fingers are shown as curling around the edges of the oval, it is made dear that this is not an insubstantial halo, but a solid object. Traces of shading indicate that this is meant to be a slightly hollowed object, such as a large dish.

Here we have before our eyes exactly what is described in Chrétien's Gral procession: a virgin holding a large dish that contains the Body of Christ, i.e. the communion wafer. Even the two squires accompanying the Grail Maiden are present in the persons of the two angels.

In search for Arthurian sources 'oral traditions' are often evoked, if literary sources fail. Could it be that such an 'oral tradition' was created from a 'pictorial tradition' by a pilgrim who had worshipped, if not at the Madonna of Bawît herself, then perhaps at one of the Byzantine icons derived from this prototype, and told about it back home in France, where what he had seen was turned into Chrétien's sublime vision of the bearer of the Grail?

Notes

1. See Richard Barber, *The Holy Grail: Imagination and Belief* (Cambridge, Harvard University Press, 2004), p. 27.
2. See Chrétien de Troyes *Perceval: or, The Story of the Grail,* trans. Ruth Harwood Cline (New York: Pergamon Press, 1983), p. 88.
3. In light of this description in celestial terms it is tempting to see the objects carried in the procession as cosmological symbols, with the brilliantly shining Grail as the sun, the silver platter as the moon, the two youths with candles as morning star and evening star, and the squire with the bleeding lance as the planet Saturn

with its ring that (seen edgewise) was apparently recognized by keen-eyed Babylonian astronomers and thought to be a piercing staff or lance. Later, Arab stargazers saw the phenomenon as the stylus of the Book of Fate transfixing the body of the baleful planet. Max Hesse, 'Iranisches Sagengut in christlichen Epos: Ein Beitrag zur Entstehung des Parzivalliedes,' *Atlantis 10* (Oct. 1937): 623-28.

4. This ichthyological remark has been seen as a reference to the Fisher King, as well as to the Christian symbol of the Fish, but in an entirely different twist a curious connection with the Isis/Osiris cult has been pointed out. After Osiris was killed by his evil brother Set, he was not only dismembered by Set, but his body parts were cast into the Nile. Isis collected these parts and tried to reassemble Osiris' body in order to revive and resurrect him. However, she found the genitals missing. They had been already swallowed by greedy fishes. According to Hellenistic tradition these denizens of the deep that in their voracity imperilled the restoration of Osiris were three – a pike, a lamprey and a salmon. See Silvestro Fiore, 'Les origines orientales de la Légende du Graal: évolution des themes dans le cadre des cultures et des cults', *Cahiers de Civilisation Médiévale Xe'XIIe siecles* Universite de Poitiers (April-June 1967), 207-19. As it turns out, the cause of the Grail king's disability was a lance thrust 'through the thighs', a euphemism for accidental castration and resultant loss of virility.
5. See 'The Origin of the Grail Legends', entry 21 in *Arthurian Literature in the Middle Ages,* ed. Roger Sherman Loomis (Oxford: Oxford University Press, 1959), pp. 274-94; and Jean Frappier, 'Perceval or "Le Conte du Graal"' in the same work, pp. 184-90; Richard O'Gorman: 'Grail (Graal),' entry in *The New Arthurian Encyclopaedia,* ed. Norris J. Lacy et al. (New York & London: Garland, 1991), pp. 212-13.
6. See Heinz Stafski, 'Die Statuette einer "Maria in Erwartung" aus dea Dominikanerinnen-kloster HI. Kreuz in Regensburg,' *Zeitschrift des deutschen Vereins für Kunstwissenschaft* XVII, Heft 1-4 (Berlin 1973), 55-62, fig. 8. I would like to acknowledge my late friend, Heinz Stafski, of the Germanisches Nationalmuseum, Nurnberg, for the photo of the Madonna of Bawît from his essay that gave me the idea about a pictorial source for the Grail maiden so many years ago.

7. N. P. Kondakov, *The Iconography of the Mother of God,* vol. I (St. Petersburg, 1914) pp. 304-307, figs. 206-209, 212, 213, 216. I am deeply indebted to the late Vera Ostoia, my friend and colleague at the Metropolitan Museum, New York, for her translation of this crucial passage.

Originally published in *Arthuriana* vol. 16, no 1, Spring 2006, pp. 61-64.

26

About the Saxon Rebellion and the Massacre at Amesbury

> It is the chief value of legend to mix up the centuries while preserving the sentiment; to see all ages in a sort of splendid foreshortening. That is the use of tradition; it is telescope history. (G. K. Chesterton)

When Arthurian literature is dealing with events before Arthur's time, the standard view is that the 'proud tyrant' Vortigern hired three shiploads of Saxon mercenaries under their leaders, Hengist and Horsa, to fight the Picts. However, the Saxons rebelled, turned against their hosts and drove the Britons out of their homeland into the mountains of Wales. Their most infamous crime was the treacherous breach of faith at the peace meeting at Amesbury, where Hengist conducted a massacre on the assembled leaders of the Britons, sparing only Vortigern.

Significantly, Gildas, as an almost contemporary, does not mention the massacre at Amesbury at all, although he describes the devastation wrought by the Saxon heathens in the most lurid details, as he might have heard in tales of his grandfathers.[1] The Saxons (a name not to be spoken!) were for him 'gallowbirds', hated by men and God. They came in three 'keels' and were let into the island by the members of the council and the 'proud tyrant', to beat back the peoples of the North, Picts and Scotti.[2]

Gildas's oft-quoted lament – 'The barbarians push us back to the sea, the sea pushes us back to the barbarians; between these two kinds of death, we are either drowned or slaughtered' – was about invasions by the Picts, before the arrival of the Saxons.[3] It seems that they turned the tide; the raiding Irish went home, and the Picts kept quiet. After the first three ships, a second and larger troop was admitted. However, when the promised supplies dwindled away, the Saxons decided to pay themselves by plunder.[4]

The first to tell of the massacre at Amesbury, and already in considerable detail, is Nennius (*c.* AD 820). In doing so, he goes back to the relations between Romans and Britons during the centuries before the end of the Roman Empire in Britain: 'After the killing of the tyrant Maximus ... the British went in fear for 40 years. Vortigern ruled in Britain, and ... he was under pressure, from fear of the Picts and Scotti, and of a Roman invasion, and, not least, from dread of Ambrosius.' When three keels with Saxon warriors arrived, led by the brothers Hengist and Horsa, they were welcomed by Vortigern and settled on the island of Thanet. They were promised supplies of food and clothing, and in their turn promised to fight bravely against the king's enemies. To augment their scanty numbers, Hengist asked permission for more warriors to come, and there came sixteen more keels, which brought his strength up to almost a thousand men.[5]

Judging from excavated boats of the period, each keel would have carried a crew of about fifty. At that point the Britons said: 'We cannot give you food and clothing, for your numbers have grown. Go away, for we do not need your help.'[6] In one of the sixteen ships had come Hengist's daughter. Hengist held a banquet for Vortigern, and his daughter, a very beautiful girl, served the wine. 'Satan entered Vortigern's heart and made him love the girl.' Vortigern, through his interpreter, asked Hengist for her hand: 'Ask of me what you will, even to the half of my kingdom.' After taking council with the elders Hengist asked for Kent. Although it was ruled by Gwyrangon, it was handed over to the heathens.[7]

As Vortigern's father-in-law, Hengist took it upon himself to suggest sending for more Saxon warriors, not only as reinforcements in the fighting against Picts but also to protect the king, Vortigern, against the growing unrest among the Britons. Vortigern consented, and Hengist's son Octha and his nephew Ebissa came with forty keels. They fought in the North and occupied lands beyond the Frenessian Sea, at the border of the Picts.[8]

Meanwhile, Vortigern's son, Vortimer, attacked the Saxons in the South, fought vigorously against Hengist and Horsa and in four battles drove them back to the island of Thanet. In the second battle Horsa and also Vortigern's other son, Cateyrn, were killed. Vortimer finally expelled the Saxons even from Thanet, and they went back to their homeland.[9]

However, Vortimer died soon after this victory, and the Saxons returned, readmitted by Vortigern, who was their friend because of his wife. Hengist asked for a meeting, unarmed, to discuss terms for a permanent treaty. But before the meeting Hengist told his followers to hide their knives in their boots and wait his signal, '*Eu, nimet saxas!*' in order to fall upon their British partners, but to spare the king, Vortigern, because he was wedded to Hengist's daughter and valuable to be ransomed. Thus, all three hundred elders of the Britons were murdered and Vortigern captured, to be ransomed by ceding Essex, Sussex, Middlesex and more.[10]

Geoffrey of Monmouth uses Nennius's basic storyline, but elaborates on it, as is his wont. For instance, when the Picts invaded the lands beyond the Humber, the ensuing battle was won thanks to Vortigern's newly hired Saxon mercenaries.[11] In order to secure a base, Hengist asked for land, as much as could be encompassed by a single thong. Cutting a bull's hide into the thinnest possible strip, he marked out a large site and built Thanceastre, 'Thong Hall'. When he got permission to invite reinforcements, eighteen ships came, with his daughter on board. At the banquet Hengist gave for Vortigern in his new hall, the beauty of the maiden smote the king, and although he was a Christian, he took the pagan girl for his wife, giving away the province of Kent as a bride price. This way he incurred the enmity of the British leaders and of his own three sons.[12] Although with the Saxons' help Vortigern was victorious in every battle, the British became wary of them and wanted him to banish them from his lands. When he refused, the British deserted him and elected his eldest son, Vortimer, to the kingship.[13]

Vortimer right away started to attack the barbarians, defeated them in four bloody battles, and drove them back to Germany. Shortly after his victory, Vortimer was poisoned by his stepmother, Hengist's daughter. After Vortimer's death, Vortigern was reinstated as king and Hengist returned with a large army.[14]

Under the pretence of arranging a permanent treaty, Hengist asked for a meeting with the elders of the Britons, unarmed, on the first of May at the 'Cloister of Ambrius'. However, treacherously, Hengist ordered his men to hide their long knives (the *seaxes)* in their leggings, and at his signal, '*Nimet oure saxes,*' they fell upon the Britons, killing four hundred and sixty. Only Eldol, count of Gloucester, managed to escape.

Vortigern was taken captive and had to ransom himself by ceding cities and fortresses.[15]

In the absence of trustworthy contemporary sources we have to rely on the semi-legendary accounts of Nennius and Geoffrey, and neither see the conflict as an unprovoked rebellion by the Saxons against their hosts. Quite the contrary, its reason was the unwillingness of the British ruling class to fulfil the conditions of the contract that Vortigern, as king, had offered to his mercenaries. In addition to that, there was active resistance by Christian zealots against the heathen Saxons. In its most blatant example, Layamon, as a follower of Geoffrey's, even goes so far as to report that the 'good king' Vortimer offered twelve pennies bounty money for Saxon heads 'for the love of Christendom.[16]

As already mentioned, the treacherous attack of the 'Long Knives' at Amesbury is not found in Gildas's diatribes. It appears almost four hundred years after its supposed occurrence in Nennius's *Historia Brittonum,* who states in his preface: 'I ... have made a heap of all that I have found, both from the Annals of the Romans and from the Chronicles of the Holy Fathers, and from the writings of the Irish and the English, and of the tradition of our elders.'

It has been pointed out that on the Continent the Saxons were accused of a similar crime against the Thuringians, as reported in *Res gestae Saxonicae,* by the monk Widukind of Corvey, *c.* 980, in time halfway between Nennius and Geoffrey. The Benedictine abbey of Corvey was located on the Weser River in the Saxon heartland of North Germany.

Widukind says that land-seeking Saxon exiles found themselves stranded in Thuringian territory and were on the point of starvation when a Saxon forager carrying gold jewellery for barter encountered a Thuringian. He asked the Thuringian to give him anything he saw fit for his gold. The Thuringian, as a cruel jest, responded that he would give him as much dirt as he could fill his cloak with. The Saxon took the dirt to his waiting tribesmen, who declared him a madman, until he explained his ruse. The Saxons now spread this dirt in a thinnest film over a huge area, claiming that thus they sat on their legally bought soil. The Thuringians protested, battles were fought, but at last both parties tired of it and agreed to hold a peace conference. The Saxons secretly brought their long knives to the meeting and massacred the Thuringians.[17]

The ruse of the thinly spread soil is a parallel to Hengist's ruse of the thin thong that secured him his fortress of Thanceastre, as reported by Geoffrey (vi, 11).[18] That story is, of course, based on the founding myth of Carthage, when Dido, as an exile from Tyre, used the same sleight-of-hand to acquire land, 'as much as could be encompassed by a bull's hide', for the building of Carthage's citadel (*Aeneid,* 425-430).[19] For this it was called Byrsa (Gr. 'hide'; Sem. 'fortress').

If we find the source of Hengist's land acquisition in classical literature, in looking for a classical source for his treacherous massacre, we need not go as far back as Xenophon's *Anabasis,* where in BC 401 at Cunaxa, before the gates of Babylon, the Greek captains (two hundred and twenty-five, with one survivor to tell the tale) were seized and killed during peace negotiations.[20]

There was just such treason at hand much closer to home and in a time that Nennius could have found in the *Annals of the Romans.* The deed was perpetrated in AD 376, at the banks of the Danube, reported by the Roman historian Ammianus Marcellinus (*c.* 330-395), himself a high-ranking military officer and a contemporary.[21]

In AD 375, the Huns had overrun the two Gothic kingdoms at the Northern shore of the Black Sea. The Eastern Ostrogoths were forced into vassalage, but the Western Visigoths managed to retreat beyond the Danube into East Roman territory. Although their warriors volunteered as auxiliaries in the Roman army, the fugitives were interned under appalling conditions. The corrupt governor of Thrace, Lupicinus, saw a golden opportunity to barter food for slaves, preferably children of the starving Goths. (Lupicinus had been in Britain as a military commander, and stopped the invasion of the Great Alliance of the Scotti, Picts, and stray Saxon raiders in AD 368)[22]

When one of the Gothic sub-tribes in his care, the Tervingi, showed signs of resistance against the treatment dealt out to them, Lupicinus invited two hundred of their chieftains under their leader, Fritigern, to a meeting (dinner included) at Marcianople. There he sprung a trap and killed them all; only Fritigern was spared, in the vain hope that he could be useful to ensure the good behaviour of the Tervingi.[23]

Understandably, this treasonous act sparked a general revolt in which Lupicinus was killed (AD 377). Its climax was the battle of Hadrianople in AD 378, where the combined tribes of the Visigoths, together with their allies, Alanic horsemen driven out of the Eurasian steppes by the Huns, practically annihilated an East Roman army led by the Emperor in person. The Emperor Valens was among slain, and Visigoths and Alans went on to conquer Rome itself a generation later, in AD 410.[24]

Could it be that in a case of telescope history the tale about a treasonable massacre with one single survivor named *Fritigern* became attached to *Vortigern* because it was perpetrated by a rogue leader with connections to Britain? *Tervingi* and *Thuringi* sounded similar enough for the purpose of the same tale to be told on the Continent, and all of it became associated with heathen Saxons, a tribe ominously named for their long knives, the *seaxes,* and of whom a Christian chronicler (even the Saxon monk Widukind) expected dastardly deeds as a matter of course.

Although probably neither Nennius's massacre in Britain nor Widukind's on the Continent ever happened at all, the stuff of the tale was simply too good to be passed over and thus became firmly entrenched in legend.

Notes

1. *Gildas,* ed. and trans. Michael Winterbottom, Arthurian Period Sources 7 (London: Phillimore, 1978), p. 27; 'The Coming of the Saxons', 24, 1-4.
2. *Gildas,* 'The Coming of the Saxons.' Ch. 23.3, p. 26.
3. *Gildas,* 'Independent Britain,' Ch. 20. 1, pp. 23-24.
4. *Gildas,* 'The Coming of the Saxons,' 23.4-5, pp. 26-27.
5. *Nennius,* ed. and trans. John Morris, Arthurian Period Sources 8 (London: Phillimore, 1980).
6. *Nennius,* 'The Kentish Chronicle, Part 2,' ch. 36-37, p. 28.
7. *Nennius,* 'The Kentish Chronicle, Part 2,' ch. 37, p. 28.
8. *Nennius,* 'The Kentish Chronicle, Part 2,' ch. 36-37, p. 28.
9. *Nennius,* 'The Kentish Chronicle, Part 2,' ch. 38, p. 29.
10. *Nennius,* 'The Kentish Chronicle, Part 3,' ch. 43-44, p. 31.
11. *Nennius,* 'The Kentish Chronicle, Part 3,' ch. 44-46, p. 32.
12. Geoffrey of Monmouth, *The History of the Kings of Britain,* trans. Lewis Thorpe, (New York: Penguin Classics, 1966), p. 157, Part Four, 'The House of Constantine', 6. 10.
13. Geoffrey of Monmouth, *History,* p. 157-60, Part Four, 4.11-12.
14. Geoffrey of Monmouth, *History,* p. 161, Part Four, 4.13.
15. Geoffrey of Monmouth, *History,* p. 161-63, Part Four, 6.13-15.
16. Geoffrey of Monmouth, *History,* p. 164-66, Part Four, 6.15-16.

17. Geoffrey of Monmouth, *History*, p. 161, Part Four, 6. 13. The British 'told the King that he should banish the newcomers from the lands over which he ruled, for pagans ought not to be in close communications with Christians, nor to be allowed to infiltrate in this way, for the Christian faith forbade it... Already no one could tell who was pagan and who was Christian, for the pagans were associating with their daughters and their female relations.' In Wace & Layamon, *Arthurian Chronicles*, trans. Eugene Mason (London: Everyman's Library, 1912), p. 135, we are told 'Vortimer, the young king ... ordered each man that loved the Christendom, that they all should hate the heathens, and bring the heads of them to Vortimer, the king, and have twelve pennies for reward, for his good deed.'
18. Widukind von Corvey, *Res gestae Saxonicae/Die Sachsengeschichte*, ed. and trans. Ekkehart Rotter & Bernd Schneidmüller (Stuttgart: Reclam, 1992), pp. 21-29.
19. Geoffrey of Monmouth, *History*, pp. 158-59.
20. *The Aeneid: Vergil's Great Epic Poem Concerning the Adventures of the Trojan Hero Aeneas*, trans. Patric Dickinson, Mentor Books (New York and Scarborough, Ontario: The New American Library, 1961), 1.425-30, pp. 16-17.
21. Xenophon, *Anabasis: The March Up Country*, trans. W. H. D. Rouse, Mentor Classic (New York: The New American Library of World Literature, 1959), p. 60. The lone survivor was Nicarchos, an Arcadian.
22. *Ammianus Marcellinus*, ed. and trans. J. C. Rolfe, 3 vols. (London, 1950-52) 31:5.6-7. See Helmut Nickel, 'Wer waren König Artus' Ritter?' *Waffen-und Kostümkunde* (1975); 1-28, esp. 27 n16.
23. On Lupicinus, see Beram Saklatvala, *Arthur: Britain's Last Champion* (Newton Abbot: David & Charles, 1967), pp. 37, 43.
24. Peter Heather, *The Goths* (Oxford/Cambridge, MA: Blackwell, 1966). Peter Heather, *Goths and Romans, 352-489* (Oxford: Oxford University Press, 1991). Herwig Wolfram, *History of the Goths* (Berkeley: University of California Press.1988; first published in German, Beck, Munich, 1979).

Originally published in *Arthuriana*, vol 16, No 1., Spring 2006, pp. 65-70.

27

Last Days of Rome in Britain and The Origin of The Arthurian Legends

One of the clichés of the history textbooks is that the Glory of Rome was blotted out by an onrushing tide of pagan barbarians, and that afterwards the Dark Ages engulfed Europe until Charlemagne and the Christian Church brought civilisation back to the world.

The trouble with this simplified version – as is the case with simplified versions in general – is that it tells only part of the story and distorts and obscures the rest. Most of the barbarians credited with the destruction of Rome were themselves Christians, who were anxious to take up the Roman way of life at the first opportunity they had and did their best to continue it for as long as they could. Such was the case with the Visigoths, the Ostrogoths, the Burgundians, and later the Franks. The Visigoths, who had sacked Rome in 410, were the mainstay of the Roman army at the Battle of the Catalaunian Plains in 451, when the West was saved from Attila's Huns.

During the Dark Ages, indeed, the basis for the political and territorial future of Europe was laid, and factors established that are still of importance today; but there was another, cultural phenomenon that appeared at that time: the birth of the romance literature of the Middle Ages.

It was during the fifth and sixth centuries – more precisely the period between 440 and 540 AD – when the great epics of chivalry, the *Nibelungenlied*, the Dietrich von Bern cycles, and above all the Arthurian legends, became attached to the historical personalities they featured.

The legends of King Arthur are by far the most important group in this entire complex, and they can claim to have been one of the most influential factors in the shaping of the most outstanding cultural feature of the Middle Ages – chivalry. To a degree it can be said that they even brought forth the concept of chivalry itself.

The earliest complete version of the Arthurian legend is presented in Geoffrey of Monmouth's best-selling *Historia Regum Britanniae*, *c.* 1135. Though several of his fellow-historians, such as William of Malmesbury, William of Newburgh and Giraldus Cambrensis, had reservations about Geoffrey's truthfulness and his sources, nevertheless the story itself and the historicity of Arthur were not questioned until the Age of Reason, when all stories of this nature were regarded as literary inventions at best. However, since Heinrich Schliemann discovered the remains of Troy, we know that a kernel of truth may exist behind the most colourful trappings of legend.

During the last hundred years, enough books and articles about every aspect of the Arthurian legends have been written to fill a medium-size library. As far as the historicity of Arthur is concerned, practically all scholars agree that the historical Arthur must have been a Romanized Celtic chieftain, who heroically tried to preserve the remnants of Roman civilisation in Britain from the onrushing tide of barbarian Angles and Saxons from across the North Sea. The fact that these Angles and Saxons were not Christians, like the Goths and Burgundians, but were still heathen and remained so for more than a century, has contributed to the popular idea of an onslaught of pagan barbarians.

Many have tried to find Celtic traditions in the Arthurian legends, but unfortunately what little material has come down to us does not always fit with the basic motifs of the medieval Arthurian story. Most of the popular writers in Arthurian matters are therefore content with a circular argument: because something appears in the Arthurian legends, it has to be an ancient Celtic tradition, otherwise it would not be in the Arthurian legends in the first place.

Very few scholars have looked into Roman traditions as a possible point of origin. This is the more surprising because it is generally agreed upon that Arthur defended Roman civilisation from barbarism. Roman sources have been acknowledged so far in three points: the name Arthur itself, the use of cavalry in his fight against the Saxons, and the incorporation of biographical details taken from the career of the usurper Magnus Maximus. The latter declared himself Imperator in 383, crossed from Britain to Gaul with the greater part of the Roman troops then stationed in Britain, and marched against Rome. He was defeated and killed at Aquileia, in 388. This episode is supposed to account for Arthur's attempt to capture Rome, as told in the later romances. The name Arthur is generally accepted to be a Celtization of the Latin Artorius. In 1924, the American scholar Kemp Malone published two dedication inscriptions found at Podstrana, near Split in Croatia. These described the military career of a local Procurator, Lucius Artorius Castus, who had served in Judaea and Pannonia before he became praefectus of the *Legio VI Victrix*, stationed in Britain at Eboracum (York) in the second half of the second century AD.

During his service in Britain Lucius Artorius is believed to have led a punitive expedition into Gaul to quell an otherwise unrecorded rebellion. After the expiration of his term of service he retired to his native Dalmatia as '*procurator liburniae*'. Malone suggested that the expedition to Gaul, and the fact that Artorius, the old soldier, did not die in Britain but simply went away (to his retirement in some sunnier clime) might be the root for the Arthurian legend later elaborated by Geoffrey of Monmouth or his source, the 'ancient book in the

Distance Slab of *Legio VI Vitrix* discovered near Cleddans on the Antonine Wall. (Courtesy George MacDonald, public domain)

Welsh language' that he claimed to have received from his friend the archdeacon Walter of Oxford.

The historical Arthur is claimed to have been a Celtic chieftain who made use of Roman cavalry tactics in his fight against the Saxons. Because the Roman army – whatever was left after the adventure of Magnus Maximus in 383 – is generally thought to have been completely withdrawn by the beginning of the 5th century. It is claimed that a local commander of genius remembered these Roman tactics and trained his tribesmen as heavy cavalry to intercept the Saxon invaders.

The Saxons were originally mercenary soldiers hired by the British to fight against the Picts in the North. In the beginning they apparently did their job very well, but after a while troubles started about payments and supplies in arrears, and the Saxon mercenaries mutinied and started to exact payment in the form of goods and land. Their hiring had been perfectly in agreement with established Roman practice; it was only their mutiny and later take-over that did not run true to pattern.

The Saxons had arrived in Britain in three keels – long-ships, of a type similar to the boat found in the bogs near Nydam in Denmark. The craft had benches for 36 oarsmen and was probably crewed by around 50 men. This means that the original invading force of Saxons was probably only about 200 men, although during the struggles that followed they were reinforced by large numbers of adventurers from across the North Sea, who sailed up and down the British coast in search of plunder, using the rivers for inland forays and disappearing before local defence forces could be rallied. Against these hit-and-run tactics the best defence would have been a brigade of fast-moving cavalry assumed to be led by the historical Arthur.

The documentary evidence for the distribution of the Roman army at the beginning of the fifth century is a neatly compiled muster roll, the *Notitia Dignitatum*, which has survived, almost complete, in early medieval copies. It shows that Britain at the end of Roman domination was under three military commanders: one *Dux Britanniarum*, one *Comes Britanniae,* and one Comes (Count) of the Saxon Shore. Among the cavalry units were the two active regiments of *cataphractarii* in Western Europe, two regiments of *Stablesiani*, one of *Taifali* and one *cuneus* of Sarmatian veterans.

Cataphractarii were heavy cavalry, armoured after Iranian prototypes with scale armour and segmented helmets. Even their horses wore armoured housings of scale armour and chamfrons of thick leather reinforced by brass studs. *Stablesiani* were medium-heavy cavalry wearing segmented helmets and body armour of mail but riding on unarmoured horses.

Taifali were a tribe of Eastern steppe riders, as were the Sarmatians. It is to the latter that we turn now. The Sarmatians consisted of a group of nomadic tribes, speaking an Iranian language. Like their relatives the Scythians, they were famous horsemen, living on the Steppes of Eastern Europe, north of the Black Sea between the Caucasus and the Hungarian Puszta. Here, in ancient Pannonia, the Romans had clashed with the westernmost tribes of Sarmatians, the Roxolani and the Jazyges.

In 175 AD the Emperor Marcus Aurelius had made a treaty with the Jazyges of Pannonia and had taken 8,000 of them as auxiliaries into the Roman army. Of these auxiliary troops 5,500 were sent to Northern Britain to fight the Picts. After their 20-year term of service in the army had expired, these Jazyges auxiliaries were not discharged and sent back to their homeland, because this was behind the Iron Curtain of the period. Instead, they were settled in Britain. Their settlement in Bremetannacum, today's Ribchester in Lancashire, was unique in the entire Western Roman establishment; they are still listed 250 years later in the *Notitia Dignitatum* as the *cuneus*, a troop – and any number of horsemen in addition to the regimented *ala* of 500 – consisting of Sarmatian veterans. The fact that they were still called Sarmatians indicates that they must have managed to preserve at least some of their tribal identity.

The Sarmatians were heavy armoured horsemen; the *cataphractarii* of the regular army were actually equipped after the Sarmatian model. The Sarmatians insisted that they all were equally nobly born, without serfs or subordinates in their tribe. Their distinctive tribal battle standard was a dragon carried on a pole and shaped like a windsock, with a head of gilded bronze and a body of red fabric that writhed like a live serpent. When the wind blew into its open jaws it made a terrifying sound. They worshipped their tribal god of war in the shape of a naked sword thrust into the earth or set upon an altar. They had, like all steppe nomads before the introduction of Islam, a shamanistic religion, and shamans were not only there to guide the welfare of the individual but the entire tribe. Finally, in connection with this shamanism they had a hashish-cult, using sacred cauldrons filled with hot stones sprinkled with hemp leaves and seeds to induce visions.

All these Sarmatian characteristics suddenly look awfully familiar: here are the armoured knights that are all equal, without distinction of sitting above or below the salt (like sitting at a round table). Here is the dragon standard of Arthur and Uther Pendragon. Here is the Sword in the Stone. Here is the wizard Merlin, and even the High History of the Holy Grail might well have one of its roots in the sacred hashish-cauldron, which incidentally was reported by Herodotus.

In addition to this it is interesting to note that the Sarmatians transferred to Britain in 175 were attached to the *Legio VI Victrix*, commanded by Lucius Artorius Castus. As we have heard, Castus had served in Pannonia, the homeland of the Sarmatian auxiliaries, before he took office in Britain, and it is quite likely that he had contact with the Sarmatians during his time in Pannonia. He may even have been personally known to some of their chieftains, who in the tradition of the Roman army were serving as officers to their tribesmen. Perhaps his name was used as a title among the Sarmatian horsemen in Britain – 'the Artorius' meaning 'the general', in the same way that the

Artorius inscription found at the coastal villa owned by him just south of Liburnia, in part translated as: 'To the Spirits of the Departed: Lucius Artorius Castus, for himself [...] twice *praefect* of the *Leg. VI Victrix*, *dux* of the three British legions against armed men, *procurator centenarius* of the Province of Liburniae [...] he himself while alive built this for himself and his family.' (Courtesy Linda Malcor and John Matthews, from *Artorius: The Real King Arthur,* photo Nenad Stanić)

name Julius Caesar became 'the Caesar', surviving until recently as Kaiser and Tsar.

The first time the name Arthur is mentioned, is in the *Historia Britonum* of Nennius, a compilation made shortly before 800 of material which the author himself says that he just brought together in a heap of all that he could find, gladly leaving the job of turning it into a real book to whoever would be ambitious and able enough to do so. Nennius draws up a list of twelve battles, in which Arthur, fighting as *dux bellorum* alongside the kings of Britain, had been victorious. It is of interest that here Arthur is not yet a king; the use of the term *dux bellorum* has been interpreted as the survival or revival of an earlier Roman military title, such as the *dux Britanniarum.*

The first of these battles was at the River Glein; the second, third, fourth and fifth at the River Dubglass in Linnuis; the sixth at the River Bassas; the seventh in the Forest of Celidon; the eighth at the Castell Gwinnion, 'where Arthur wore the image of the Blessed Virgin Mary on his shoulders, and there was great slaughter among the heathens by the grace of our Lord Jesus and the virtue of Our Lady'. The ninth battle was in the City of the Legions; the tenth at the mouth of the River Tribruit; the eleventh at Mount Agned or, according to other versions, at Bregomion; and finally, the twelfth was at Mount Badon This last battle is the only one that is mentioned in a contemporary source, in the writings of Gildas, who claimed to have been born in the year it was fought.

Unfortunately, Gildas does not mention the victorious commander in this battle by name, in all probability for the good reason that he was only too well known. Another early source, the *Annales Cambriae*, consists of a list of remarkable dates, including that of the Battle of Mount Badon, 'where Arthur carried the cross of our lord Jesus on his shoulders', for the year 518; and the Battle of Camlann 'where Arthur and Medraut were killed', is recorded for the year 538. Since the Battle of Camlann is missing from the battle list of Nennius, it has been suggested that this battle list might be an adaptation of a song of praise composed in honour of Arthur during his lifetime.

There have been many attempts to identify the sites of these battles. Though the names seem precise, the exact sites were already forgotten by the time Nennius listed them. The River Glein might be the Glen near Boston; the River Dubglass must have been somewhere near Lincoln in Linnuis; the River Bassas might have been the Wass, a tributary to the Glen; the Forest of Ceildon was most likely somewhere in Scotland, in Caledonia, though the forest of Chiltern has been proposed, too. The Castell Gwinnion most likely was the Roman castellum Vinovia or Vinonia, today's Binchester; the City of the Legion was almost certainly Chester.

The River Tribruit seems to have been the Clyde, according to an ingenious bit of scholarly guesswork. There is no actual river known by that name, but in the twelfth-century romance 'Perceval' by Chrétien de Troyes, Perceval's sword is forged by the smith Trebuet at Clotoatre.

Clotoatre is recognizable as the French version of something like Clutwater and Clot was the Anglo-Saxon form of the modern Clyde. Mount Agned has been claimed to be either the Castle Hill of Edinburgh, or the site of Trimontium, a Roman fortress near Newstead on the river Tweed; the alternative site -– Bregomion – could well be Bremetannacum Gordianum, today's Ribchester in Lancashire. The twelfth and most important battle however, the one at Mount Badon, is the most elusive, and there are a number of places, such as the city of Bath, and the Iron Age hill fort of Badbury Rings, that have been claimed as its place of origin.

Going over the battle list, it appears that most of these battles were fought at rivers – seven out of twelve – and this would be only natural if the enemy were bands of sea-borne pirates rowing up the waterways on their inland forays. But more significantly, there are three place names, Castell Gwinnion, Vinonia/Binchester, the City of the Legions that is most likely Chester, and Bregomion that might be Bremetennacum/ Ribchester, which have in common that they used to be garrisons of Roman heavy cavalry, either *cataphractarii*, or – as in the case of Bremetennacum – Sarmatians.

If the site of the eleventh battle at Mount Agned/Trimontium is accepted, there is archaeological evidence in the form of excavated horse armour and equestrian equipment that Trimontium, too, was a garrison of *cataphractarii*. This predominance of battles fought on river sites and names of Roman cavalry garrisons in this battle list supports the assumption that the historical Arthur, whoever he was, had a cavalry force at his disposal, with which he intercepted and fought the Saxon pirates.

One or other of these battles, such as the one that took place in the Forest of Celidon, or the one at Mount Agned, might have been against the traditional enemies in the North, the Picts. The motifs of Uther

Pendragon's banner and the Sword in the Stone, as preserved in the later Arthurian legends, make it likely that this cavalry force was Sarmatian.

The Sarmatians of Bremetennacum, as already mentioned, were a unique establishment in Western Europe. They were a military settlement, not simply a garrisoned unit of the Roman army. Therefore, they presumably were not withdrawn from Britain when the regular units of the Roman army left at the beginning of the fifth century, never to return. Their original task had been to breed horses for the Roman cavalry, at the same time guarding the rich country at the mouth of the river Ribble against the raids of Irish pirates. Around 450 AD, however, these Irish raids came to an end, due in part to the Christianization of Ireland by St Patrick. Therefore, the Sarmatian guardians of the river Ribble area would have been free for combat duty on the East coast, where there was a new and worse danger in the shape of the Saxons.

The thirteenth battle, the Battle of Camlann, where Arthur and Medraut were said to have been killed, has been a particular bone of contention among scholars. Some have located it at Camelford in Cornwall, at the river once called Cambula, now Canal. Others put it on Salisbury Plain, while a third possibility is the Roman fort of Camboglana, now Birdoswald, on Hadrian's Wall, not far from Carlisle. Apart from the identity of Medraut, who fell in the same battle and later turned into the traitor Mordred in the medieval romances of Arthur, there is the consequence of Arthur's death to be considered.

In the earliest surviving stories Arthur is said to have been taken to the Island of Avalon after the Battle of Camlann. Avalon is claimed by most scholars to be an aspect of the ancient Celtic Otherworld. Its name, translated as the Island of Apples, is indeed reminiscent of the Islands of the Blessed of antiquity, and with the Apples of the Hesperides. If Avalon is the Celtic Otherworld, then it would have been seen as a mythical island somewhere in the Western Sea. There are legends about such an island, floating and made of glass, which to the suspicious modern mind sounds very much like the sighting of an iceberg. As a consequence of Arthur being carried to the Island of Avalon there arose the legend that he was not dead at all but was brought there to be cured of his wounds, and from where he would return to free his people – by this time narrowed down to the Welsh – from their oppressors.

For the greater part of the Middle Ages it was proverbial that nobody knew where Arthur lay. It was therefore startling news when, in 1191, the monks of Glastonbury Abbey announced that they had found

Arthur's tomb, complete with a cross of lead bearing a Latin inscription proclaiming that here was the grave of the famous King Arthur '*in insula Avalonia*'.

The burial itself is reported to have been in a hollowed-out oak, containing the skeleton of a huge man as well as that of a woman, a lock of whose golden hair fell to dust when one of the monks tried to snatch it up. This looks rather like a Bronze Age burial as we know it from finds in Germany and Denmark. The claim that this tomb was that of Arthur and Guinevere, however, looks like an ingenious ruse on the part of the monks of Glastonbury, who were desperately in need of a new pilgrimage attraction after their original one, the famous St Mary's Chapel, burned down in 1184.

At the same time the monks of Glastonbury were able to furnish proof that Arthur was dead and buried, thus discrediting the Welsh legend of his possible return from Avalon, a development that was gratefully accepted by the English kings, who had been struggling to conquer Welsh independence for a considerable time.

The legend of Arthur's tomb in Glastonbury is still carefully maintained – the site of his tomb is shown in the ruins of the Abbey, though the actual tomb, as well as the Abbey, was destroyed during the Reformation. In order to get around the awkward fact that Glastonbury is situated far inland and could not well be claimed to be an island, it was said that in early medieval times it would have been surrounded by marshes and ponds, thus turning it into an island after all. Glastonbury was not considered in connection with Avalon before the discovery of the inscribed cross.

Considering the other site for the Battle of Camlann – the Roman fort at Camboglana on Hadrian's Wall – it is interesting to note that about 20 miles to the west, at the end of the great Wall at the mouth of the river Solway, there used to be another Roman fort, Avallava, or Avallana, now Burgh-by-Sands. The distance from Camboglanna to Avallana is just about as far as a seriously wounded man could be transported; in any case it is only half the distance than that between Salisbury Plain and Glastonbury, and one fifth of the distance from Camelford and Glastonbury. If the mortally wounded 'historical Arthur' would have been brought to the harbour-fort Avallana and shipped south to safety, this might have become the nucleus of the transport-to-Avalon story. This would be especially so if the ship arrived without him, because he had died on the way; or not all, because it sank in a storm.

On the other hand, if our assumption is true that Arthur's knights were Sarmatian cavalrymen, then it should be pointed out that it was a Sarmatian custom to bury their important dead on riverbanks, in order to make the site unrecognisable after the next spring flooding and in this way to prevent any robbing of the graves.

The best known example of such a river-burial is that of Alaric, King of the Visigoths, who died in 411 after the sack of Rome, and who was buried in the bottom of the dammed-up river Busento, without doubt on the advice of his Alanic allies (the Alans were a branch of the Sarmatians), who amounted to about one third of his army and formed its cavalry arm. Indeed, the area surrounding the ancient harbour-fort of Avallana is still miles of low-lying marshland and sandbanks, with warning signs all around that this area could be flooded up to five feet at high tide. The marshes around Avallana would have been the perfect place to bury the 'historical Arthur' in an unmarked grave, and to recall afterwards that he was not dead at all but would return one day from the Otherworld.

Apart from these archaeological and documentary pieces of evidence about the influence of Late Roman auxiliary troops on the origins of the Arthurian legends, there are mythological and philological connections, too.

In these fields two other scholars, J. H. Grisward, and in particular C. Scott Littleton, Professor at the Occidental College, Los Angeles, have achieved some remarkable results through their research. In 1969, Grisward found that among the Ossetians, a tribe in the Caucasus and the last surviving speakers of a Sarmatian dialect, there is a legend of a national hero named Batradz, who at his death ordered his surviving followers to throw his magic sword into a nearby body of water. At first the companions could not bring themselves to dispose of the wonderful sword, and only at the third attempt did they throw it in – just as Sir Bedivere hesitated to throw Excalibur into the mere in the medieval Arthurian legends.

Among the Ossetian stories there are other motives that have a strangely familiar ring for someone acquainted with the Arthurian legends, such as the story of the hero Soslan, who had a body of steel and was born from a rock, and who later set about to gather the scalps and beards of his enemies to make himself a fur coat. This is not only vaguely reminiscent of the Sword in the Stone, but also of the Arthurian tale of the giant Rhyons, who collected the beards of kings to trim his cloak.

(The use of scalps for trimming cloaks, incidentally, is already mentioned by Herodotus of the Scythians).

Furthermore, the Ossetian heroes, who called themselves the Narts, have a prized cup, the Nartamonga, which is kept in the custody of the clan Boratae. In the tales concerning the Holy Grail, the brother of the Grail-king is called Mangon or Amangons, and in some versions it is the knight Sir Bors who achieves the Grail.

The name of the sword Excalibur is derived from Caliburnus, as it is called by Geoffrey of Monmouth, and this seems to be made up from the Graeco-Latin *chalybs* 'steel' and *eburneus*, which means 'radiant white (as ivory)'. The word *chalybs* is actually derived from the name of the Kalybes, a Sarmatian tribe of smiths who lived in the Caucasus.

Other names that should be mentioned here are Pendragon, Bedwyr and Kay, which have equivalents in most languages and dialects in Eastern Europe and Central Asia, such as *aba-tarqan*, *er-targhyn* (leader) in early Turkish; *batur bahadur*, and *bagatyr* (hero), *Bodvar* (fighter) in Hungarian, Turkish, Russian, and Old Swedish, and *kai* (warrior) in Iranian.

Finally, there are among the Arthurian tales connected with the Holy Grail two – the story of Perceval, and the story of Sir Balin and Sir Balan – that have a number of motifs in common with the Ossetian myths: such as that the hero carries two swords, that he is in exile, that he fights with his brother without recognising him; that he fights a red knight; that one of his two swords breaks; that a king appears who has been deprived of his virility by a wound received in battle, and finally that of a hero lying under a tree with his head in a lady's lap.

The same assortment of motifs is to be found in the one of the earliest surviving epics of the *Nibelungen* cycle, 'Walther and Hildegunde', which is set in part at the court of Attila the Hun, as well as in the Turkish-Khazak epic of *Er-Targhyn and Ag-Zhunus the Beautiful* and in the Khirgiz epic of *Manas of the Noble Heart*. The earliest representation of a scene from this complex of stories appears on a pair of gold scabbard-mountings, obviously made for two matching swords, from the 3rd century BC and found in Siberia.

Aside from these influences from the Sarmatians imported to Britain by the Romans, there are elements in the Arthurian legends that were directly taken from Roman traditions, such as the several possible locations ascribed to the Round Table: Carlisle, Chester, Caerleon and Winchester. These four sites are four of the five places with major

Roman amphitheatres. In fact, the ruins of the Roman arena in Caerleon are still called 'King Arthur's Round Table' in local tradition. The fifth amphitheatre, that of Verulamium/St. Albans, does not appear on this list because it was already in Anglo-Saxon occupied territory at the time of the historical Arthur.

The motif of Arthur wearing 'the image of the Blessed Virgin Mary on his shoulders', as reported in the battle list of Nennius on the occasion of the eighth battle, at Castell Gwinnion, could be based upon a Roman tradition also. Presumably the expression 'on his shoulders' is a mistranslation of the Welsh words *ysguid,* 'shoulders' and *ysguit*, shield. Roman generals could have an image of the emperor affixed to their shields, such as that shown on an ivory relief depicting the West Roman commander-in-chief Stilicho, who had a double portrait of both the emperor and empress on his shield. At the time of Arthur, however, Britain was not under the authority of the West Roman emperor anymore, and therefore a religious image, such as the one of the Virgin Mary described by Nennius, would have been the perfect solution to conform to the established tradition.

Even the Saxons, despite being consistently shown as the villains in all the Arthurian tales presented as history, contributed some important features to the growing body of Arthurian lore. For instance, in the homeland of the Angles, the province Angeln at the border between Denmark and Germany, there are several peatbogs that yielded large deposits of early weapons, particularly richly decorated swords. These bogs were once sacred lakes into which these precious weapons were thrown as sacrifices. In all probability the story of the Lady of the Lake, who presents Arthur with the magic sword Excalibur, is reminiscent of a priestess in charge of such a sacred lake who would have on occasion retrieved one of the deposited swords to present it to an important person.

A passage in Geoffrey of Monmouth's *Historia* describes Arthur's armour and weapons in detail, but neither the leather corslet worthy of such a great prince, nor his great round shield, nor his helmet surmounted by a golden dragon crest, would have been worn by any knight of Geoffrey's days, the second quarter of the twelfth century. Geoffrey must have had a reliable older source because this description conforms closely to actual objects of a much earlier time: a leather lorica in Roman style, a round shield with a dragon emblem, and particularly the helmet with the golden dragon crest – so like that discovered in 1939 at the excavation of the famous Anglo-Saxon ship-burial at Sutton Hoo.

To sum up, we have seen that the later stories of Arthur are the offshoot of many influences, most of them based on facts from the latest days of Rome in Britain, particularly from the distribution of Roman civilisation via the legions, and among them some influences that had travelled around half the world with the riders from the Steppes, who wound up in Britain as the *cataphractarii* of the *praefectus* Lucius Artorius Castus – otherwise known as the Knights of King Arthur

Select Bibliography

Alcock, Leslie, *Arthur's Britain: History and Archaeology AD 367-563*, Penguin, 1971, Pelican, 1973

Brengle, Richard L, *Arthur, King of Britain,* New York, 1964

Chambers. E. K., *Arthur of Britain*, London, 1927; New York 1966

Eadie, J. W., 'The Development of Roman Mailed Cavalry' *Journal of Roman Studies* 57 (1967) pp.161-173

Fletcher, Robert H. *The Arthurian Material in the Chronicles,* New York, 1958

Gamber, Ortwin, 'Dakische und sarmatische Waffen auf den Reliefs der Trajanssaule', *Jahrbuch der Kunsthistorischen Sammlungen in Wien* 60 (1964), pp. 74 ff.

______ 'Grundriss einer Geschichte der Schutzwaffen des Altertums', *Jahrbuch Kunsthistorischen Sammlungen in Wien,* 62 (1966), pp 7-70.

______ 'The Sutton Hoo Military Equipment – an Attempted Reconstruction,' *Journal of the Arms and Armor Society* 5 (1966) pp. 265-289

______ 'Kataphrakten, Clibanarier, Normenreiter', *Jahrbuch der Kunsthistorischen Sammlungen in Wien* 64 (1968), pp. 34 ff.

Grisward, J. H. 'Le motif de l'epée jetée au lac: la mort d'Arthur et la mort de Batradz', *Romania*, 90 (1969), pp. 289-34

Harden, D. B. *Dark Age Britain,* London, 1956

Haskins, John, 'Targhyn, the Hero, Aq-Zhunus the Beautiful and Peter's Siberian Gold', *Ars Orientalls* 4 (1961) pp. 153-170

Jettmar, Karl, *The Art of the Steppes*, London, 1967

Littleton, C. Scott and Linda Malcor, *From Scythia to Camelot: A Radical Reassessment of the Legends of King Arthur, the Knights of the Round Table, and the Holy Grail,* Garland Publishing, New York & London, 1994

Malone, Kemp. 'Artorius', *Modern Philology*, XXII (1924), pp 367 ff.
Morris, John. *The Age of Arthur*, London, 1973
Nickel, Helmut. 'About the Sword of the Huns and the "Urepos" of the Steppes', *Metropolitan Museum Journal*, 7 (1973). pp 131-142
______ 'The Dawn of Chivalry' *From the Lands of the Scythians*, Special Issue of The Metropolitan Museum of Art Bulletin no.5, 1973/74; pp.150-152
______ 'Wer waren König Artus' Ritter?: Über die geschichtliche Grundlage der Artussagen,' *Waffen-und Kostümkunde* (1975) pp.1-28
Phillips, R. D., *The Royal Hordes: Nomad Peoples of the Steppe*, London, 1965.
Richmond, I. D., 'The Sarmatae, Bremetennacum Veteranorum and the Regio Bremetennacum', *Journal of Roman Studies*, X (1945) pp. 16-29
Robinson, H. Russell, *The Armour of Imperial Rome*, New York, 1975
Seeck. Otto (ed.) *Notitia Dignitatum*, Berlin, 1876
Sulimirski, Tadeusz, 'The Forgotten Sarmatians', Chapter 12 in *Vanished Civilizations*, London/New York, 1963
______ *The Sarmatians*, London & New York, 1970
Tatlock. J. S. P. 'The Dragons of Wessex and Wales', *Speculum*, 8 (1933) p. 233 ff.
Vinaver, Eugene, 'King Arthur's Sword', *Bulletin of the John Rylands Library, Manchester*, 40 (1957-58), pp. 513-526

Originally published in *Lucius Artorius Castus and the King Arthur Legend: Proceedings of the International Scholarly Conference from 30th March to 2nd April 1212*, Književni Krug, Split, 1214.

28

About The Knight with Two Swords and The Maiden Under a Tree

The second book of Sir Thomas Malory's *Le Morte d'Arthur* is 'The Tale of Balin', who was known as 'the Knight of the Two Swords'. There is a thirteenth-century French Arthurian romance of a similar title, *Meriadeuc, Li chevaliers as deus espees* (Meriadeuc, the Knight of the Two Swords). However, Sir Balin and Meriadeuc are not the only Arthurian knights carrying two swords. Chrétien's Perceval, as well as Wolfram von Eschenbach's Parzival, were given a second sword by the Fisher King at the Grail castle in addition to the swords they had taken from the Red Knights whom they killed at Arthur's court. Gawain, in *Diu Crône,* receives a second sword from the Grail King. Sir Palomides, the Saracen Knight, bore two swords according to this exotic custom, and even King Arthur himself had two swords (although not at the same time), the sword in the stone and the sword given to him by the Lady of the Lake, which was named Excalibur.

Heroes carrying two swords are found not only in Arthurian tales but also in epics spread across the Eurasian continent from the Germanic Nibelungen cycle to the Chinese history of the Three Kingdoms. There is archaeological evidence that Scythian elite warriors of the Eurasian steppes carried two swords, and historically a pair of swords was carried not only by Japanese samurai, but a curved sabre together with a straight pallash or a mail-piercing estoc was standard equipment for Polish and Hungarian hussars in the seventeenth century.[1]

Intertwined in the tales of the Knight of Two Swords is a set of up to fifteen motifs, some of them of a strangely unrelated nature, some even unreasonable in the context:

1. The hero is in exile or temporary disgrace.
2. He acquired his second sword in a way that often involved a woman.
3. One of the hero's swords will break.
4. The hero has to fight [a] his brother [b] his best friend, or [c] one of his vassals.
5. The hero encounters a Red Knight or is a Red Knight himself.
6. A king or knight is lamed, wounded 'in the thighs', i.e. castrated or impotent.
7. A fight is decided by putting out an enemy's eye or cutting off his hand.
8. There is an episode of fishing or at least of meeting a fisherman.
9. There is a visit to the Grail Castle.
10. There appears a maiden seated under a tree, holding a sleeping or dead man's head in her lap.
11. The maiden is [a] killed [b] in danger of being killed or [c] raped, or [d] begs to be killed to keep her from being raped.
12. There is a connection with the Near East, with Saracens, Hungarians, or Huns.
13. The hero has to ask a fateful question.
14. The hero encounters [a] a lion or [b] the image of a lion.
15. There is an episode about [a] cutting off beards or [b] hair, or [c] 'searching' of hair for lice.

Although not all of these fifteen motifs are encountered in every single one of the epics about Heroes with Two Swords, motif 10, the woman under the tree holding a man's head in her lap, is ubiquitous. This is the more remarkable because motif 10 can be assigned either to the hero or to his foe, and even to persons without any direct impact on the plot. Other motifs are reassembled and often switched around like blocks of Lego. In the following retellings, motifs are indicated by their numbers in brackets.

The earliest surviving epic featuring the Hero with Two Swords and all of the above motifs, except the Grail, is the earliest known part of the Nibelungen cycle, *Waltharius* (c. 900 AD), by a monk of St. Gall,

Switzerland.[2] It tells, in 1,456 Latin hexameters, the story of three hostages [1] at the court of King Etzel, the historic Attila the Hun [12]. These hostages are the Visigothic prince, Walthari of Aquitaine, the Burgundian princess Hildegund, and Hagano (Hagen), a noble youth of the royal house of the Rhenish Franks. Hagen manages to flee. Walthari and Hildegund, his betrothed from childhood, escape soon after. In preparation for their flight, Walthari arms himself in Hunnish fashion – *pro ritu Pannoniarum* – with a double-edged long sword, *spatha,* belted to his left hip, and a single-edged shortsword, *semi-spatha,* at his right [2]. His trusty steed's name is Leo [14].[3]

As the fugitives make their way along the Danube, Walthari catches fish for food [8].[4] Having crossed the Black Forest, they come to the Rhine, where Walthari pays a ferryman with two fish caught at the headwaters of the Danube. The ferryman goes to sell the unfamiliar fish to the king's kitchen, where he tells of the stranger with the beautiful girl. The young and brash Frankish king, Gunthari, decides to waylay them and confiscate the treasures he is sure they must be carrying. His recently returned kinsman, Hagen, guesses the identity of the strangers and strongly objects.

Meanwhile, Walthari and Hildegund have reached the Vosges Forest. Walthari decides it would be safe to get some sleep at last, after all the days he had been on guard. He takes off his armour and hangs it in a tree. Under this tree, he lies down, with his head in Hildegund's lap, [10] and asks her to keep watch, but to wake him only gently if she sees danger coming. Soon enough, Hildegund sees thirteen horsemen approaching and she wakens Walthari. He dons his armour and gets ready for a fight. At this point Hildegund clutches his knees and begs him to kill her that she might not fall into the hands of – as she thinks – these Huns and be raped [11]. However, Walthari recognizes the helmet crest of his old friend, Hagen, and is sure of a friendly reception.

Unfortunately, the rash and greedy king Gunthari forces a fight on Walthari. Hagen, refusing to draw sword against his friend, watches the ensuing fight from a distance. Walthari had put Hildegund and the horses safely in an easily defendable narrow gorge, where attackers can get at him only singly. The poet gives a blow-by-blow account of the battle, in which virtually the entire arsenal of early medieval warriors comes into play.

After the seventh encounter there was a lull in the fighting. To cool off, Walthari took off his helmet with its red plume [5], but the next attacker rushes him before he could don it again. In a sweeping stroke he shears off two locks from Walthari's head [15] and mocks him for getting bald. The fighting continues until eleven of the attackers are killed. Finally, Hagen has to enter the fight [4], because one of the slain was his sister's son. Through the ruse of a feigned retreat, Gunthari and Hagen lure Walthari out in the open and attack him from two sides. Gunthari soon goes down with a terrible wound in his thigh [6], but Walthari's sword shatters on Hagen's hard helmet [3].[5] In disgust, Walthari throws away the now useless hilt, and Hagen lops off his outstretched hand [7]. Undaunted, Walthari transfers his shield to his right arm by hooking the stump through the straps, with his left hand he grips the shortsword we remember he has belted to his right hip – *semi-spatham, qua dextrum cinxisse latus memoravimus ilium* – and with a slash at Hagen's face gouges out one eye [7].[6] After that, the heroes call it quits. While Hildegund bandages their wounds and serves refreshing wine in a gold cup, Walthari and Hagen renew their friendship with good-natured banter.[7]

The earliest (before 1191) Arthurian epic of a Knight with Two Swords is Chrétien's unfinished *Perceval, or The Story of the Grail.* Here, Perceval leaves his grief-stricken mother and arrives at Carduel, Arthur's court, during the celebration of the victory over King Rien of the Iles, who, it is understood, had demanded Arthur's beard as token of vassalage [15].[8] Another foe of Arthur's, the Red Knight [5] of the Forest of Quinqueroi, insults the queen, and Perceval slays him by a javelin cast into the eye slit of his helmet [7]. Perceval takes the Red Knight's horse, armour and sword, and goes forth as the Red Knight himself [5]. One day he comes to a river, where a nobleman and his servant are in a boat fishing [8]. The nobleman invites Perceval into his nearby residence, which turns out to be the castle of the Grail [9]. The lord of the castle, the Rich Fisher, is 'lamed' [6].

A squire arrives and hands the lord a sword, as a gift 'from his lovely blonde niece' to present it to whomever he likes; the lord presents it to Perceval [2]. A warning comes with the sword that it will break on an occasion that only he who forged it knew [3]. At the Grail procession, Perceval fails to ask the crucial question [13] and is expelled from the Grail castle [1]. In the forest he meets a weeping maiden sitting under an oak tree, with the head of a slain knight in her lap [10]. The maiden is a cousin of Perceval's, the slain knight was her lover, but the slayer was actually out to kill her [11]. The maiden recognizes Perceval's new sword, and names its maker, Trebuchet, as the only one who could repair it, if it is broken. Eventually, when Perceval fights the slayer, the Proud Knight of the Moor, the grail sword shatters on the Proud Knight's helmet [3]. Perceval defeats him with the sword he took from the Red Knight.

Wolfram's Parzival[9] is the son of Herzeloyde, Queen of Wales, and Gahmuret, who had won her hand in a tournament, but went away as a knight errant to be killed in the service of the Baruch of Baghdad [12].[10] Parzival leaves his mother in order to become a knight errant seeking adventure [1]. Herzeloyde dies of a broken heart [11]. On the very first day of his adventure quest, Parzival meets a weeping damsel in the forest, holding a dead knight in her lap [10]. She turns out to be Parzival's cousin, Sigune, mourning her slain lover, Schionatulander. Parzival vows to avenge the slaying, but Sigune, sensing his naiveté, misdirects him away from danger. At nightfall, Parzival meets at a river a fisherman [8], who gives him shelter for the night and the next morning guides him to Nantes, Arthur's capital. Before its gate Parzival encounters Ither von Gaheviez, the Red Knight [5], who had challenged the Knights of the Round Table. Parzival kills Ither by a javelin cast into the eye slit of his helmet [7], takes the Red Knight's horse and armour, and goes forth as the Red Knight himself [5].

One day Parzival comes to a lake, where a richly clad nobleman is fishing from a boat [8]. The angler directs Parzival to a nearby castle that turns out to be the Grail castle [9]. The lord of the castle is the angler from the lake, and he is lamed by a wound 'in the thighs' [6]. At the banquet, the Grail [9] is carried in procession by the Grail maiden, and the lord of the castle presents Parzival with a splendid sword [2]. However, Parzival fails to ask the spell-breaking question [13] and is expelled from the Grail castle [1]. He meets Sigune again, sitting under a linden tree, still cradling the now embalmed body of her dead lover in her lap [10]. She recognizes Parzival's second sword and tells him that it was fashioned by the smith Trebuchet, that it will break at a second blow [3], and that it can be repaired by submerging it in a magic well.

In a parallel story line, Parzival's friend, Gawain, on a green meadow between Schanpfanzun and Logroys meets a lady sitting under a tree holding a wounded knight's head in her lap [10]. Gawain, knowledgeable in leechcraft, saves the knight's life. At the Castle of Lit Marveile, Gawain has to fight a lion [14] and cuts off its paw [variant of 7].

Many adventures later, Parzival encounters and fights a strange knight, who turns out to be his heretofore unknown half-brother, Feirefiz [4], whom his father Gahmuret begat with Belakane, the black Queen of Zazamanc, while abroad in the service of the Baruch of Baghdad [12]. Parzival's grail sword breaks on Feirefiz's helmet [3]. Feirefiz and Parzival make peace as soon as they recognize their relationship. Eventually, Parzival becomes the Grail King and begets Lohengrin, the Swan Knight. Feirefiz marries the Grail Maiden and takes her to his kingdom of the Three Indies, where they become the parents of Prester John.

Meriadeuc, Li chevaliers as deus espees[10] starts with a Red Knight [5] coming to King Arthur's court at Cardueil as messenger for King Ris of Outre-Ombre, who demands Arthur's beard as the still missing part of his mantle of kings' beards [15].[11] King Ris had as his captive the Lady of Cardigan, but offers her freedom, if she would dare the Adventure of the Gaste Chapele. By achieving this adventure the Lady acquired a magic sword that she could not unbuckle after she had belted it on. King Ris released her from captivity, and she went to find a knight who could help her out of her predicament.[12] At Arthur's court, a newly dubbed knight 'without a name' was the only one to free her, and he carried this second sword[13] along with the one King Arthur had given him at his knighting [2].

Later, when King Ris with nine companions went scouting in Arthur's Forest of Cardueil, they were intercepted and severely wounded by the Knight of the Two Swords, who sent them to Arthur's court as prisoners. One of Ris's knights had a broken hip [variant of 6]. As a knight errant, the Knight of the Two Swords has to fight his friend Gawain twice [4]. One day, he meets a weeping lady, sitting in a forest glen with the head of a dead knight in her lap [10]. Among the other adventures are the Fontaine des Merveilles, encounters with the Wild Hunt and with a grievously wounded knight [variant of 6], who can be healed only by a stroke of a magic sword by a knight without a name. The Knight of the Two Swords heals the suffering knight, and there appears miraculously on the blade his own name, Meriadeuc, which he could not answer when questioned earlier [13]. Towards the end, Meriadeuc has to defeat yet another enemy of King Arthur's, Le Roux [5] of Val Perilleus.

At the beginning of 'The Tale of Sir Balin', Balin is at King Arthur's court, but just released from imprisonment for slaying a kinsman of Arthur's [1]. A damsel arrives, belted – like the Lady of Cardigan – with a sword from which only the best knight present could free her. The predestined one is Balin, and in spite of dire warnings by the damsel he decides to keep this sword [2] in addition to his own that had been returned to him after his release from the dungeon. At this point the Lady of the Lake appears and demands of the king that Balin's head be given to her as reward for her having presented Arthur with his second sword Excalibur. Instead, Balin beheads the Lady [11], and is banished from the court [1]. During his travels as a knight errant Balin comes back into the good graces of the court when he and his brother Balan defeat and capture Arthur's enemy, King Riens, who had demanded Arthur's beard for his cloak [15].

Later, Balin pursues Garlon, a knight who rides invisible and had killed a damsel's good knight. Arriving with the damsel at the castle of the Grail king, Pellam [9], who is Garlon's brother, Balin kills Garlon, breaks one of his swords [3], and smites the Dolorous Stroke, which cripples the Grail king [6]. When the castle collapses on him, it kills the damsel [11] and everybody in it, except Balin and Pellam.

Then Balin meets Garnish of the Mount, a knight who is hopelessly in love with the daughter of Duke Hermel. At the Duke's castle, in a fair little garden, they discover the Duke's daughter lying under a laurel tree with a knight in her arms [10]. The love-stricken Garnish kills the maiden [11], her lover, and himself. At last Balin comes to a ford held under an 'ill custom' by a Red Knight [5] with a plain red shield without a cognizance. The Red Knight is actually Balin's brother, Balan, under a spell. Balin's shield is damaged beyond usefulness after all his adventures, and a friendly knight offers him his own sturdy shield for the fight. Thus, neither Balin nor Balan are able to recognize each other and fight to the death [4]. Too late, Balin asks the Red Knight's name [13], and only when they are dying do they find out each other's identity. In an obvious parallel to Arthur's Sword in the Stone, Balin's sword is set into a block of marble by Merlin, to wait for its release by Galahad, the future achiever of the Grail adventure [9].

In the divergent Grail story, *Diu Crône* [The Crown], by Heinrich von dem Türlin (before 1240), it is Gawain who achieves the Adventure of the Grail [9] by asking the right question [13] at his second visit to the Grail castle, after having failed the first time.[14] His host, 'the old lord', is lame [variant of 6], and gives Gawain a beautiful broadsword [2]. At the end of the story, he tells Gawain as the denouement that years ago Parzival had failed at the Grail procession, and the company of the Grail castle were living dead, because of God's wrath vented on

Parzival's clan for fratricide. Gawain was their longed-for redeemer, and after this revelation, the lord and the castle vanished forever. There is an abundance of strange and supernatural events, such as when even Gawain has to play the Beheading Game with the magician Gansguoter.

One day, in the forest, Gawain has to fight a Red Knight [5] who was whipping along a bevy of naked maidens, who then sank into the ground [11].[15] Although there is no explicit fishing episode, a scaly Fish-Knight comes to Arthur's court, riding a seal-like mount [variant of 8]. During his quest, Gawaine has to slay no fewer than three lions [14], and there are three episodes of the Rest under the Tree. In the first, a wounded knight, Lohenis of Rehaz, is lying under a linden tree, with his head in a maiden's lap [10]; in the second, Queen Ginover is abducted, and her abductor, Gasozein, insists on resting under a linden tree with his head in the queen's lap [10].[16] Finally, at a riverbank, Gawain finds a bloody, torn-out tress of blond hair [15] tied with a string of pearls. It leads him to a maiden in the claws of a water monster. The maiden begs Gawain to kill her [11] if he cannot save her. Gawain rescues her by cutting off the fiend's arm [7]. Exhausted, he falls asleep under a tree and is cared for by the maiden [10].

The Spanish *Libro del Caballero Zifar*, *c.* 1300, has the set of motifs connected to the story line of the Knight of Two Swords spread out over two generations.[17] The story itself is loosely based on the legend of St. Eustachius, and narrates the fates of the members of the same family, the Knight Zifar, his wife Grima, and their sons Garfin and Roboán. The Knight Zifar was guiltlessly unlucky, very much like Balin. He was under a curse that any steed he rode would drop dead after ten days. In the long run this bizarre affliction became too expensive for his liege lord, and Zifar had to leave his service and go into exile [1]. One day, after he had travelled on foot for three days, because the horse he rode for ten days had died, Grima persuades him to rest at a spring in the woods and to lay his head in her lap [10] so that she could look for lice in his hair [15]. When Zifar fell asleep, a lioness [14] came to the spring and snatched one of the children. Alarmed by Grima, Zifar jumps on her horse to save the child, but cannot catch up with the lioness. Of course, this horse drops dead in due time, and Zifar, Grima, and the remaining son arrive on foot at a nearby port. There, the boy gets lost in the maze of streets and in searching for him Grima is kidnapped by pirates.

Alone, Zifar meets a fisherman [8], El Ribaldo, who joins him as a squire, Sancho-Panza-style. Nine years later, the Knight Zifar becomes King of Mentón and will be united with his wife and sons, who in the meantime had many adventures of their own.[18] As king of Mentón, Zifar has to deal with a rebellion [4]. His sons, Garfin and Roboán, take part in the fighting; Garfin cuts off the hand, still clutching the sword, of the rebel, Count Nason [7], and Roboán kills the count's nephew by a sword thrust through the helmet visor into the eyes [7]. Later, Roboán departs seeking adventure [1]. At the banks of the river Tigris [12] Roboán receives a second sword from the Emperor of Tigrida [2]. For the ceremony he is bathed by beautiful maidens. However, he is exiled [1] when he asks a question the Emperor refuses to answer [13]. After many adventures, Roboán reaches the Fortunate Isles, marries the Empress who rules there, and becomes Emperor himself.

The Spanish *Poema del Cid* was written around 1140, more or less at the same time Geoffrey of Monmouth wrote his *Historia.*[19] The *Poema* celebrates the deeds of Rodrigo Diaz de Bivar (*c.* 1043-July 10, 1099), called *El Cid (Arab, el said,* 'Lord') *Campeador* ('Champion'), and it is particularly interesting that, though it was written within living memory of the events it deals with, it already contains fictitious episodes. El Cid was only a member of the minor nobility but rose to be *alférez* (chief commander) of the forces of King Sancho II of Castile, who was assassinated in 1072 by his brother Alfonso, prompted by their sister, Princess Urraca, who had an incestuous affair with Alfonso. Nevertheless, El Cid keeps faith with the new king, Alfonso, who even marries him to his own niece, Doña Ximena, of the high nobility clan of Beni-Gómez. However, court intrigues force El Cid into exile [1].

El Cid 'of the great beard' was in the habit of swearing by his beard that never had been touched by an enemy. During the battle of Cabra (1079), he plucked the beard [15] of his arch enemy and in-law, Count Garcia Ordonez of the Beni-Gómez clan [4]. While he was an exile and outlaw, El Cid fought the Christian Count of Barcelona, Ramón Berenguer, took him prisoner, and exacted as ransom the famous sword Colada ('of White Polish').

Fighting and killing the Moorish King Búcar [12], he gained his second sword, *Tizón* ('Firebrand') [2]. Although El Cid vastly increased Alfonso's kingdom by conquering Valencia, his enemies at court strove to disgrace him.[20] Under pretence of friendship, two princes of the Beni-Gómez clan,

Diego and Fernando Gonzalez, the Heirs of Carrion, succeed in marrying El Cid's two daughters, Doña Elvira and Doña Sol. Graciously, El Cid presents Colada and Tizón to his new sons-in-law. The next day, while El Cid was sleeping, his pet lion escaped from its cage [14], and the Heirs of Carrión shamefully fled. Fuming about being disgraced in the eyes of El Cid, the Heirs of Carrión decided to avenge themselves on his daughters. On their way back from Valencia to Carrión they sent their retainers ahead and stayed with their brides in the oaken grove of Corpes, where 'under the tall trees they took their pleasure ... in their arms' [variant of 10]. Afterwards, they maliciously whip their brides with saddle straps, while the abused princesses beg to be killed by Colada and Tizón rather than be thus outraged [11].

Their revenge satisfied, the Heirs of Carrión abandon their maltreated brides in the grove, half-dead from the beatings and half-naked in their torn silken chemises. The princesses are found and rescued by one of El Cid's knights. In order to avoid a civil war, El Cid seeks and finds redress at the king's court.

Another Knight of Two Swords, who was a historical person, is Dietrich von Bern, the Germanic equivalent of King Arthur, complete with his twelve *Gesellen* (companions), the equivalent of the Round Table. The historic Dietrich was Theodoric the Great, King of the Ostrogoths (*c.* 455-August 30, 526). In the pseudo-history of the Dietrich cycle he becomes exiled [1] from his kingdom in Italy, and is for thirty years a member of the court of King Etzel [12], the historic Attila the Hun (d. 453), although the 'Scourge of God' had died two years before Theodoric was born.[21] In one of the earliest surviving epics of the Dietrich cycle, the rambling *Eckenlied of* the first half of the thirteenth century,[22] a youthful Dietrich as a knight errant is confronted in the mountain forests of the Alps by the hero Ecke ('Sword Edge'), who is so tall that no horse could carry him. Ecke was the lover of Seburg, one of the three weather-mongering elfin queens residing in a fairy castle on top of Mount Jochgrimm. Seburg had given Ecke a splendid sword, and named it in his honour, *Eckesax*.[23] By her art, she knew of Dietrich nearby in the forest, and desired to see him of whom she had heard so much praise. Thus, she sent out Ecke to bring Dietrich to Jochgrimm.

Dietrich, like Gawain, is not averse to avoiding unnecessary bloodshed if reason can win the day. Therefore, he agrees to come along willingly; he even asks Ecke to join his band of *Gesellen*. Ecke, however, insists on a fight, because he wants to drag Dietrich before his ladylove as a conquered foe. In a bitter battle Ecke strikes a mighty blow with Eckesax that splits Dietrich's shield right through the red lion [14] he bears as his heraldic device,[24] but at the end, Ecke is slain. Dietrich takes Eckesax as his hard-won trophy, and carries it along with his own sword, Nagelring [2].

Later that day, Dietrich hears a woman's pitiful cries for help. A naked wild woman of the woods is chased by a knight on horseback [11][25] and Dietrich comes to her rescue. The horseman, who has his hair braided in two tresses reaching to the ground, is Ecke's brother, Vasolt. Seeing Eckesax borne by Dietrich, he immediately attacks to avenge his brother's death. In the fight, Dietrich severs one of Vasolt's cherished tresses [15]. After the loss of the second tress, Vasolt yields and swears fealty to become one of Dietrich's *Gesellen,* and then departs. At nightfall, Dietrich, exhausted and grievously wounded, has to lie down at the foot of a tree in the forest. The grateful wild woman treats his wounds with healing herbs and holding him in her lap keeps watch over him throughout the night [10]. In the morning, she tries to awaken him, gently, not to startle him when Vasolt returns and in spite of his oath of loyalty treacherously attempts to kill Dietrich, who reluctantly has to fight him once more and kill him [4].

Abbreviated versions of this story complex are found in Hungarian lore, in the legend of St Ladislaus and in the folk ballads about Anna Molnár, the miller's wife [12]. In the legend of St Ladislaus (King of Hungary, 1077-1095), a Hungarian princess is kidnapped by a warrior of the heathen Kuman tribe [11]. Believing that he had put a safe distance between himself and possible pursuers, the abductor decides to rest in the shade of a tree. He puts his head in the princess' lap [10] to let her search for lice in his hair [15].

The gentle probing of her fingers on his scalp lulls him to sleep, so that the knightly saint, Ladislaus, can catch up with the pair. In the following fight the princess even takes an active part by hacking the leg of the Kuman with a discarded sword [6]. In the folk ballads, Anna Molnár, the miller's wife, runs away with a soldier [1]. The soldier leads her to a shady linden tree, where he wants to rest. He asks Anna to take his head in her lap [10] and look for lice in his hair [15]. He expressly forbids her to look up in the tree. Of course, as soon as the soldier is asleep, Anna looks up and sees the corpses of eleven girls hanging from the branches. In fright, she bursts out in tears. One teardrop falling on the face of the soldier wakes him, and he tells her that she will be the twelfth [11].

There are multiple endings to the basic story: either the wayward woman gets killed, or her brother comes to the rescue, or she outsmarts the soldier and kills him with his own sword.[26] Though not expressed in so many words, the motif of the Rest under the Tree is here still connected with the motif of the Knight of the Two Swords, insofar as it was understood that Hungarian medieval warriors – like Walthari – as well as Hungarian Hussars up to the eighteenth century customarily carried two swords [2]. Similar ballads of abductions and elopements with a Rest under a Tree, including the detail of looking for lice in the abductor's hair, are known all over Eastern Europe as far as Siberia, where the tree can be a magic iron larch tree with nine branches and if the abductor is a prince, his lice are blue in colour as a status symbol.

A variant story is told in the Khazakh epos of Targhyn and Aq-Zhunus the Beautiful [12]. Though it is believed to be in its present form not earlier than the fifteenth century, it is certainly based on a much earlier tradition.[27] Here, the hero Targhyn is exiled [1] for the killing of a clansman [4]. He takes refuge with Aqsha-khan, the most powerful prince on the Crimea, and in time he becomes the commander of the Khan's forces. Inevitably, the Khan's beautiful daughter, Aq-Zhunus, falls in love with him, but she had been betrothed to the khan of a neighbouring tribe. Targhyn and Aq-Zhunus elope, and her enraged father promises her hand to whoever brings his wayward daughter back.

The only warrior who owns a horse that could catch up with Targhyn's steed, Tarlan, is the aged Qart-Qozhaq. He luckily finds Aq-Zhunus alone, but she ridicules his attempts to earn his just reward. In most unflattering terms, she refers to his advanced age and his resulting impotence [variant of 6]. Many adventures later, Targhyn leads an army of the Nogai tribe against the Kalmucks, who flee without giving battle. Scouting after them, Targhyn climbs a tall tree to espy their path of retreat. However, a branch breaks under his weight, and he crashes to earth, dislocating his spine. Unable to move, Targhyn has to remain lying under the tree, cared for by Aq-Zhunus [10] but abandoned by the Nogai. Lamenting his fate to perish as one who fell from a tree instead of heroically falling in battle, Targhyn in desperation seizes his own back and wrenches the dislocated spine back into position, going on to fight many more battles.

In Chrétien's first Arthurian epic, *Erec et Enide*,[28] we find that a question [13] about the identity of Iders fils de Nuit leads Erec to the

Adventure of the Sparrowhawk, for which he has to borrow a sword [variant of 2] and armour from an old, lame nobleman [variant of 6], the father of Enide. Later, when Erec takes Enide along on his honour-forced quest [1], he commands her on pain of death [11] not to speak to him [variant of 13]. But, when they encounter one band of robber knights after another, Enide dares to warn Erec of these approaching dangers in spite of this threat. Erec defeats eight foes, the seventh by cutting off his arm [7] and hands their horses to Enide to herd them along as best she could.

At nightfall, they take shelter under a lonely tree in an open field. Erec orders Enide to sleep, but she insists that after all his efforts he should sleep, while she keeps watch [10]. (Hartmann von Aue, in his German adaptation of Chrétien's *Erec,* lets Erec lay his head in Enide's lap [10], to rest after his victory in the tournament at Tulmein castle.)

In another adventure, Erec meets a maiden in a forest, her clothes rent, weeping and tearing her hair [15], because two giants had captured her lover, the knight Cadoc de Cabruel. Erec kills one of the captors by a lance thrust into the eye [7]. Later, he has to fight Guivret le Petit, whose saddle is decorated with golden lions [14]. Afterwards, they discover that they are old friends [4]. In the adventure of 'La Joie di Cors' Erec encounters in an enchanted garden a damsel under a sycamore tree together with a Red Knight [5 & 10]. The damsel had laid a pledge on the Red Knight not to leave her unless defeated in combat. A row of forty-four stakes bearing helmeted heads attests to his prowess. During their fight, both combatants are blinded by sweat and blood running into their eyes [variant of 7] to a degree that they have to drop their swords and continue by wrestling. After the Red Knight's defeat, the enchantment of the garden is lifted, and Erec and the Red Knight, Mabonagrain, find that once, in their youth, they were friends [4].

Of the three 'romances' in the *Mabinogion – The Lady of the Fountain, Peredur Son of Efrawg* and *Geraint Son of Erbin*[29] – even champions of their Welsh and Celtic origins have to admit that there are many details that have been taken over from Norman/French sources, especially Chrétien's works. *Peredur* contains a number of motifs found in *Perceval.* These definitely belong to the Knight of Two Swords complex, although Peredur only temporarily gets hold of a second sword, and this only in an oblique way [2]. After having left his mother, Peredur comes to Arthur's court, and by a javelin cast in the eye [7] kills a knight who had insulted the queen. Later, he comes to a lake, where a richly clad but lame man is watching youths fishing [8]. In his castle, the lame nobleman [6] tests Peredur's strength by letting him smite an iron column with a sword. Twice the sword breaks [3] and can be mended, but it remains broken after the third stroke and nothing more is heard of it.

Then follows a procession [variant of 9] of a youth carrying a bleeding spear and two maidens carrying a salver with a man's head swimming in blood. Peredur fails to ask the fateful question [13]. In the forest, he meets a shrieking woman with a dead knight in her arms [10].

At another castle, Peredur meets a maiden in a gown of brocaded silk that is so tattered as to let her lily-white skin shows through, a detail found in *Erec et Enide*. At yet another castle, he kills its porter, a sleeping lion on a chain [14]. Eventually, Peredur meets Edlym Red-sword, the Red Knight [5], who becomes his companion. In an encounter with Cei, he breaks Cei's arm [7], but later. Cei pierces Peredur's thigh with a spear [variant of 6], In spite of having promised numerous maidens that 'he loves them best', Peredur marries the Empress of Constantinople [12].

In Chrétien's *Cligés* the hero is the Greek Emperor's son [12] and is in love with his uncle's bride, Fenice.[30] In order to get out of this potentially dangerous triangle, Cligés leaves for Arthur's court [1]. Fenice feigns her own death [11]. On his return from Britain, Cligés, who also is a Red Knight [5], hides her for more than a year in a tower with a secret walled garden. In the middle of the garden is a pear tree grafted and trained to form a bower. One day, a knight is out flying his hawk, which strays into the secret garden. The knight climbs over the garden wall to recover his bird, and sees Cligés and Fenice under the tree, lying asleep and naked in each other's embrace [10]. By chance a pear drops next to Fenice's head, and the lovers awaken. Even in this awkward situation, Cligés has his sword at hand and cuts off the leg of the fleeing intruder [6] when he climbs back over the wall.

The Rest under the Tree is a recurrent motif in the fifteenth-century Byzantine epic, *Digenes Akrites,* which is thought to be based on a tenth-century archetype. The epic survives in a Greek and a Russian version and is fragmented into scores of folk ballads.[31] It consists of eight 'books' that tell the story of a lonely hero guarding the marches of the East Roman Empire [12] against raiders and cattle reivers.

Digenes, the son of an Arab emir who in a raid carried off the daughter of a Greek general, was 'twyborn', of two races and two faiths.

Eventually, Digenes eloped with Evdokia, the daughter of a Greek governor of the Imperial Doukas clan. Among Digenes' many exploits there are four victorious encounters with lions [14]. In the sixth 'book,' he meets at a spring in the desert a disarrayed maiden weeping under a palm tree. Primly adjusting her veil on Digenes' arrival, she tells him that she is an Arab emir's daughter. In the standard fashion of romance she had fallen in love with a Greek captive of her father's. Having provided horses, supplies, and treasure, she eloped with her lover. For three days they stayed at the oasis of the palm tree [10], but then, ten days before, the ingrate left her, taking horses, supplies, treasure, and even her clothes with him.

Digenes offered to return her to her lover, but they were attacked by a band of a hundred Arab raiders, irresistibly attracted by the sight of a beautiful maiden in the seemingly negligible protection of one lone warrior. Digenes easily beat them off, but before leaving the oasis he 'succumbed to temptation' under the palm tree [11]. Later he bitterly rued this betrayal of his wife, Evdokia. One other day, at the banks of the Euphrates, Digenes had to fight Maximo, an Amazon princess, who carried two swords [2], a double-edged long sword at her belt and a single-edged yataghan at her saddle. Her shield bore the device of a lion's head [14]. Maximo received a wound on her hand [7] and dropped her sword. She yielded herself conquered and offered 'you shall win me all,' but Digenes refused because he had 'a lawful wife noble and fair'. However, he invites the warrior maiden to rest with him under a tree's shadow [10].

In *Devgenij,* the Russian version of *Digenes Akrites,* and in the ballads, the hero puts his head in the lap of the warrior maiden, Maximinia [10], to let her search for lice in his hair [15]. For the Rest under the Tree, Maximo takes off her armour, 'since the heat was great.' In her gossamer shift 'all her limbs displayed ... her small paps just peeping from her breast', she meekly approaches Digenes: 'Hail, master mine, I am your slave,' and he yields to temptation again [11]. Afterwards, smitten by remorse, he kills her [11].

Digenes Akrites has been claimed as the archetype of the epics with the Rest under the Tree as their central motif. John Mavrogordato, translator and editor *of Digenes,* sees a possible connection with *Waltharius* because of Maximo and Walthari's two swords. However, for the fifteenth-century *Digenes* there can be forwarded only a hypothetical tenth-century epic as its possible source. *Waltharius,* on the other hand, is securely dated to *c.* 900 A.D., and is therefore, so far as we know, by far the earliest literary example of the motif complex of the Hero with Two Swords and the Rest under the Tree. Remarkably, it is *Waltharius* that introduces the fishing motif that is found in the Grail stories, *Perceval/ Parzival* and also in *Peredur,* as the motif of the Rich Fisher in the Grail stories.

As mentioned in Chapter 19, The earliest representations of the Maiden under the Tree with a Man resting his Head in her Lap are on two matching gold plaques in the so-called Siberian Treasure of Peter the Great, in the State Hermitage Museum, St Petersburg. These 'anecdotal' plaques, Altai/ Sauromatian, *c.* 400 BC, have long been seen as illustrations of a lost epic. Their peculiar P-shape indicates that they were scabbard mountings for a pair of swords.[32]

Drawings of scabbard mountings for a pair of swords. Gold, Altai/Sauromatian. *c.* 400 BC. State Hermitage Museum. St. Petersburg. Siberian collection of Peter I. Si 1727. 1/161.

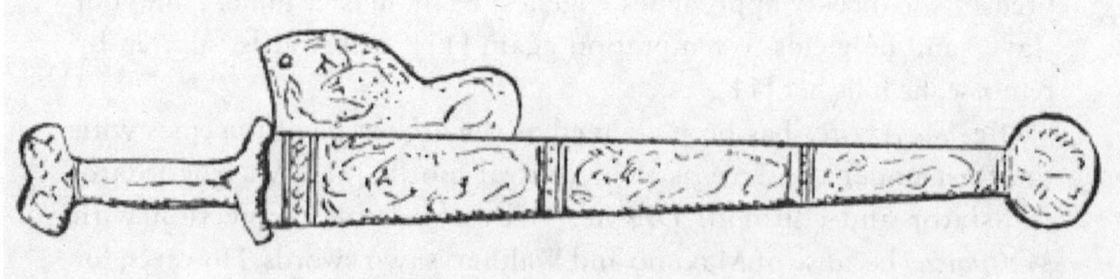

Drawing of a Scythian sword with similar mountings.

There can be little doubt that the Rest under a Tree, either as an abduction episode or as an elopement of lovers, must have been a main motive of the 'Ur-Epos' of the Eurasian steppe nomads whose elite warriors carried their swords in pairs. Fortunately, far from being lost, with *Waltharius* and/or oral sources as intermediaries, this 'Ur-Epos' has survived in Western European epic literature, and not least in Arthurian legends, as the tales about Knights with Two Swords.[33]

Notes

I wish to thank my friend, Gunar Freibergs, Los Angeles Valley College, for invaluable advice and especially for supplying me with 'A Fast Horse, an Epic Battle, "and Thou under a Tree": Romantic Adventure in Scythia and on the Rhine,' his unfortunately not yet published paper tracing *Waltharius*' roots, read at the annual meeting of the Medieval Association of the Pacific at the University of San Diego, San Diego, California, on March 17, 1996.

1. As for Far Eastern examples: the hero Liu Peh of the history of the Three Kingdoms carries a pair of swords, and even in popular Vietnamese folk art we find the heroine of a sixth-century war of liberation against the Chinese, Ba Trieu, represented riding a white elephant and wielding a sword in either hand. The samurai's pair of swords is called *daisho*, 'long-short'. There was also an archaic sword type, *ken*. In many Eurasian languages, the name for 'sword' is closely related: *chen* (Chinese), *khanda* (Hindu), *kindjal* (Caucasus). The Scythian sword was called *akinakes* by the Greeks. Its components, *kin* and *kes*, possibly meant a pair of long and short weapons (the Hungarian word for 'knife' is *kes*). For an actual find of a warrior with two swords, see the 'Golden Man of Issyk', frontispiece in C. Scott Littleton and Linda A. Malcor, *From Scythia to Camelot: A Radical Reassessment of the Legends of King Arthur, the Knights of the Round Table, and the Holy Grail* (New York & London: Garland Publishing, 1994).
2. Dennis M. Kratz, trans, and ed., *Waltharius and Ruodlieb*, Garland Library of Medieval Literature, Series A, vol. 13 (1984); 'Waltharius', pp. 4-71; Helmut Nickel, 'The Dawn of Chivalry,' in

The Metropolitan Museum of Art Bulletin Special Issue: From the Lands of the Scythians, vol. XXXII, no. 5 (1975), pp. 150-152, ill.

3. Walthari's horse (perhaps a palomino?) was called *Leo*, 'Lion,' *ob virtutem*, 'because of [his] valour.' We do not know what the Huns called their trusty steeds, but the Hungarian word for 'horse' is *lo* (!).
4. Fishing, for fugitives, is a strangely time-wasting way to get supplies. In Wolfram's *Titurel II*, 154-159, a fragment telling the pre-history of *Parzival*, Schionatulander is fly-fishing at a crucial moment, wasting precious time. In *Waltharius* the fishing at least serves the plot in a contrived way, bringing the fugitives to the attention of King Gunthari. Within the motif complex of the tales of the Knight with Two Swords, the fishing motif seems to have been once of great significance. When this was no longer understood, it became vestigial and in the Christian context of the Grail story was made into the person of the Rich Fisher, or it cropped up here and there as a helpful fisherman without any real importance to the plot.
5. Thigh wounds often are euphemisms for castration. Gunthari is King Gunther of the *Nibelungenlied*, whose failure in his bridal night with Brunhild sets the events in motion that lead to the catastrophe at Etzelburg.
6. The lone hero defending the narrow pass is, of course, standard in heroic literature, ever since Horatius Cocles (the one-eyed) on the ridge. In the Ni*belungenlied*, Hagen will defend the gate of the hall at Etzelburg. It has been pointed out that in Germanic mythology, Odin/Wotan is one-eyed, and the sword-god Tyr/Ziu has only one (left) hand.
7. *Waltharius* contains all the motifs to be found in the complex, with the exception of the Grail. It would be too much of a wild stretch of imagination – tempting as it is – to see a prototype of the Grail maiden in Hildegund carrying the golden cup of revitalizing wine.
8. Ruth Harwood, trans, and ed., *Chrétien de Troyes: Perceval, or The Story of Grail*. New York: Pergamon Press, 1983.
9. A.T. Hatto, trans, and ed., *Wolfram von Eschenbach: Parzival*. New York: Penguin Classics, 1980. Herzeloyde (in modern German 'Herzeleid') means 'grief,' but Gahmuret's name is derived from Guyomars/Gayamurd, a culture hero in the Persian national epos *Shahnahme* (*c.* 1000-1010 AD). Parallels between *Parzival*, the *Shahnahme*, and its continuation, *Barsuname* (!), were first pointed

out by Max Hesse, 'Iranisches Sagengut im christlichen Epos: Ein Beitrag zur Entstehung Parzivalliedes', *Atlantis* IX: 10 (October 1937): 623-628. In *Perceval* and especially in *Parzival*, with its strong Christian tendency, the influence of the iconography of the Madonna in Pieta on the motif of the Maiden under the tree is unmistakable. Also, Max Hesse points out that in the Shahnahme the Rustam kills his magically armoured foe Isfendijar with an arrow shot in the eye.

10. Ross G. Arthur & Noel L. Corbett, trans, and ed., *The Knight of the Two Swords: A Thirteenth-Century Arthurian Romance* (Gainesville: University Press, Florida, 1996).
11. Ris/Riens/Ryons was in the habit of demanding the beards of vassal kings for purfling his cloak. Trimming vestments with scalps and/or flayed beards was a custom of the Scythians, as recorded by Herodotus. In 175 AD, 5500 Sarmatian (relatives of the Scythians) auxiliaries of the late Roman army were stationed in Britain as heavy cavalry.
12. In order to get to the Gaste Chapele, the Lady of Cardigan had to force her way through thickets of brambles that tore her clothes to shreds. On her return, helpful ladies of the court had to pull out what was left of her gown and chemise from under the tight-fitting sword-belt, wash her, and then push a clean chemise gown back under the belt again.
13. Arthur's Sword from the Stone breaks in the fight with King Pellinore, the father Perceval, who becomes one of the achievers of the Adventure of the Grail, Arthur's second sword was given to him by the Lady of the Lake.
14. J. W. Thomas, trans, and ed., *The Crown: A Tale of Sir Gawein and King Arthur's Court by Heinrich von dem Türlin* (Lincoln and London: University of Nebraska Press, 1989).
15. Heinrich is obsessed with strange and supernatural events, especially if of a risqué nature. He enjoys featuring damsels in distress as dis-dressed, although he equally enjoys describing in detail if ladies are wearing rich clothes. See Chapter 24.
16. In this most ribald version of the Rest under the Tree, Gasozein, with his head in Ginover's lap, thrusts his hands under the queen's dress, grasps her 'bare hips' and lets his hands 'wander to the gate of the castle on Lady Love's mountain'. Fortunately for everyone concerned, Gawain happened by before things went too far.

17. Charles L. Nelson, trans, and ed., *The Book of the Knight Zifar* (The University Press of Kentucky, 1983).
18. Kidnapped aboard the pirate ship, Grima tries to throw herself into the sea, but her sash gets caught in the rigging. Dangling in mid-air, she is hauled back on board and the pirates start a fight about who would be first to rape her [11]. Thus, they kill each other to the last man. While the ship was drifting rudderless, Grima had ample time to search the hold and found it full of treasures, especially precious textiles, enough for dresses for two hundred ladies. She indulged herself in dressing up lavishly and therefore made a favourable impression on the local authorities when at last she came to the port of Galán, where she promptly founded a convent with the pirates' treasure.
19. W.S. Merwin, trans, and ed., *Poem of The Cid* (New York: Mentor Classic, New American Library, 1959).
20. The most famous relic in the Cathedral of Valencia is a Late Roman agate bowl, reputed to be the Holy Grail.
21. Dietrich's epithet 'von Bern' does not refer to the capital of Switzerland, but is a medieval German rendering of Verona. In one of the epics of the Dietrich cycle. *Rabenschlacht,* about Dietrich's pseudo-historic re-conquest of his lost kingdom and its capital Ravenna ('*Raben*'), King Etzel (Attila) sends along his two sons, named Scherpfe = 'Sword Edge' and Ort = 'Sword Point'!
22. Francis B. Brevart, trans, and ed., *Das Eckenlied* (Reclam. Universal-Bibliothek Nr. 8339 [5], Stuttgart, 1986).
23. The sword's name, *Eckesax,* implies that it was single-edged, as was the machete like *seax* of the Saxons in Arthurian literature.
24. In most other epics of the Dietrich cycle, notably the Norse *Thidrek Saga,* Dietrich's red shield bears a golden lion, surmounted by a crown. See Edward R. Haymes, trans, and ed., *The Saga of Thidrek of Bern,* Garland Library of Medieval Literature, series B, vol. 56 (1988), p. 111.
25. In German folklore, the wild people of the woods are covered with thick pelts; they live without need for clothing or the use of fire. Wild women are the prey of the spectral huntsmen of the Wild Hunt. Thoughtful woodcutters hack a cross on the stump of a felled tree, thus marking it as an asylum for a wild woman when chased. Vasolt acts here as the Wild Hunter, but other traditions have it that Dietrich, like King Arthur, is the leader of the Wild Hunt.

26. Lajos Vargyas, 'Forschungen zur Geschichte der Volksballade im Mittelalter: II. Das Weiterleben derlandnahmezeitlichen Heldenepik', in *Acta Ethnographica Academiae Scientiarum Hungariae* 10 (1961) pp. 242-293, ill.

    Sometimes the maiden is given three choices of being killed: by hanging, drowning, or having her head cut off. In most cases she has to undress, but resourcefully uses this state of seemingly utter helplessness to thwart the designs of the would-be murderer. He makes her strip to climb the tree for her hanging, but then she claims not to know how to climb. As soon as the abductor himself climbs up, in order to hoist her up, she grabs his sword that he had left leaning at the trunk of the tree and is ready to kill him when he comes down. Before the drowning, she also is ordered to strip, because her fine clothes should not wind up rotting at the river's bottom. Thus unhampered, she wrestles the villain into the river and drowns him. For decapitation, as the noblest way to die, the murderer wants her to strip so that bloodstains would not ruin her dress, because he saves the clothes of his victims for his sister (!). Demurely, the intended victim asks him to turn his back, 'because it is not seemly to watch while a maid takes off her clothes.' As soon as he complies, she yanks his sword out of its scabbard and kills him. In one stunning reversal, she thoughtfully suggests to the murderer to take off his own clothes, because 'maiden blood makes such bad stains.' To undress, he has to unbuckle and lay down his sword, and while he is entangled in his clothes, she cuts off his head.

    The Rest under the Tree with the knight's head in the maiden's lap, sometimes with the 'searching' for lice in the hair, and often with three choices for the Killing of the Maiden, is found in West European ballads, of the type of the Dutch *Heer Halewijn* and the English *Lady Isobel and the Elf Knight,* although in these the detail of the knight having two swords is lacking.
27. John F. Haskins, 'Targhyn – the Hero, Aq-Zhunus – the Beautiful, and Peter's Siberian Gold', in *ARS ORIENTALIS: The Arts of Islam and the East,* vol. 4 (1987) pp 153-170, ill. Again, it would be understood that the Hero, as a member of the warrior elite, would have carried a pair of swords according to ancient custom.
28. See W. W. Comfort, trans, and ed., 'Erec et Enide', in *Chrétien de Troyes: Arthurian Romances* (New York: Everyman's Library, 1913), pp. 1-90. Chrétien does not wish to go into details of the lady's

surpassing beauty, her jewellery and clothes, but Hartmann von Aue, in his *Erec,* describes the damsel's clothes as an ermine mantle and a robe of samite 'like brown glass with sable at the wrists'. This sumptuous but apparently also sheer robe represents a contrast and also a parallel to Enid's threadbare gown that she wore at her first meeting with Erec, her swan-white skin showing through the holes. Hartmann mentions that the head on the last stake is that of the renowned knight, Thibaud the Esclavonian, 'born in Winden', i.e. modern Slavonia. Another one of the heads on the stakes is that of Gurzgri, father of Schionatulander! See Thomas L. Keller, trans. and ed., *Erec,* Garland Library of Medieval Literature, Series B, vol. 12 (1987), p. 124.

29. Gwyn Jones & Thomas Jones, trans, and ed., *The Mabinogion* (Amsterdam: A Dragon's Dream Book, 1982).
30. W. W. Comfort, trans, and ed., 'Cliges,' in *Chrétien de Troyes: Arthurian Romances* (New York: Everyman's Library, 1913), pp. 91-179.
31. John Mavrogordato, trans, and ed., *Digenes Akrites* (Oxford, Clarendon Press, 1956).
32. Helmut Nickel, 'About the Sword of the Huns and the "Urepos" of the Steppes', in *Metropolitan Museum Journal* 7 (1973) pp 131-142, ill.; Helmut Nickel, 'The Dawn of Chivalry,' in *Metropolitan Museum Bulletin* [Special Issue], XXXII.5 (1975): 150-52, ill.
33. *Waltharius* has been called everything from 'a masterpiece of early German heroic literature' by generations of German *Literaturhistoriker,* to 'a schoolboy's exercise' (this certainly says a lot about the quality of Swiss schools) by John Mavrogordato. Ever since *Waltharius* was brought to the attention of Germany's reading public by Victor von Scheffel's translation (1857), teachers of German literature, my own *Deutschlehrer* in high school included, praised *Waltharius* as a precious relic that rescued from perdition an oral heroic epic, 'ur-germanisch' in spirit, in spite of its being written in Latin. Actually, as I tried to point out above, *Waltharius* seems to be the key link between Eurasian and Western European – especially Arthurian – epic traditions, and the 'Ur-Epos' of the steppe nomads, told and retold in many tongues (a good story is a good story, no matter which language) round thousands of camp fires. Finally, a very faint echo of the 'Ur-Epos' could be found in *Le Morte d'Arthur,* Book VIII, chapter XXIX, where Sir Palomides, the Saracen knight

rescues Bragwayne, who had been tied to a tree and left to die. (Is this the inspiration for Sir John Everett Millais's provocative painting, *The Knight-Errant,* of 1870?) At a tournament, as recorded in the *Romance of Tristan* (transl. Renee Curtis, Oxford University Press, 1994, pp. 163-165), Sir Palomides bore black arms and two swords to show that he was prepared to take on two opponents at the same time. In the fictitious Arthurian heraldry of the fifteenth century Sir Palomides bore as his heraldic device two scimitars in a chequy field.

Originally published in *Arthuriana*: Vol 17 Number 4, Winter, 2007, pp. 29-48.

29

About The Lace with the Knot in Sir Gawayne and the Green Knight

Among the connoisseurs of romances of chivalry, whether they were the poets themselves or the courtly audiences who eagerly listened to them in the castle's hall or read them in the ladies' bowers from carefully lettered scrolls or even as books produced by the black art of the printing press, it was an article of faith that the first, and, of course, foremost of all orders of chivalry was that of King Arthur's Knights of the Round Table. It is also accepted today as unquestionable fact that the Most Noble Order of the Garter was established by King Edward III as a re-foundation of King Arthur's Round Table.

In the single surviving manuscript copy of *Sir Gawayne and the Green Knight*, British Museum ms. Cotton Nero A. x, the famous motto of the garter 'HONY SOIT QUI MAL Y PENCE' is added right after the poem's final episode, where it is told how the knights of the Round Table merrily accept as their common badge the green lace, the humbling token that Gawayne brought back from the quest.

Most modern commentators, though, point out that apart from this one occurrence, a common badge of the Knights of the Round Table in nowhere else to be found.[1] In the Penguin Book edition of *Sir Gawain and the Green Knight* (1972) it is even stated categorically by its editor, J. A. Burrow, that 'The Arthurian order of the Green Lace, if such it is, does not correspond in detail to the English order of the Garter or to any other fourteenth-century order.' There is, however, good reason to believe that it was exactly such an order that the *Gawain*-Poet had in mind when he wrote about the Green Lace.

This green lace is the girdle of the Green Knight's lady, given to Gawain as a love token and a supposedly protective charm. It is described in the poem in careful detail:

> Ho laȝt a lace lyȝly Þat leke vmbe hir sydez,
> Knit vpon hir kyrtel vnder Þe clere mantyle,
> Gered hit watz with grene sylke and with golde schaped,
> Noȝt bot arounde brayden, beten with fyngrez (1830-33)

Gawain himself wears the lace first, too, as a belt in his encounter with the Green Knight, but on his return to Arthur's court, he has it arranged in an entirely different and highly distinctive manner:

> And Þe blykkande belt he bere Þeraboute
> Abelef as a bauderyk bounden bi his syde,
> Loken vnder his lyfte arme, Þe lace, with a knot,
> In tokening he watz tane in tech of a faute. (2485-88)[2]

'He still carried about him the belt, in token of his fault.' The difference of detail to the Order of the Garter as pointed out by most commentators is that here in the poem it is a green silken belt slung over the shoulder that becomes the badge of the Round Table knights, while that of the Order of the Garter is a ribbon of blue velvet buckled around the left knee. However, there was indeed a secular order of chivalry, in fact, the earliest such organization in Western Europe, which had as its badge exactly such a band looped over one shoulder. This was the Order of the Band, also known as the Order of the Scarf or the Sash, founded by King Alfonso XI 'the implacable' of Castile and Leon (reigned 1325-1350), in the year 1330 (Boulton 46-95).

The anonymous chronicler of *La Crónica del Rey Don Alfonso el Onceno,* written about 1344, gives a detailed account of how in 1330 a delegation from the Basque dominion of Alava offered the lordship of that land to King Alfonso. During his stay in Alava's capital of Victoria, the king bethought himself that in times past the knights of Castile and Leon excelled in knighthood, but lately had not practised it anymore. In order to revive their interest in chivalrous pursuits, he decided to install an *ésprit de corps* among the knights and squires of his household by giving them a uniform of a white surcoat with a black band slung from the left shoulder to the right hip.

> And they were called the Knights of the Band, and they had an ordinance amongst themselves of many good matters, which were all works of chivalry... And thus it happened afterwards that the knights and squires who had done some good deed of arms against the enemies of the king, or attempted to perform such deeds, were given the band by the king.

Later the colour of the surcoat was changed to red and that of the band to gold after the red and gold livery colours of the kings of Castile, whose canting arms were: *Gules, a triple-towered castle Or.* The Knights of the Band formed an elite unit within the chivalry of Spain, fighting together under the Banner of the Band in battle, and teaming up together at tournaments, including *tablas redondas,* such as held at Valladolid in 1333. The explicit mentioning of Round Table tournaments is a clear indication of the Arthurian character of this order.

The Band itself was a strip of cloth one hand's breadth wide and was regarded as such an important symbol of chivalrous integrity that halving the Band was a severe penalty for breaches of chivalrous behaviour, such as failure to come to a tournament called by the king, or quarrelling or feuding with fellow members of the order. The penalty period, during which the halved Band was to be worn, could vary from two months up to ten full years, depending on the severity of the offence.

The Order of the Band was carried on by the successors of King Alfonso XI until the death of King Enrique IV in 1474; it was discontinued under Queen Isabella 'the Catholic'. A heraldic device possibly related to the Order of the Band was the so-called *banda engolada.* This device, typical for Spanish heraldry and found nowhere else, was a bend, that is a diagonal stripe across an armorial shield, held on either end in the maws of dragons' heads. This *banda engolada* was employed as a royal device by the late fourteenth century. In 1375 Don Juan de Castella, the natural son of King Pedro 'the Cruel' (reigned 1350-1369), bore in his shield a *banda engolada* of green edged in gold (!) (Louda table 48) This particular case is interesting, not only because this unusual colour scheme happens to correspond to that of the Green Lace exactly, but it also occurs at the same time period during which *Sir Gawayne and the Green Knight* is thought to have been written. This is also just the time when the connections between Spain and England were particularly strong.

In 1367, at the Battle of Najera, the Black Prince fought as the ally of the deposed King Pedro against the usurper Enrique de Trastamara. While Pedro's mixed Spanish-English contingents wore as their distinctive badges red crosses on white, the traditional English design of St George, doubtlessly in recognition of the reputation of his famous ally, Enrique's men pointedly wore yellow bands, presumably on red coats. After the recovery of his throne, King Pedro resumed the Band as a royal Castilian badge and maintained the Order of the Band. His daughters, Constance and Isabel, became married to two of the Black Prince's younger brothers; Constance (in 1371) to John of Gaunt, Duke of Lancaster, who spent much time and effort on his claim to the throne of Castile, and Isabel (1372) to Edmund of Langley, Duke of York. Also, John of Gaunt's daughter, Catherine, married Enrique III of Castile in 1387.

The Knights of the Band wore their Band over their left shoulders slanting down to the right hip. Presumably this was done for practical reasons, in order to leave the right, the sword arm, unencumbered, and also to ensure that the Band would not be mistaken for a popular heraldic ordinary, the bend, on a knight's surcoat. The bend was a diagonal stripe on a shield, starting from the dexter corner (the right-hand side from the shield bearer's point of view); a bend sinister (starting from the left-hand corner) was generally regarded as a token of some disgrace or blemish, such as illegitimacy.

In his description of the Green Lace, the *Gawain*-Poet takes care to point out that the Green Knight's lady had her girdle tied with a knot (1831: 'Knit vpon hir kyrtel'), which means that it had no buckle like an ordinary belt. Also, on his return to Camelot, Sir Gawain has the lace draped diagonally (2486: 'Abelef') over his shoulder and tied under his left arm 'with a knot'.

Contemporaneous with the Order of the Band and the Order of the Garter was a Company of the Knot, officially known as the Company of the Holy Spirit of Right Desire, founded in 1352 by King Ludovico of Naples-Sicily (Boulton 211-40), who had come to his throne as the second husband of Queen Joanna 'the Terrible'. Though this order was in existence for only about ten years, until the death of its founder, it, too, is of interest in an Arthurian context. In its goals and iconography, it actually strongly resembles an attempt to re-found the Order of the Knights of the Grail. The badge of the Knot was worn in three different stages or classes – the Knot Tied, the Knot Untied, and the Knot Retied – indicating whether its wearer had achieved the goal of Right Desire or was still striving for fulfilment.

These knots worn as everyday badges seem to have been brooches of gold wire pinned to the breast above the heart, but on Fridays they were replaced by a knot of simple white cord in memory of the passion of Christ. The full-dress costume worn by the Knights of the Knot was entirely white, with the dove of the Holy Spirit embroidered on their surcoats. The Dove was also emblazoned on their white shields and on the company's white banner. This is rather reminiscent of the turtledove as insignia of the Templeisen, the Grail Knights in Wolfram von Eschenbach's *Parzival.*

The knotted lace has a parallel with deeper meaning in Gawayne's own emblem of the pentangle, the 'endeles knot' (629-30). Again, it is only in *Sir Gawayne and the Green Knight* that Gawain has this peculiar badge assigned to him. In most other medieval sources, his arms are either: *Argent, a canton gules,* or *Purpure, a double-headed eagle Or, armed and beaked azure* (Brault 37-52; Pastoureau 69-70; Nickel 16-19).[3]

During the third quarter of the fourteenth century, the shield as the main defence of a knight in battle had been made obsolete by the development of plate armour, though in the tournament, shields were still used for additional protection as well as for their decorative value in the display of the knight's armorial devices. These tournament shields were of a shape different from the knightly shields used in battle, and in the middle of the fourteenth century it became *de rigueur* for the fashion-conscious knight to have a garniture of shields, a 'shield for War' and a 'shield of Peace', as noted earlier. The 'shield for War' was of the traditional triangular shape and bore the knight's family arms, while the 'shield of Peace' was a squarish targe with a *bouche*, a cut-out in its upper dexter corner for a lancerest. In contrast to the 'shield for War' this 'shield of Peace' displayed the knight's personal badge.

Gawain's arms changed as described above from the first in the thirteenth and fourteenth centuries the second in the fifteenth century. Both these arms were meant to be family arms of the Orkney clan, because they were shared, with the appropriate marks of difference, by King Lot and all his sons. The pentangle, on the other hand, is a strictly personal badge with its detailed interpretation (620-64) to show that it represented Gawain as being perfect in his five senses, in the dexterity of his five fingers, in his reverence of the five wounds of Christ, in his love for the Queen of Heaven and her five joys, and finally in his five virtues 'fraunchyse,' 'felaȥschyp,' 'clannes,' 'cortaysye,' and 'pité', as noted in Chapter 10. Such a personal badge would be placed on the 'shield of Peace,' to be taken along on a quest, but not on campaign or into battle.

It was considered to be highly desirable that the family arms of a knight would be canting, i.e. representing a pun or rebus on his name; the castle (*Castillo*) of Castile mentioned above is one of the classical examples for this practice. It would be essential, though, to know on which language the pun was based. The family arms of the Orkney clan, with its *canton gules,* seem to be a rebus in French, the language of courtly society in medieval Western Europe. The head of the Orkney clan was Gawain's father, King Lot. 'Lot' means 'section' in French, and therefore a *canton* was an elegant way of expressing the clan's head name, because a *canton* can be considered as a section of a shield!

Though badges sometimes became hereditary in certain families or were tied to certain dignities or offices (the three ostrich feathers of the Princes of Wales are perhaps the best-known example), the personal badge of a knight was usually chosen by himself for reasons of his own. Its significance or possible symbolism was for him to know, along with perhaps a few close friends, and whoever did not belong to this in-group was left guessing.

The eagerness with which the *Gawain*-Poet hastens to explain the significance of the five-pointed 'endeles knot' on Gawain's shield in such detail makes one wonder whether there might be another, deeper meaning not spelled out behind the choice of this unusual geometrical figure for Gawain's 'deuys'. After all, if it was only to represent fivefold perfections or virtues, a five-fingered hand or gauntlet, a five-pointed star or five figures in any colour on the shield would have served. The three red bends on Sir Lancelot's silver shield are a case in point; they are meant to show that he possessed the strength of three ordinary men.

A more secretive explanation for the golden pentangle could be based on the tradition, recorded in surviving rolls of arms of the Knights of the Round Table, that Gawain's battle cry was 'Orcanie', the name of his home country, Orkney. The golden pentangle, the 'endeles knot,' therefore could make a wordplay based on 'Orkney' as *Or-knit* with the heraldic term *Or* for golden and *knit,* a knot (remember that in Chaucer's and the *Gawain*-Poet's time the *k* was still pronounced). Finally, in her essay 'Examples of the Use of the Golden Ratio in Medieval Arthurian Literature' Joan Helm pointed out (7-14) that the line segments of a pentangle intersect each other in the Pythagorean Golden Ratio (A is to B as A plus B is to A. If A is 1, then B will be 0.618; in relation to A; if B is 1, A will be 1.618 times the length of B) and that of the descriptions of Gawain's 'deuys' on his helmet and of the golden pentangle on his shield are bracketing the line 618 of the poem!. Thus, when Pythagorean mystical numbers come into the play, would it be too far-fetched to suspect that the golden pentangle, as the 'endeles knot' and Seal of Solomon, a magic symbol of the most concentrated power, was yet another rebus in the almost-homophone 'arcane', 'Orcanie'?

In any case, with the choice of the 'endeles knot' as Gawain's badge, the *Gawain*-Poet created an image that counterpointed the knotted Green Lace, which for his knightly audience called to mind the (for them) presumably well-known Order of the Band and Order of the Knot with their presumably equally well-known Arthurian inspirations.

Notes

1. Modern Arthurian authors, on the other hand, following Rosemary Sutcliff's lead in *Sword at Sunset,* where Arthur's warband takes sprigs of heather or daisies as good luck pieces and/or badges before battle, have given badges to Arthur's knights on occasion.
2. Quotations from the poem are from the Tolkien-Gordon edition, revised by Davis.
3. In the mid-fifteenth century rolls of arms of the Knights of the Round Table, attributed to Jacques d'Armagnac, Duke of Nemours, Agravaine, the unpleasant brother of Gawain, is given the arms: *Purpure, a double headed eagle Or, with a fess vert overall* (!).

Select Bibliography

Boulton, D'Arcy Jonathan Dacre, 'The Company of the Holy Spirit of Right Desire, Commonly Called the Company of the Knot: Mainland Sicily (Naples), 1352/3-1362?' *The Knights of the Crown: The Monarchical Orders of Knighthood in Later Medieval Europe, 1325-1520.* New York: St. Martin's, 1987. 211-40.

______ 'The Order of the Band: Castile-Leon, 1330-1474?' *The Knights of the Crown: The Monarchical Orders of Knighthood in Later Medieval Europe, 1325-1520*. New York: St. Martin's, 1987. 46-95.

Brault, G. J., *Early Blazon: Heraldic Terminology in the Twelfth and Thirteenth Centuries, with Special Reference to Arthurian Literature.* London, Oxford, 1972

Burrow, J. A., ed. *Sir Gawain and the Green Knight.* New York: Penguin, 1972

Helm, Joan, 'Examples of the Use of the Golden Ratio in Medieval Arthurian Literature.' *Quondam et Futurus*. 9.1 & 2 (Fall, 1988 / Winter 1989) pp 7-14.

Louda, Jiri and Michael Maclagan, *Heraldry of the Royal Families of Europe*, New York: C. N. Potter, 1981.

Pastoureau, Michel, *Armorial des Chevaliers de la Table Ronde.* Paris: Le Léopard d'Or, 1983.

Sutcliff, Rosemary, *Sword at Sunset.* London, Hodder and Stoughton, 1963.

Tolkien, J. R. R. and E. V. Gordon; rev. Norman Davis, *Sir Gawain and the Green Knight*. Oxford: Clarendon, 1968.

Originally published in *Quondam et Futurus* Vol 1., No. 1., Spring, 1991 pp. 15-24

30

Arms and Armour in Arthurian Films

Among the aspects of Arthurian film that deserve special attention is its treatment of arms and armour. After all, Arthurian films are mainly about knights, and knights would not be knights without their armour. This essay will examine some typical approaches to the subject among these films and try to explain how arms and armour were handled, not only as far as selection of the period style is concerned but also in actual use of weapons in battle and tournament.

In reviewing costume and armour in cinema Arthuriana, one must keep in mind that these films face problems different from those encountered by the average costume drama. Most historical films deal with an exactly datable timespan – say, Imperial Rome for *Ben-Hur* or the fifteenth century for the campaigns of Henry V and Richard III— and therefore costumes, furniture, and weapons can be designed that should be reasonably accurate for the periods in question, provided that the designers did their research.

Arthurian films, by contrast, are not necessarily bound to such a fixed style period. Actually, the scriptwriter, the director, and the costume designer are free to choose from a timespan of almost a thousand years, if their ambition would call for historical accuracy. Given the legendary nature of the Matter of Britain, though, any flight of fancy concerning costume and setting could be equally well justified.

The version of the tales of King Arthur best known to the general public is Malory's *Le Morte d'Arthur,* written down in the fifteenth century, and for this reason costumes and setting in Late Gothic style might be considered to be appropriate. On the other hand, it is also well known today that the 'historical Arthur' would have lived and fought at about the year A.D. 500, and a filmmaker aiming at historical verisimilitude would thus prefer a Dark Age background. Then again, most of the major Arthurian romances were composed during the twelfth and thirteenth centuries, and costume designers might see 'around 1200' especially attractive as the right style period, because of its romantic association with the Crusades. All these period styles could be shifted onto an imaginary plane by adding fanciful touches to otherwise quite realistically rendered costumes as *Verfremdungseffekt* (Brecht's alienation effect), a trick amply used by nineteenth-century illustrators.

The medieval romances of chivalry are legitimate ancestors of both Western novels and the Western movies, where the Lone Cowboy riding into town is the Questing Knight, the Sheriff and his posse are King Arthur and the companions of the Round Table, the villain in the showdown on Main Street is the Black Knight at the tournament, and the rancher's daughter is the Princess, whose fair hand is the prize at the happy end.

Every moviegoer knows and accepts the 'white hats/black hats' rule of the Western horse operas. For the 'knights in shining armour' films, the same rules apply in an appropriately modified form. The evil significance of the Black Knight is self-evident;[1] for balance, the hero, who normally is also the star, not only has to ride a white horse whenever possible but also has to wear an open-face helmet in order to make absolutely sure that the audience gets a good look at the star's radiant brow, while the villain is hiding his sinister countenance behind a closed visor. Every so often, the hero is found fighting through raging battles without benefit of any helmet at all. Such a scene is usually made plausible by a fine touch of realism, when the hero's helmet gets knocked off his head as soon as the battle is under way.

All designers of costumes or armour, even those who rely largely on their own imagination, must necessarily have some models in mind upon which their creations are based. One of the problems with these models is that there are very few actual objects in the field of arms and armour that have survived from the periods in question. Practically ninety-nine per cent of existing armour dates from after A.D. 1500. For this reason, a visit to even a major museum can be only of limited help, and therefore book illustrations would be the logical (and also the most accessible) source for such models.

Purists among designers could find their prototypes in the standard reference works of costume and armour, but those searching for the realm of myth and fantasy, if they would be willing to look for inspiration outside of their own imagination, presumably would prefer to glean their inspiration from the glorious illustrations provided by Howard Pyle, Arthur Rackham, Aubrey Beardsley, or N. C. Wyeth. The inspired use of such splendid material would contribute greatly to the success of a film.

Once in a while, a film is straightforwardly based upon fully prescribed pictorial material, which makes it both easy and difficult for the designers, who have to stay faithful to their source but have to use their own imaginations to flesh out the parts not preformed in the prototype. This is the case with *Prince Valiant* (1954), which was an adaptation of the comic-strip classic by Hal Foster. Foster, in his painstakingly precise drawings, had created his own vision of the Middle Ages, which even beyond the circle of his fans is widely taken for medieval reality. The setting of his *Prince Valiant* is as imaginary as the hero himself. Foster created him in the best tradition of medieval minstrels, who kept inventing new heroes and new adventures within the well-known and well-beloved Arthurian framework. This was done to enhance their performances and to catch the attention of their audiences in castle halls and county fairgrounds. The costumes and armour designed by Foster are of a medievalistic nature, vaguely 'around 1200' with some highlights from earlier times, such as the Late Roman/Byzantine period, and of course – as would be expected in a story about a prince of Thule – with a generous dose of romantic Viking imagery.

The film designer of *Prince Valiant* faithfully adhered to the style created by Foster, down to such details as the armorial bearings of Sir Gawain (a highly, but quite un-heraldically, stylized golden falcon on his green surcoat, doubtlessly chosen to fit the interpretation of Gawain's Welsh name, Gwalchmai, 'Hawk of May'). It is interesting that, as far as I know, not one film designer ever made use of the 'real' arms of the Knights of the Round Table that can be found recorded in romances, as illuminations in manuscripts, and even as regular rolls of arms from the thirteenth century onward. In all fairness, though, it has to be said that before Pastoureau's *Armorial,* published in 1983 (which mentions non-French material only in passing), reference to Arthurian arms was found mostly in scattered articles in heraldic journals.

The knights at the Great Tournament in *Prince Valiant* wear thirteenth-century-style mail armour with bucket-shaped *heaulms* and flowing armorial surcoats in bright colours. Shields are of the triangular 'knightly' type, emblazoned with the champion's heraldic bearings, but Prince Valiant's own shield, with his badge of the red horse's head of Thule, is circular, to hint at his 'Viking' heritage. A stickler for technical detail would insist that his shield is structurally closer to that of a Greek hoplite (a heavy-armoured citizen soldier of classical antiquity) than to that of a Norseman. (Perhaps this design can be explained as a Mediterranean influence through his association with Aleta, the Queen of the Misty Islands in the Aegean Sea.)

Shields in most films are not made of wood covered with leather, as actual medieval shields were, but are stamped out of sheet metal. Such construction has the advantages of faster and less expensive manufacture, of a neat and shiny look, and also of a pleasing acoustic effect, because these metal shields, when hit by sword or mace, give forth a resounding 'bang' instead of the less gratifying dull 'thud' of wood.

The costumes of the invading and marauding Sea Rovers evoke the standard Viking image with shaggy furs and horned helmets; their chieftain, in his conspiratorial meeting with the Black Knight, Sir Brack,[2] has a winged helmet as mark of his rank. (Unfortunately, no archaeologist so far has unearthed a Viking helmet with horns, let alone with wings.)

As light campaign gear fit equally for battle or quest, Hal Foster's knights are equipped with spiked steel caps with mail curtains hanging down to protect nape and neck. Because the manufacture of mail is a time-consuming business – it means linking together by hand thousands of tiny rings – the costume designer of the film in what must have been a brilliant brainstorm was able to circumvent considerable labour expenses by simply obtaining a number of *khula-khud,* spiked helmets with camail of a traditional pattern (Robinson, *Oriental Armour* 31-52, 93-115), which were produced en masse in busy family armorers' shops in Persia and India up to the first half of the twentieth century. Made expressly for the tourist trade, they were sold in all the bazaars of the East, and they are still cluttering up antique shops and auction sales. These helmets resemble Foster's noble knightly gear quite admirably, as long as one does not look too closely for tell-tale Oriental features, such as the paired plume-holders on either side of the moveable nasal.

An even more popular Arthurian film was *Camelot* (1967). Admittedly, one reason for this popularity would be the fact that its model, the Lerner and Loewe musical *Camelot,* has become nostalgically linked with the presidency of John F. Kennedy (Knight 26-31). However, the lavishness of the film's production also guaranteed its success. In the illustrated souvenir booklet for *Camelot,* the costume designer, John Truscott, states that he 'tried to make the film seem sophisticated but with elements which contradict sophistication'. Truscott also claims that 'materials were collected from all over the world.' Though this comment evidently refers to the fabrics for the costumes to be made, it also applies to the armour in a surprising way.

Armour of knights and men-at-arms, a total of 361 suits, was designed to give *Camelot* a 'timeless' medieval look, but with generous use of *Verfremdungseffekt,* in order, in the words of director Joshua Logan, to 'eliminate all the clichés that have surrounded castle-and-crusade pictures since the beginning of films'.

The armour of the men-at-arms, to be seen only more or less on background figures in mass scenes, is vaguely fourteenth century in style, with mailshirts, iron-studded leather jackets, and simple bassinets. The knights, as befitting their superior status, wear much more elaborate armour. Their articulated arm and leg defences are also of the type in use since the fourteenth century (Blair 62-67), but the cuirasses and helmets of the main actors, Sir Lionel, Sir Sagramore, Sir Dinadan, and even of King Arthur himself, are derived from Central Asian and Chinese prototypes of the Wei, T'ang, and Ming periods (Robinson, *Oriental Armour* 32, 137-39, 151); a superlative *Verfremdungseffekt* indeed!

In particular, Sir Lionel's lamellar helmet with its mask visor is clearly styled after an original of *c.* A.D. 500, found in an Avar warrior's grave at Kertch in the Ukraine and now in the Historical Museum, Moscow (Robinson, *Oriental Armour* 55-56; Kirpicnikov 101-02). Presumably in order to make the bumptious Sir Lionel even a little more ridiculous-looking, his visor is not hinged at the brow, to fold upward, as it should, but is made to open sideways, like the door of a pot-bellied iron stove.[3]

The bardings and trappings for the noble steeds of the three champions at the tournament, in contrast, are in sixteenth-century European style. Their horses' chanfrons are magnificently crested: Sir Lionel's with a golden swan with spread wings, Sir Sagramore's with a splendid rack of stag's antlers, and Sir Dinadan's with a huge pair of curling ram's horns. These ram's horns are the clue for where the inspiration for these crests must have come from.

Chanfrons with ram's horns as ear protectors are on display in two museums in Madrid. One example is conspicuous as the first in an array of a dozen equestrian figure of knights in full armour, man and horse, in the Great Hall of the Real Armeria, the ancient armoury of the kings of Spain (Cortes pls. I and IV); the other has pride of place in the Armour Gallery of the Army Museum (*Museo del Erjecito* 35). Ram's horns as protectors are the *leitmotif* for horse armour made by a prolific Nürnberg armorer, Kunz Lochner (*c.* 1510-67). The armour in the Army Museum is his work. When *Camelot* was filmed on location in Spain, using real castles in Spain for its scenery (the Castillo de Coca is Camelot, the Alcazar of Segovia is Lancelot's Joyous Guard), the designer seems to have found his inspirations for his horse armour in the Madrid museums. Having decided to adapt the impressive ram's horns for the chamfron crest of Sir Dinadan's charger, it would be only one further step to create the antler rack and the swan crest for the other champions.

Lancelot's silver armour (he rides a white horse, of course) is topped by his helmet crest of a silver fleur-de-lys, to show not only that he is terribly pure but presumably also that he is French. The same 'French' fleur-de-lys, set in a glory of rays, is displayed on his silver shield.[4] This shield has a bouche in its upper dexter corner, a cut out that served as a support for the lance in the charge.

A knight's shield was his main defence in the days of mail armour, which was too flexible to be shock resistant. To make the most out of the shield's protection, knights, especially in the formal combat of the tournament, charged each other left (shield) side against left side, their lances pointing diagonally across their horses' necks.

Unfortunately, fight coordinators in films are generally unaware of the technical function of the shield as a shock breaker. In sword fights, they let their combatants happily flail away, sword clashing against sword (the surest way to ruin a good blade), with their shields held out of the way as a mere ornamental nuisance, and in jousts the combatants all too often point their lances straightforward, meeting their opponents on their right sides unprotected by the ignored shields. Sad to say, in the wayside encounter of Lancelot with King Arthur, and also in his jousts with Sir Lionel and Sir Dinadan, the jousters charge each other right (but wrong) side against right side. Only Sir Sagramore manages to get on the proper side of the tilting barrier, a fine point appreciated by Queen Guinevere.

Another technical point regularly missed by illustrators of knightly tales and fight coordinators alike is that of the broken lance. Inevitably, the loser in the joust falls off his horse ingloriously, his broken lance dangling limply, while the victorious champion's shaft is boldly pointing up – and forward at a triumphant angle – perhaps for us moderns understandable from the point of view of Freudian symbolism, but quite wrong technically. A shattered lance was the best proof that the jouster had hit his opponent with the greatest force possible; a mere glancing blow or a miss would have left the shaft intact. It was a score point recorded by the heralds, whether a jouster broke his lance, even if neither combatant fell. Contemporary depictions invariably show the victor's lance broken, and the loser's intact (Cripps-Day xxvii-xxx; Nickel, 'Tournament' 216-17, 248).

In *Camelot,* King Arthur's great sword Excalibur is the sword he drew from the stone, as indicated by the Gothic script etched on its blade: 'Whoso Pulleth Out This Sword of the Stone Is Rightwise King Born of All England.' The Sword's cruciform hilt vaguely resembles that of a fifteenth-century sword with a grip of 'one-hand-and-a-half'. In an interesting pattern of mutual influence between the arts, the famous still photo of King Arthur enthroned, his fists clenched around the guard of Excalibur, was adapted as the cover picture for the third novel, *Arthur,* in Stephen R. Lawhead's Pendragon Cycle (1989). The graphic artist exchanged Richard Harris's frowning brow for a more youthful countenance, and slightly, barely noticeably, altered the appearance of Excalibur by putting a purple gem in its guard because the novel mentions an 'eagle-carved amethyst' on its hilt.

The amethyst in Excalibur's hilt has become an established detail, passed on and elaborated upon among Arthurian writers for fifty years, ever since Wart in T. H. White's *The Once and Future King* (1939) pulled at the Sword in the Stone, and 'the light all about the churchyard glowed like amethysts.'[5]

T. H. White's *The Once and Future King* has been the basis not only of *Camelot* but also of the Disney version of the story in *The Sword in the Stone* (1963), As an animated film, it is of course subject to rules totally different technically and aesthetically from those films already discussed. Therefore, nobody would expect anything resembling historical accuracy in such an esoteric subject as the arms and armour of the knights meeting at the Tournament toward the end of the picture. It is hard to swallow, though, that the cartoonist quite blithely let the Golden Knight couch his lance with his left hand and carry his round shield in his right![6]

Monty Python and the Holy Grail (1975) is among satires 'in a class by itself' (Lacy and Ashe 281). At first glance, the armour of its knights looks exactly like the medievalistic standard equipment of top-to-toe mail, helmets, and shields. In particular, the armour of King Arthur himself is not noticeably different from that which can be seen on dozens of effigies in dozens of churches and cathedrals all over what used to be Arthur's kingdom of Logres. The giants Robert de Vere, Earl of Oxford (d. 1221), or of William Longespeé (d. 1228), in Salisbury Cathedral, might well have served as direct models.

The jokes, in Monty Python fashion, are in silly details, such as Sir Bedevere's helmet with a visor open like a picture frame, funny armorial bearings like those of the Knight of the Red Herring or of Sir Robin Coeur-de-Poulet, the high-kicking ballet of the knights at Camelot, and of course the outrageous notion of having the knights galumph about on pretend horses. The armour of the Black Knight is probably styled after that of a sculpture of a knightly saint on the facade of Wells Cathedral (Blair 22; Norman 13).

It would be interesting to know whether the black cross on the white shield of the knight in the fore of the battle array at Arthur's attack of the Grail Castle was chosen because this was the badge of the Teutonic Knights. This detail could well be one of those sometimes surprisingly subtle Monty Python gags, most likely arranged by Terry Jones, who also happens to be the author of an iconoclastic book about Chaucer's 'parfit knyght' and his connection with the Order of the Teutonic Knights (Jones 49).[7]

The French film *Perceval le Gallois* (1978) takes its armour from the twelfth century. Not having seen this film, I know of it only from still photos. Reviewers have, however, praised it highly, because of its beautiful stylization using two-dimensional scenery props to create visual effects like the illuminations in a medieval manuscript (Lacy and Ashe 283). The film designer's puristic use of manuscript illustrations as his models is clearly evident in his treatment of armour. Those mail shirts not yet covered by surcoats, and the huge round-topped shields with simple heraldic charges painted in the Romanesque style of the late twelfth century are taken directly from miniatures in a devotional manuscript, the *Hortus Deliciarum* of the Abbess Herrad von Landsberg (*c.* 1185).

The precious original, once one of the treasures of the City Library of Strasbourg, was destroyed in a fire when this formidable fortress city was shelled in 1870 during the Franco-Prussian War, but we do have carefully made hand-coloured lithograph copies of the miniatures from the early nineteenth century (Engelhardt n.p.; Martin 36-39).

Incidentally, when in *Camelot* King Arthur has his talk about Lancelot with King Pellinore,[8] he is toying with two armoured puppets, which are so close in style to marionettes shown in one delightful miniature of the *Hortus Deliciarum,* where puppeteers are playing *ludus monstrorum*, that it is hard to think this similarity entirely coincidental (Nickel, 'Little Knights' 170-83).

Though *Perceval le Gallois* has been much lauded for how closely it follows Chrétien de Troyes, it seems on the other hand to follow the 'white hat' tradition, by letting its title hero ride a white horse, instead of a red sorrel or roan, as he should after he becomes the Red Knight. Very properly, the designer did not give Perceval's charger the flowing trappings so beloved by designers of 'castle and crusade' films, because these trappings were not yet in fashion in Chrétien's time (*c.* 1170-80). The first representations of knights on horses with trappings are from 1196.

While *Perceval* has its setting in the twelfth century of Chrétien de Troyes, the television series *The Legend of King Arthur* (1979) tries hard to evoke the background of the 'historical Arthur' *c.* A.D. 500. At times, it succeeds even a little too well in pointing out the rough edges of the Dark Ages; all too often, the Knights of the Round Table look rather more like the Stratford Inn's bane, Larry, his brother Darryl, and his other brother Darryl, from CBS's *Newhart*, than like shining champions at the foremost court of chivalry.

The armour designer for this series gave his knights body armour of the lamellar type, made up of small rectangular iron plates arranged in overlapping rows and laced together with leather straps. This was authentic Dark Age armour, introduced by the steppe tribes that came from the East during the Great Migration period (Robinson. *Oriental Armor,* 4-10, 25-27, and *Armor of Imperial Rome* 163; Kirpičnikov 104-07; Gamber, 'Kataphrakten' 7-44). In order to give the armour the 'primitive' look appropriate for the Dark Ages, however, the designer seems to have turned these laced-together lamellar cuirasses inside out, so that the strap endings of the lacings dangle loosely (and messily) on the outside for the desired effect.

Primitive starkness was also uppermost in the designer's mind when the film's helmets and shields were created. The helmets with mask visors, cheek pieces, and neck guards are deliberately crude versions of the magnificent original from the fabled Sutton Hoo ship burial of the seventh century (Grohskopf 60ff; Gamber, 'Some Notes' 208-16; Bruce-Mitford 217-80; Nicolle 13). The helmet, now in the British Museum, is richly embellished by an overlay of embossed silver; its crest in the shape of a dragon is stretched across the helmet bowl from its brow to the nape of the neck.[9] The helmet's most remarkable element is a visor wrought as a face mask with bristling moustache and garnet-inlaid lips. In the television series, the helmets are of the same type, with visor masks, but of starkly plain dark iron and without any decoration.

Shields in the series are circular, with a central boss sometimes surrounded by five or six smaller bosses that would serve both as reinforcement and as ornamentation. Like the helmets, shields bear no distinguishing marks to tell one from the next. To tell friend from foe by painting shields with such markings was the reason for the rise of heraldry, necessary after the introduction of visored helmets that made faces unrecognizable. For this reason, it is a truly amazing feat that Bors recognizes Lancelot's shield in the bundle that a groom, on Elaine's orders, tries to hide from him.

Arthur's legendary battle standard is a golden dragon; it probably was a windsock-like draco (a cavalry ensign of the Late Roman army), with a metal head and a fluttering fabric body (Tatlock 233; Esin 15; Nicolle pl. 1. C; Robinson, *Armor of Imperial Rome* 17). In novels and films alike, Arthur's dragon banner is usually interpreted as a flag with a dragon's image. One of the exceptions is the dragon standard, only fleetingly seen, that is shown in the *Legend of King Arthur* television series. Here it is a sculptured dragon of metal, sitting on a crosspiece on top of a pole, in the style of the eagles and other signa of the Roman legions (Robinson, *Armor of Imperial Rome* 32, 34).

Quite likely, 'for some tastes the most successful of the Arthurian films in English is *Excalibur*' (Lacy and Ashe 281). Its ambition is to tell the entire Arthurian story, including the Grail quest, in one fell swoop. It places extraordinary emphasis on the representation of armour, to a degree unusual even among Arthurian films. *Excalibur* in fact indicates the rise, the glory, and the fall of Arthur's kingdom by changes in the appearance of the knights' armour. Not only are the knights in full armour practically all the time – Uther Pendragon keeps his armour on even while he rapes Ygraine – but armour is ingeniously used to convey messages about the deeper meaning underlying the events. Stylistically, the film's armour is, with two exceptions, based on fifteenth-century models, but makes imaginative use of the *Verfremdungseffekt* of fanciful deviations from the traceable prototypes.

In the opening scenes, the kingless interregnum and the no less brutal period of Uther Pendragon's rule are symbolized by warriors in black armour of monstrous shape, with oversize shoulder-pieces and elbow-cops, heavily studded with knobby rivets and wicked spikes. Helmets have bizarre visors of animal forms; Uther Pendragon's own is shaped as the snout of a wild boar. Here symbolism makes a clever play on the term 'pig-faced' for this type of pointed visor (Blair 69), with the transformation of his helmet into a realistic boar's snout, Uther Pendragon's unbridled lust, both for power and for Ygraine, is unmistakably expressed in a literal and visual way. By contrast, Duke Gorlois's armour is recognizably based on an existing armour (*c.* 1450-60), now in the Historical Museum at Berne, Switzerland (Thomas and Gamber 51; Martin 122). As the wronged husband of Ygraine, Gorlois is the 'good guy' and therefore does not qualify for the weirder bizarreries marking the more sinister characters.

After the foundation of the Round Table, the Knights appear in truly 'shining armour,' beautifully polished and styled in the best tradition of the illustrations of Arthur Rackham, as for instance in his 'How Sir Launcelot fought with a friendly dragon' (Pollard and Rackham pl. 10).[10] Rackham's illustrations inspired entire episodes of the film, such as the hanged knights in the tree (Pollard and Rackham pl. 96) and the climactic last fight at Camlann, derived from 'How Mordred was slain by Arthur, and how by him Arthur was hurt to the death' (Pollard and Rackham pl. 16).

The symbolic value of the armour becomes fully evident when the gradual breaking up of the Companionship of the Round Table is demonstrated by the rusting of the armour worn by the questing knights, until Perceval, after the achievement of the Grail, sheds his corroded armour altogether and returns almost naked, dressed only in loose breeches resembling the loincloth of Christ.

Equally, Lancelot's guilty conscience is brought out in the open through the medium of his armour. When resting in the forest, he is attacked and wounded with his own sword by a nightmare enemy, who turns out to be his own still shiny armour come to ghostly life. To demonstrate the fundamental difference between the brutal lust of Uther's rape of Ygraine and the guilty but pure love of Guinevere and Lancelot, armour is deftly utilized as symbolic props. Uther, disguised by Gorlois's armour, ravishes the naked Ygraine, after having ripped the clothes off her body; by contrast, Guinevere joyfully joins Lancelot in the enchanted forest glade, where the lovers embrace in almost chaste nakedness, with Lancelot's armour cast aside, never to be put on again.

As a detail borrowed from Gottfried's *Tristan,* where King Mark is still noble and forgiving and not the despicable coward as in Malory (Surles 60-75), Arthur, in the only scene in which he rides a white horse, finds the guilty lovers asleep in the forest and, with broken heart, plants Excalibur between them, by this token giving up everything worthwhile in his life.

One of the most spectacular scenes in *Excalibur* is the ride of the Knights of the Round Table to meet their destiny at Camlann in a blaze of glory. Their armour shining again, they follow King Arthur on his steed bedecked in golden scale armour, the huge banner of the Dragon floating above. There are few sights more stirring than a knight in sparkling plate armour galloping forth holding aloft a streaming banner of red and gold – and this sight is seen through a screen of apple trees in full bloom.

Interestingly, the scale armour of Arthur's steed is styled after original cataphract (heavy-armoured cavalry) armour found in the Late Roman fortress Dura Europos, Mesopotamia, and now on display in the Higgins Armory Museum, Worcester, Massachusetts. Fragments of such armour have been excavated at Newstead, the site of the Late Roman cavalry fort of Trimontium between Hadrian's and the Antonine Walls; they are now in the National Museum of Antiquities, Edinburgh. This scale armour for horses was introduced by steppe nomads taken into the Late Roman army as auxiliaries from A.D. 175.[11] The same steppe nomads, Sarmatians and Alani, introduced their tribal dragon banners as cavalry battle standards into the Roman army (Gamber, 'Kataphrakten' 35ff; Robinson, *Armour of Imperial Rome* 186, 190-95).

Arthur's knights ride to Camlann in shining armour, but the forces of evil, as represented by Mordred's followers, are in dark armour with bizarre elements. Their ensigns are ragged banners topped by skulls, identical to those from the period before Arthur's reign, signalling the lawless times to come.[12] The two glaring exceptions that do not fit the fifteenth-century image of armour in *Excalibur* are Mordred's golden helmet and cuirass and the moulded breastplate Morgana wears in her last scene of the film.

Mordred's golden helmet with its facemask and embossed curly hair is styled after Late Roman parade helmets in the Oriental fashion (Robinson, *Armour of Imperial Rome* 114-26, and *What Soldiers Wore* 26). One of the three helmets with visor masks found at Newstead might well have been its prototype. Mordred's cuirass is also of Roman pattern (Robinson, *Armour of Imperial Rome* 147). With its embossed nipples, navel, and pectoral and abdominal muscles, it was designed to give the impression of heroic nudity.

In antiquity, warriors of the most diverse cultures – Greek, Etruscan, Germanic, Celtic – went into battle naked, believing themselves to be invulnerable by virtue of invocation of the special protection of a deity. In societies where magic was accepted as fact, it must have been a mighty deterrent to face such an enemy flaunting his powerful 'medicine'. More practical fighters, who wanted nothing left to chance with something as important as their own lives, preferred to wear such a muscle cuirass, which had the look of a naked body but gave solid real protection in addition to the magical one. Morgana's words when she is arming Mordred – 'No weapon forged by man can harm you, when you wear this armour' – clearly indicate its enchanted quality. It is only Excalibur, the magic blade from the Lady of the Lake (no man!), returned to Arthur by Guinevere in their reconciliation scene before Camlann that breaks the spell and kills Mordred.

Morgana's armour, mainly an abbreviated breastplate that looks as if it was designed by and for Cher, covers few of her vital parts and even fewer of her erogenous zones. When wearing it, she weaves her last and fatal spell, indicating thereby that her armour was meant to equal the ritual nakedness of witches. Judging by the expanse of skin exposed, she must have felt supremely confident in its magic defence value, probably against 'weapons forged by man', though it proved to be useless against Merlin's greater power that led her into her own trap.

Addendum

After this essay was written and published in 1991, several Arthurian films of importance were made and released. Three of them – *First*

Knight, The Fisher King, and *Indiana Jones and the Last Crusade* – are of note in discussing arms and armour.

The most interesting of the three as far as arms and armour are concerned is *First Knight* (1995). Here, Lancelot is not the son of a king, but a lowly wandering sellsword. As said before, in the main part of this essay, film directors like the ring of blade against blade, and fight coordinators seem to be unaware of the defensive value of shields. Therefore, right at the film's beginning, we see Lancelot lustily whacking away with local champions at a county fair. Again and again, after a whirlwind clash of blades without any regard of the ruination of their edges, he wrests the sword from his opponent's hand and sends it flying. He fervently denies using any tricks, but – unnoticed by the bumpkins at the fair – his sword does have a trick guard with a forward hook to catch an opponent's blade.

The small crossbows one-handedly wielded like pistols by the bad guys are, of course, without any true medieval models, and their use cheapens the film.

The costumes in *First Knight* were designed in decidedly Italian style by Costumi dell'Arte of Rome, and the armour was made by Terry English, who also made armour for *Sword of the Valiant* (1982), an attempted reinterpretation of the story of Gawain and the Green Knight. There he recreated credible armour in late fifteenth-century style for Gawain and for most of his opponents (the antlered headdress and leafy elements of the Green Knight's armour excepted). By contrast, the armour worn in battle by the Knights of the Round Table in *First Knight* (breast- and backplates over mail shirts, and ill-fitting arm defences) is only vaguely medievalistic.

Foot soldiers wear reinforced leather jerkins, spangenhelms, and round shields more or less like those of the Vikings in the *Ancient Warriors* television series. Archers and spearmen in *Sword of the Valiant* wear bascinets, kettle hats, and rivet-studded brigantines; such gear is generally accepted as armour of 'medieval' soldiers. (Indeed, these foot soldiers do look strikingly like figurines from the 1969 *Men-at-Arms of the Fourteenth Century* series of Imrie/Risley miniatures come to life.)

There is, of course, always a considerable amount of artistic liberty to be expected with the costuming in historical, and even more so with pseudo-historical, films, but the 'undress' uniform of the Knights of the Round Table in *First Knight,* which they wear when questing or sitting around the Round Table, is something terrible to behold. One can only hope that the black-and-blue of their tunics was chosen by the Italian designer in all innocence and in ignorance of the English vernacular; their weird trappings certainly do not have anything to do with knightly gear of any period. As token armour for this 'undress' uniform, the knights have to wear on their forearms metal tubes that look as if made from tin cans, and on their left shoulders peculiar moulded shield shapes that are blank metal for the knights, but decorated in relief with a golden Celtic crowned cross for King Arthur. (This cross is also the device on his blue banner.)

These little shields are presumably a misinterpretation of Italian pictorial sources. The protection of the shoulder joint against heavy blows of sword or mace was a serious technical problem as long as the tough but flexible mail shirt was the only body armour in use. Cup-shaped shoulder guards, probably of *cuir-bouilli,* came into use in the middle of the fourteenth century. At that same time, it became fashionable in Northern Italy to wear surcoats with triangular flaps hanging down from the shoulders. These triangular flaps were somewhat of a shield-shape and, therefore, lent themselves to the display of heraldic charges. It is not clear whether they were reinforced and actually protective armour or were merely decorative. In any case, the very few representations of knights with these elements (Boccia and Coelha figs. 1, 2, 5, 13, 15) show wearers in profile, which might have given the designer the mistaken impression that there was only one 'shield' on the left shoulder.

Shortly after *Cinema Arthuriana* was published in 1991, *The Fisher King* appeared on the silver screen. This essay is not the place to review its highly arbitrary interpretation of the Grail story; suffice to say that the sporadically appearing Red Knight is the only element of the film that has anything to do with arms or armour. This Red Knight, though, is a figment of the imagination of the Grail-seeking Robin Williams, and, as a symbol of the massacre that pushed Williams over the edge, he obviously has no connection whatsoever with his prototype in Chrétien or Wolfram. True to his violent symbolism, his armour is exaggeratedly enhanced by dagged fluttering helmet mantlings and horse trappings that create a flame-like silhouette, in a style reminiscent of the artwork of Darrel Sweet and Julek Heller.

Indiana Jones and the Last Crusade is a Grail quest revved up by the usual chases over water and land. Near the end of the film, the last surviving Knight Guardian of the Grail makes an appearance in mail armour and surcoat of around 1200. Somewhat illogically, the clue to the whereabouts of the Grail is provided by an inscription engraved on a crusader's shield in a crypt in Venice (found after Indiana Jones vandalized a medieval marble floor); it goes without saying that the shield is of the sheet metal type, essential for historical films. Armour in the modern military sense is provided by World War I-type tanks clattering around, supposedly in 1938. Indiana Jones's competitors in the search for the Grail are the Nazis, who are on the quest for purposes of evil. Their use of the badge of Rommel's World War II Afrikakorps is rather premature for 1938.

Finally, there is the 1994 educational film *Knights and Armor,* made for the A&E Television Network. The historical armour shown here is from the best European collections, the Hofrüstkammer of Vienna, the Landeszeughaus of Graz, and the Wallace Collection of London among them. There is in the film the obligatory reference to King Arthur and his Knights of the Round Table. In one of the film's spirited fighting scenes, a re-enactment in mail with 'Norman' helmets and 'Norman' shields, the shields are properly used as shock breakers and are actually emblazoned with the arms of Arthurian knights from the 'Armagnac' armorial, Sir Calogrenant (*Gules, a serpent or*) and Sir Galegantin of Wales (*per pale of or and sable, a lion vert overall*). Too bad, though, that these 'Norman' shields are of sheet metal, and that Sir Galegantin wields his trusty sword in his left hand and his shield in his right. That he is bested in this fight shows, although unintentionally I am sure, the danger of neglecting the niceties of proper medieval combat.

The Mists of Avalon, Marian Zimmer Bradley's feminist retelling of the Arthuriad, came to television in the summer of 2001. As essentially macho subjects, arms and armour play a relatively subordinate role in the telefilm, and as is too often the case with medievalistic films (see the latest remake of *Henry V*), those responsible for costuming have no clue about knightly combat. In blissful ignorance of the accepted rules of chivalry, the left-handed Lancelot is picked for the role of the best knight of them all.

Spaced out over the telefilm's four hours, there are three major battles, two ambushes, and three swordfights. The script makes constant reference to the rescue of British-Roman civilization from the barbarism of the always-bellicose Saxons, who are represented as shaggy savages clad in rough tunics and animal hides and fur. The civilized Christian Romano-Britons wear standard Hollywood early medieval garb, but interestingly, the true British 'of the Old Religion' gambol around their Beltane fires half-naked in animal skins with horned and feathered headdresses. By strange coincidence, in the spring of 2001, Univision aired a Spanish-language costume drama, *Ramotta,* where 'Yaqui mission Indians' did almost identical war dances in almost identical outfits.

In *The Mists,* the Saxons bear round shields with bosses (quite historical as familiar from Viking films) and wear little armour, and mercifully no horned or winged helmets. Their weapons are swords (although none of their eponymous *seaxes),* spears, and axes. In particular, one huge double-axe makes a repeatedly spectacular (albeit totally unhistoric) appearance. Saxon battle ensigns are tattered skins mounted on rickety sticks and painted with Pictish clan symbols. (The murals of stag and boar seen in the sacred places of the 'Old Religion' are copied from reliefs on the silver cauldron found at Gundestrup in Denmark.)

The Romano-British elite warriors, such as Arthur's knights, wear neat leather armour reinforced with small metal plates, riveted on in the manner of Victorian misinterpretations of 'Norman' mail armour represented in the Bayeux Tapestry. For ceremonial wear, Arthur has a 'Roman' armour of breastplate and skirt straps. Men-at-arms have to do with plain leathers with sewn-on washers. Helmets are simply conical; some have 'Norman' style nasals. The most elaborate helmet belongs to Duke Gorlois and is styled after the visor helmets found in the Viking age Swedish royal burial mounds at Vendel and Valsgaerde. The helmet serves as Uther's disguise for the seduction of Igraine after he kills Gorlois and takes his armour. Shields are oval, in the late Roman style, with central bosses, but in most sword combats the champions prefer to fight without them. (The ring of the blade is still more dramatic than the dull thud against a wooden shield.)

Castle architecture and women's costumes are more or less 'Norman'. Interestingly, the only credible 'Norman' armour with conical helmets with nasals, and with 'Norman' shield of pointed almond-shape, is worn by two toy knights with which Morgaine and Arthur play as children. These puppets are evidently inspired by the figurines that King Arthur toys with in *Camelot* during his talk with King Pellinore mentioned above: they are derived from the miniature *ludus monstrorum* in the twelfth-century manuscript *Hortus Deliciarum,* where two puppeteers stage just such a fight using puppets (Nickel, 'Little Knights' 170-83).

Shields in *Mists of Avalon* lack any markings to indicate heraldry. To indicate they are Christian, the Roman-Britons do carry a banner with the Chri-Rho labarum. The dragon emblems of Uther and Arthur are displayed golden on red banners or blue as tattoos on their sword arms. Some of the dragon banners are on crossbeams similar to Roman vexilla, but most are mounted (upright with a short bracing rod on top) like sashimono of Japanese samurai, a detail that raises some interesting questions about transcontinental cultural influences in the so-called Dark Ages. Excalibur is first a cross on a stone altar. It is changed into a gleaming sword by an apparition of the Lady of the Lake in Arthur's hour of need during one of the battle scenes, and after Camlann, when it is thrown into the Lake of Avalon by Morgaine, in mid-air it turns into a blindingly radiant cross as the Mists of Avalon lift forever.

In conclusion, it can be said, not surprisingly, that the ways to approach the subject of arms and armour in Arthurian films are as many as there are costume designers, but that a blending of historical realism and fantasy seems to be the most successful, insofar as it corresponds to the image of the 'knight in shining armour' every Arthurian carries in his or her heart.

Appendix

One of the first educational films ever made, *A Visit to the Armor Galleries,* was a project completed in 1923 by Bashford Dean, Curator of the Department of Arms and Armor, The Metropolitan Museum of Art, New York, and his assistant and eventual successor, Stephen V. Grancsay. This film attempted to dispel popular myths about armour that existed already before they became cast in concrete by Laurence Olivier's *Henry V* and the television series about Henry VIII, where knights are hoisted into their saddles with derricks.

Armour is heavy, as can be expected from its being made of iron, but it is not so heavy that a knight would be unable to get up when thrown to the ground. A mailshirt with long sleeves weighs about twenty-five pounds; a full cap-a-pie plate armour of the fifteenth century, not more than sixty-five pounds. This weight, if properly 'custom-made' and fitted to the body, represents no encumbrance for a well-trained man. In the film, the 'knight' in fifteenth-century Burgundian armour gets up on his steed for a ride in Central Park (with the Belvedere Castle as an appropriate backdrop, the skyline not yet cluttered up with high-rises), falls to the ground and gets up again, all unaided, though he had no previous training.

Terry Jones, in his *Chaucer's Knight* (273-74), states that in the filming of *Monty Python and the Holy Grail* most of the knights wore 'imitation chain-mail made out of knitted wool, which was uncomfortable enough, but Graham Chapman, as King Arthur, wore a genuine metal chain-mail coif and found the weight of it unbearable for more than short periods.' He also remarks that during the making of Eric Rohmer's film *Perceval le Gallois* 'real chain-mail' was used. From my own experience, I can say that though a mailshirt is heavy it can be worn without major discomfort for hours, if this is done with a proper undergarment, a padded and quilted acton or pourpoint, which would prevent chafing on pressure points. It is also important to wear a tight sword-belt to take up the drag of the loose-hanging skirts, and to minimize the weight on the shoulders. Part of the problem with Graham Chapman's coif was that it was hanging loosely over the shoulders, with its full weight pulling down from the top of the head. Original coifs were cunningly tailored to fit around head, neck, and shoulders so as to distribute the weight; a padded skullcap was worn under the coif against the painful pressure of the steel rings (and catching of hair).

One designer of theatrical costumes in Berlin had 'mail' made out of cheap brown-paper string in use after World War II, knitted with extra-thick needles by a group of nice old ladies whom his atelier had under contract. For the proper metallic effect, these shirts were dyed black and brushed with silver paint. Helmets and breastplates were hammered out of aluminium. Aluminium was also the material for the armour worn by Ingrid Bergman in her *Joan of Arc.*

This armour in its entirety and the prototypes for the helmets and body defences worn by the other 'knights' were manufactured by the late Leonard Heinrich, then armorer of the Metropolitan Museum (one of the great moments in the Department of Arms and Armor was when Ingrid Bergman came for measurements and fittings). 'White' medieval armour was highly polished, and Master Heinrich did wonders with the aluminium elements. It turned out, however, that they were too dazzling under the lights, and – alas – had to be dulled.

Armour's main drawback is not so much that it is heavy as that it is hot. Wearing a quilted *acton* against the chafing of the metal elements, and a closed helmet in summer temperature, can be trying indeed, quite aside from the heat of the metal under the sun's rays. For the tournaments staged as part of annual summer community events at The Cloisters (the medieval branch of the Metropolitan Museum in upper Manhattan's Fort Tryon Park), we therefore had 'mailshirts' made out of silver lamé covered with colourful surcoats to eliminate the need for breastplates; shields of masonite; and helmets of fibreglass cast from originals in the Museum's collections. Because of this lack of body armour, 'safety' lances – slim cones of rolled-up brown paper, slipped onto thin mailing tubes for handles – were used to be aimed against the shields only.

The jousts were done by John Franzreb, the stuntman who broke the Round Table in *Camelot* by jumping his horse onto it. He was, incidentally, also the White Knight in the old Ajax cleanser commercials. Ajax's white horse did participate in the Cloisters tournaments, too, though not as a charger in the jousts, but – for reasons of advanced age – as the palfrey of the Lady of the Lake.

Notes

For generously given assistance in locating material for this essay, I would like to express my thanks to my friend and colleague, Karl Katz, Consultant for Film and Television, and to Nadine Covert, Program for Art on Film, at New York's Metropolitan Museum of Art. Special thanks are due to Terry Geesken, Film Stills Archive, Museum of Modern Art, New York.

1. There are of course exceptions to this rule. In the film *The Black Knight* (1954), the Black Knight is the hero. The occasional Black Knight as a 'good guy' goes back to the Black Knight in *Ivanhoe,* who turns out to be Richard Coeur-de-Lion in disguise, and lastly to the real-life Black Prince, Edward, Prince of Wales (1330-76), who is considered, at least in English-speaking circles, to be the Flower of Chivalry.
2. A still photo of Sir Brack at the Tournament was used for the back-cover illustration of the paperback edition of the fifteenth-century

romance of chivalry *Tirant lo Blanc* by Joannot Martorell and Marti Joan de Galba, translated by David H. Rosenthal (New York: Warner 1984).

3. Helmet visors opening sideways are a standard element in Howard Pyle's illustrations of *Otto of the Silver Hand* (1888). Here, though, they are not supposed to be used humorously, because they are found on the helmets of both the 'good guys' and 'bad guys'.
4. Interestingly enough, the fleur-de-lys (which for us is the heraldic figure par excellence) does not occur in any of the fictitious arms attributed to the Knights of the Round Table before the eighteenth century.
5. The amethyst in Excalibur's hilt occurs also in Rosemary Sutcliff's *Sword at Sunset* (1963), Sanders Anne Laubenthal's *Excalibur* (1973), and Stephen R. *Lawhead's Arthur* (1989).
6. One of the questions invariably asked at any guided tour of the Armor Galleries or after a lecture is 'What happened if a knight was left-handed?' There seems to be no answer to this problem; all armour that I know of was designed for the conventional combat with the opponents charging each other left (shield) side against left side. Even the sixteenth-century stalwart, Gotz von Berlichingen 'of the Iron Hand,' had himself an artificial right hand made after he lost it in battle, rather than fight with his left. However, in the collections of the Metropolitan Museum's Department of Arms and Armor, there is one seventeenth-century Polish sabre made for a left-hander.
7. One of the climactic events in 'castle and crusader' dramas is a duel between knights fighting with two-handed swords, though these swords were strictly foot soldiers' weapons of the sixteenth century. Even in carefully researched films, such as *Joan of Arc* with Ingrid Bergman, for which the Armor Shop of the Metropolitan Museum furnished prototypes for helmets and body armour, the fight coordinator could not resist the temptation to slip in such a duel. Therefore, the two-handed swords clashing away in the encounter with the Black Knight at the ford in *Monty Python* are practically unavoidable.
8. King Pellinore, with his bald head, flowing moustaches, and befuddled manner, is obviously modelled after the White Knight in Lewis Carroll's *Through the Looking-Glass,* as illustrated by John Tenniel. The spikes of the horse's armour and the horse-headed

visors of the White Knight's and the Red Knight's helmets are like some armour to be found in *Excalibur.*

9. The armour found at Sutton Hoo corresponds in detail – parade lorica, circular shield, dragon-crested helmet – to the description that Geoffrey of Monmouth gives of Arthur's in his arming before the battle of Badon (*History* ix, 4) indicating that Geoffrey must have had some 'ancient book' as his source for Dark Age arms. Armour in Geoffrey's own time (*c.* 1136) was quite different with mailshirts, triangular shields, and crestless helmets.
10. Rackham's illustrations seem to have been the source for the costumes in NBC's 1989 Christmas telefilm, *A Connecticut Yankee in King Arthur's Court,* with Keshia Knight Pulliam, the cute kid from *The Cosby Show,* as the Yankee who teaches karate and other black arts to Queen Guinevere and her ladies.
11. Of the 8,000 Sarmatians serving in the Roman army as the first heavy armoured auxiliary cavalry, 5,500 were sent to North Britain to fight Picts, attached to the *Legio VI Victrix*, *praefectus* Lucius Artorius Castus. As late as A.D. 428, a kibbutz-like settlement of Sarmatian veterans is documented at Ribchester, Lancashire.
12. The armour, A 78, in the Waffensammlung, Vienna, Austria, with its helmet sporting a mask visor shaped as an eagle's beak and batwing side elements, seems to have been the inspiration for some of the sinister armour worn by characters at Uther's time, and also for some of Mordred's followers. Arthur's knights in their 'shining armour' have similar, non-functional batwing elements attached to their visors. Perhaps the costume designer got his inspiration from the catalogue of the Innsbruck exhibition of 1954, the only publication in which the 'Gorlois' and the 'batwing' helmets are illustrated together (Thomas and Gamber 51, ill. 1; 67-68, ill. 48 and 49).

Select Bibliography

Blair, Claude, *European Armour.* London: Batsford, 1959.

Boccia, Lionello G., and Eduardo T Coelho, 'Colaccio Beccadelli: An Emilian Knight of about 1340', Robert Held, ed. *Armors and Armor Annual.* Northfield, Illinois, Digest Books, 1973.

Bruce-Mitford, Rupert, 'The Sutton Hoo Helmet-Reconstruction and the Design of the Royal Harness and Swordbelt', *Journal of the Arms and Armour Society* 10 (1982) pp. 217-80.

Combs, Carl, *Camelot.* New York: National Publishers, 1967. Souvenir booklet.

Cortes, Javier, *Guia Illustrada de la Real Armeria de Madrid.* Madrid: Blass, 1950. Museum guide.

Cripps-Day, Francis Henry. *The History of the Tournament in England and in France.* London: Quarich, 1918.

Engelhardt, Christian Moritz, *Der Herrad von Landsberg, Äbtissin von Honberg und Odilienberg im Elsass, Hortus Deliciarum.* Stuttgart and Tubingen, 1818. Portfolio.

Esin, Emel, 'Tös und Moncuk.' *Central Asiatic Journals* (1972): 14-37.

Gamber, Ortwin, 'Kataphrakten, Clibanarier. Normannenreiter'. *Jahrbuch der Kunsthistorischen Sammlungen zu Wien* 64 (1968) pp 7-44.

______ 'Some Notes on the Sutton Hoo Military Equipment.' *Journal of the Arms and Armour Society* 10 (1982), pp. 208-16.

Grohskopf, Bernice, *The Treasure of Sutton Hoo.* New York: Atheneum, 1970.

Harty, Kevin J., 'Cinema Arthuriana: A Bibliography of Selected Secondary Materials', *Arthurian Interpretations* 3 (Spring 1989) pp. 119-37.

______ 'Cinema Arthuriana: A Filmography. *Quondam et Futurus* 7 (Spring 1987): 5-8.

______ 'Cinema Arthuriana: Translations of the Arthurian Legend to the Screen.' *Arthurian Interpretations* 2 (Fall 1987): 95-113.

Jones, Terry, *Chaucer's Knight: The Portrait of a Medieval Mercenary.* New York: Methuen, 1980.

Kirpičnikov, A. N, 'Russische Waffen des Jahrhunderts', *Waffen und Kostiimkunde* 2 (1986): 85-129.

Knight, W. Nicholas, 'Lancer: Myth-Making and the Kennedy 'Camelot', *Avalon to Camelot* 2 (1986) pp. 26-31.

Lacy, Norris J., and Geoffrey Ashe, *The Arthurian Handbook.* New York, Garland, 1988.

Martin, Paul, *Waffen und Rüstungen – von Karl dem Grossen bis zu Ludwig XIV.* Frankfurt am Main, Umschau, 1967.

Museo del Ejercito, Madrid, n.d. Museum guide.

Nickel, Helmut, 'The Little Knights of the Living Room Table.' *Metropolitan Museum Bulletin* 25 (1966): 170-83.

______ 'The Tournament: An Historical Sketch'. Howell Chickering and Thomas H. Seiler, eds., *The Study of Chivalry*, Kalamazoo, Western Michigan University, 1988.

Nicolle, David, *Arthur and the Anglo-Saxon War*, London: Osprey, 1984.

orman, Vesey A. B., *Arms and Armor*, New York, Putnam, 1964.

Pastoureau, Michel, *Armorial des Chevaliers de la Table Ronde*. Paris: Le Léopard d'Or, 1983.

Pollard, Alfred W., and Arthur Rackham, *The Romance of King Arthur and His Knights of the Round Table*, 1917. Reprinted, New York: Weathervane, n.d.

Robinson, H. Russell, *The Armor of Imperial Rome*, New York, Scribner, 1975.

______ *Oriental Armor*, London, Jenkins, 1967.

______ *What Soldiers Wore on Hadrian's Wall*, Newcastle-upon-Tyne: Graham, 1976.

Surles, Robert L, 'Mark of Cornwall: Noble, Ignoble, Ignored', *Arthurian Interpretations* 3 (Spring 1989): 60-75.

Tatlock, J. S. P., 'The Dragon of Wessex and Wales', *Speculum* 8 (April 1933): 223-35.

Thomas, Bruno, and Ortwin Gamber. *Die Innsbrucker Plattnerkunst*. Innsbruck: Museum Ferdinandeum, 1954. Exhibition catalogue.

Originally published in *Cinema Arthuriana: Twenty Essays*, rev. ed. 2010 [2002] Edited by Kevin J. Harty. Reprinted by permission of McFarland & Company, Inc., Box 611, Jefferson NC 28640. www.mcfarlandbooks.com.

31

The King's Arms, the Queen's Legs, and the Cat's Miau

Humour and Satire in Arthurian Heraldry

There is a hoary heraldists' joke that says that everyone knows the King's Arms, but nobody ever saw the Queen's Legs. Arthurian heraldry has a superabundance of kings' arms, but the leg of a noble, even royal lady can be perceived, too, if the story of the origin of the Most Noble Order of the Garter is to be believed.

In the days when knighthood was in flower, heraldry was a deadly serious business. Coats-of-arms and helmet crests were the only means of telling friends from foe when faces were hidden behind visors, but even then the fighting man's grim sense of humour manifested itself in occasionally quite light-hearted blazons. For armorial bearings it was desirable to be 'canting', i.e. to represent a rebus of the owner's name; this quite often resulted in outrageously punning charges. Where reality and fantasy intermingle, such as in the pageantry of the tournament or the extravaganzas of romance, funny, piquant, and even frivolous badges and devices can be expected almost as a matter of course.

The Most Noble Order of the Garter, it is generally accepted, was founded by King Edward III as a lofty attempt to revive the Fellowship of the Round Table, but its badge is said to have originated from a jocular whim, when King Edward III picked up a garter that had dropped from the shapely leg of the Fair Maid of Kent, Joan, Countess of Salisbury. Also,

Ye King's Arms
Ye Queen's Legs

the Round Table at Winchester, most likely built by order of Edward III, in significant self-mockery has a place reserved for Sir Dagonet, King Arthur's jester.

It seems that the earliest use of an heraldic charge used for comical effect appears in, of all places, the first complete epic about the Holy Grail, Wolfram von Eschenbach's *Parzival* (*c.* 1205). There, King Hardiz of Gascony at the tournament in the plain of Kanvoleis bears the forepart of a griffin on his own shield and banner, but to the four troops of knights in his retinue are assigned banners with griffins' hindquarters!

In addition to this straightforwardly earthy jest Wolfram also works an elaborate heraldic witticism into the rousing speech that the champion Gahmuret gives to his wavering ally and fellow knight-errant, Kaylet of Toledo, before entering the fray of the tournament of Kanvoleis. Gahmuret is a vassal of the Baruch of Baghdad, his device is an anchor; Kaylet has a *serapandratest*[1] in his shield and an ostrich for his crest (Timpson 281; Wolfram ch. 2, 43-45). Therefore Gahmuret exhorts him:

> Let us make common cause. Does not your Ostrich stand up as ever, scorning his Nest? Then you must carry your Serpent's Head against Hardiz's Demi-Griffin! I will cast my Anchor into the surge of his attack with intent to land but he will have to pick his way ashore over his horse's tail down on the sand!'

Kaylet's ostrich crest has a triple meaning, one of them used satirically. The reference to the ostrich without a nest fits a roving knight-errant, though Kaylet is 'in civilian life' the king of Spain, and is based on the medieval belief that ostriches built no nests at all, but laid their eggs into the sand.[2] Another belief was that ostriches could eat and digest anything, and for this reason it was an heraldic convention to identify a bird as an ostrich by an iron object – a nail, an arrowhead, but most frequently a horseshoe – in its beak (Staehelin 49-57). In Kaylet's case, this represents a clear allusion to Toledo's famous iron industry. Finally, the ostrich plume was a symbol for unshakable steadfastness, because no matter how hard the wind blows, it cannot be ruffled (Palliser 365-68). Therefore, Gahmuret's pep talk directed at the somewhat less than determined Kaylet, the bearer of the ostrich crest, must have been a jest greatly appreciated by a knowledgeable audience.

The other German Grail romance of the early thirteenth century, Heinrich von dem Türlin's *Diu Crône* ('The Crown'), also delights in fabulous heraldry. Some of the charges of the participants at the great tournament at Sorgarda Castle have a familiar ring, such as the griffin's claw of Gawein's opponent, Fiers de Arramis, [3] or the anchor that the champion Kavomet of Arabia wore. Heinrich makes ample use of heraldic fun, such as when he lets the Anchor (Kavomet) be thrown into the waves of combat, and not hold in the storm. The Eagle (Laamez of Babylon) swooped down to earth instead of up in the air, and the Chain (Aschalone of Syria) was stretched out full length on the ground. Though the device of the White Elephant, borne by Aschalone's kinsman, Varuch of Syria, certainly was not so funny for Heinrich's contemporaries as it seems to us, the Owl of the good knight Cleir de Voie must have been assigned to him with tongue firmly in cheek[4] (17914-18476).

In an attempt to bring some semblance of order to the often-bewildering heraldry of the Round Table, a roll of arms of its knights was compiled in the middle of the fifteenth century, naming up to 175 individual knights and even adding thumbnail sketch biographies in the more elaborate editions (Blangy, Pastoureau).

This armorial, *Les Noms, Armes, et Blazons des Chevalliers et Compaignons de la Table Ronde,* was intended as an appendix to the *Livre des tournoys: La forme des tournois au temps du roy Uter et du roy Artus* by King René d'Anjou (*c.* 1455). It is attributed to the Arthurian enthusiast, the Duke of Nemours, Jacques d'Armagnac, who was married to a niece of King René. Interestingly, many of the arms, particularly those of minor characters, are clearly lifted from a contemporary (*c.* 1440) handbook of heraldry, *Le Traitié du Blazon d'Armes* by Clement Prinsault (Douet d'Arcq 258-342) that its author had dedicated to Jacques 'filz de monseigneur le due de Nemours' (Dennys 214).

The arms in this armorial, as a hint at their fictitious nature, display an inordinate use of unusual tinctures, such as purpure and vert, but in addition to that there are quite a few cognizances that are scurrilous, comical, or satirical, and most likely were inserted for comic relief. It is most unfortunate, though, that the arms of Sir Dagonet, King Arthur's jester, which logically should have met all three of the above qualifications, are not in this list, and regrettably neither are they mentioned by Malory.[5]

One of these tongue-in-cheek arms is that of the knight known only by his surname 'li Blons Amoureux' (possibly identical with 'the count of Honolan, who had such a fine head of hair,' mentioned in Chrétien's *Erec*). 'Li Blons' bears as the charge on his sable shield and as his crest a silver comb full of strands of golden hair (Sandoz 415, no. 95; Pastoureau 51, no. 33). Two other coiffure-related crests are those of Keu d'Estraux (Sir Kay le Strange): *un bras armi d'argent tenant deux cheveux d'or et de sable,* and of King Guivret le Petit: *un bras armé tenant une brosse, le tout d'or* (Pastoureau 79, no. 107; 73-74, no. 92).

By representing the golden ring in the canting arms of Le Valet au Cercle d'Or, *de pourpre au cercle d'or lié de sable,* as a barrel hoop such as was used as inn signs, the author of the *Armorial* was making a bit of fun of the valet's high-sounding name (Pastoureau 104, no. 173; Sandoz 414, no. 73). Sir Mador de la Porte, the accuser of Queen Guinevere in the poisoned-apple episode, is given seven red-cheeked apples in his sable shield; in some variant manuscripts these have been turned into seven keyholes in allusion to his name and office as Keeper of the Gate at Arthur's court (Pastoureau 85-86, no. 123; Sandoz 411, no. 40; Scott-Giles 31).

Heraldic animals tend to be fierce beasts, such as dragons, griffins and lions rampant, but in the heraldry of the Round Table we encounter some very unusual creatures. King Pharamon of Gaul, for instance, bears three golden toads in his sable shield (Pastoureau 96, no. 151; Scott-Giles 338; Sandoz 420). This charge was obviously inspired by the medieval legend that Clovis, King of the Franks, had three golden toads as his device in his azure shield as long as he was a heathen, but these toads were miraculously changed into fleurs-de-lys when he was baptized (Hinkle 38, Smith 131). Sir Courant de Roche Dure bears three white rabbits to indicate the fleetness of foot of the 'Runner of Hard Rock' (Pastoureau 59, no. 55; Sandoz 418, no. 134), but why Sir Persides le Gent should have a green grasshopper as his crest and grasshoppers as his shield supporters remains a mystery (Pastoureau 96, no. 150).

Sir Broadas l'Espagnol bears a golden crayfish in his sable shield and also has crayfish as crest and supporters, which make his full arms look rather like the Lobster Quadrille (Pastoureau 53, no. 38; Sandoz 419, no. 143). Sir Busterin le Grand, who is said to have been rather smaller than medium size, bears on a golden field within a border company (a single row of squares) of argent and gules a black mouse, probably as a good-natured ribbing about his surname 'le Grand' (Pastoureau 55, no. 44; Sandoz 418, no. 139).

A very elaborate play on words seems to be behind the arms of Sir Argoier le Fel. He bears: *d'or a trois cotices de sable posées en bandes*, has as his crest a squirrel nibbling a nut and as his supporters two damsels 'au naturel' (Pastoureau 45, no. 16; Sandoz 415, no. 97). The Bestiaries describe the squirrel as a very choleric animal (Randall 21). For this reason it would be a fitting crest for a knight surnamed 'le Fel'. His surname seems also to have determined the choice of the other elements in his arms. *Fel* is an almost-homophone for *fil* = 'thread', and the three thin cotices or *fillets* can be seen as mere threads.[6] At the same time a pun can be made with *cotices* and *cotte* = 'gown' in the sense of 'very little dressing', which would account for the state 'au naturel' of the two *filles* who are supporting the arms of the scoundrelly Sir Argoier.

Similarly, Sir Mordred, naughty boy that he is, has two naked blackamoor girls (*mores*) flanking his shield as his supporters (Pastoureau 91, no. 139).

In looking at the 'Armagnac' armorial itself, and not at lists in alphabetical order, one can get the feeling that the author permitted himself a sly jest here and there by putting a couple of shields side by side to create visual puns. This is almost certainly the case when in the standard version of the manuscripts no. 99, the arms of Mandin l'Envoisie: *de gueules a la sirène d'argent se peignant, écaillée de pourpre,* are followed by no. 100, the arms of Gringalais le Fort: *de sable a la licorne d'argent accornée et accornée d'azur.* The mermaid, symbol of carnal lust and seduction according to the Bestiaries, is thus placed next to the unicorn, symbol of chastity and purity. English readers may be amused by the nos. 59 and 60, the arms of Amant le Bel Jousteur: *de sable au visage de jeune fille blonde au naturel,* followed by those of Ganemor le Noirsent: *de gueules au loup d'or armé et lampassé de sable.* This visual double-entendre of the wolf after the maidenhead was most likely unintentional, though. In any case, it works better in English than in French.

On occasion, scurrilous charges occur unintentionally by scribal error, when copying from an un-illustrated source. For instance, 'deux gemelles' (twin bars) in Keu d'Estraux's shield are in one manuscript (Berlin, Kupferstichkabinett, MS. 77 A10) mistaken for 'deux gueules,' two gaping maws.

The mid-fifteenth century romance of chivalry, *Tirant lo Blanc*, by Joannot Martorell and Marti Joan de Galba, though not strictly an Arthurian romance, contains numerous episodes with Arthurian themes, including pageants where King Arthur and Queen Guinevere make personal appearances. This romance, which Cervantes in *Don Quixote* declares to be 'the best book in the world', abounds with fictitious heraldry, and much of it is quite deliberately comical and scurrilous. The infidel king of Bougie, for instance, is wearing a 'gold bejewelled monkey' as his crest (Martorell, ch. CCCXL). At their knighting, Tirante's two squires, Richard and Deiphobus, received arms and splendid new surcoats. Deiphobus's surcoat was all over embroidered with opium poppies, and the motto: WHAT PUTS OTHERS TO SLEEP WAKES ME UP; Richard's device was 'heavily embroidered with gold thread', but the author fails to say what it was, and therefore his motto: I CANNOT MAKE HEAD OR TAIL OF IT, is quite apt (Martorell, ch. CXXXII).

In a scene that sheds a rather interesting light on the concept of courtly love, Tirant boldly enters the chamber where his adored Princess Carmesina has just got out of bed and is combing her golden tresses. Her damsels watch indulgently how he kisses their mistress on breasts, eyes, and mouth again and again, but they quickly intervene, when his hand strays under her chemise. In parting, however, he succeeds to slip his right leg between her thighs and takes her comb with him. The next day, at a grand tournament graced by 'those ladies who had loved most truly,' among them Queen Guinevere and Isolde, Tirant shows up with only his left leg armoured; on his right he wears the stocking that came so near to the goal of his desire, now richly embroidered to honour this event. His helmet is surmounted by four gold rods that support a copy of the Holy Grail, containing Carmesina's comb, a crest that looks very much like an elaborate version of that of Le Blons Amoureux in the 'Armagnac' armorial[7] (Martorell, ch. CLXXXIX).

Arthurian fictitious heraldry has been called 'une caricature du système heraldique véritable' by Michel Pastoureau, the author of the so far most comprehensive work on the subject, *Armorial des Chevaliers de la Table Ronde*. This is of course especially true of armorial bearings and badges invented for satirical purposes.

One the best examples is the riddle Chaucer created in his spoof of an Arthurian romance, 'The Tale of Sir Thopas', with the arms of his hero:

His shield was al of gold so reed,
And ther-in was a bores heed,
A charbocle bisyde.

This at first glance straightforward blazoning has caused a lot of confusion among his editors, an effect that Chaucer as an expert on heraldry doubtlessly had intended and would have greatly enjoyed. Most modern interpreters ignore the colour of the field, and say that the shield charge was a boar's head with an escarbuncle or even 'a precious stone' next to it.

The *escarbuncle* is a heraldic charge developed out of the reinforcing strips radiating from the shield boss, in French *rais d'escarbouncle*; Middle High German, Buckelrîs, literally 'branches (rîs) of the shield boss (buckel) in pre-heraldic days. By a wrong etymology and because of its 'rays' it was connected with Latin *carbunculus* = 'little (live) coal, garnet,' which explains its alternative interpretation as a precious (red) stone. Needless to say that the position of an escarbuncle or a 'precious stone' next to the boar's head would be a heraldic atrocity that would make any heraldist wince.

However, the clue to the puzzle lies in Sir Thopas's own name, which is itself a heraldic technical term. In addition to the usual terms for heraldic tinctures – or for gold/yellow, argent for silver/white, gules for red, etc. – late medieval heralds invented some rather fanciful terminologies in order to give their blazons a more pompous wording. Thus, the tinctures could be indicated by the names of gemstones, the planets, and even the days of the week, with the virtues thrown in for good measure. (See Chapter 23.)

In Prinsault's *Traitié* the tincture Or (gold/yellow) can be expressed 'en vertues' as *Noblesse,* 'des planètes' as *Le soleil,* 'des jours' as *Le Dimanche,* and 'en pierrerie' as *La topaze* (Douet d'Arcq 258). Sir Thopas's name is therefore simply a fancy heraldic term for gold.

Topasion is also 'the fyrste stone ... sygnyfyenge golde in armys' in the very first heraldic handbook printed in English, *The Book of St Albans*, 1486, and *Carbuncle* is 'a shynynge stone, sylver it is called in armys.'

In *Le Morte d'Arthur* Malory describes the arms of Sir Pryamus, whom Gawaine encounters in Tuskane during the War with Lucius (Malory V. 9), as 'The knyght bare in his shelde thre gryffons of gold in sable *charbuncle,* the chyef of syluer'. The mysterious *charbocle* in Sir Thopas's shield is thus meant to be neither the figure *escarboucle* nor a gemstone, but is the colour of the shield charge, the boar's head, that is blazoned 'bisyde,' i.e. in profile.

However, in the *Augmented Version of Prinsault's Treatise* it is the tincture *Or* that 'en pierrerie' is meant to be represented by *l'Escarboucle*! (Douet d'Arcq 324; Nickel 20). Using the 'pierrerie' term for Or/gold as the hero's name, Chaucer with a straight face is poking fun at the confusing high-faluting terminologies of his fellow heraldists, and succeeds gloriously to befuddle everybody. Since Sir Thopas's shield is 'of gold so red', the audience is left to wonder whether it is golden (Thopas = *Topasion)* or possibly red, and because of the equally absurdly ambiguous *charbocle,* whether the boar's head would be silver on red, red on gold, silver on gold, gold on gold or red on red.[8]

The *Book of St Albans* insists that heraldry was introduced during the Trojan War, and therefore is older than the Ten Commandments (Berners, f j). The medieval epics of the Matter of Greece, such as *Le Roman de Troie* and *Le Roman de Thèbes*, are full of blazonry and also heraldic jests. When in the *Roman de Troie* a Lacedaemonian champion bears a gnat (in natural size) as his shield charge, boasting that he will come close enough to his enemy in combat that he should have a good look at his gnat, this is a parallel to Sir Busterin's mouse. In the *Roman de Thèbes*, however, as a much juicier jest, the hero Eteocles bears a shield of ivory with an azure canton, but has painted on its inside, next to the handgrip, 'par gaberie ... les jambes de s'amie'! [9]

The piquant shield device of the legs of Eteocles's lady love as well as Queen Guinevere's thigh that according to the *Merlin Continuation* bore her badge of true royalty, a birthmark in the shape of a crown (Griffith 261), and the gartered leg of the Fair Maid of Kent (who would have been Queen of England, if her husband, the Black Prince, had not died a year before his father Edward III) should be evidence to contradict the heraldists' jest mentioned in the beginning of this article.

In Mark Twain's *A Connecticut Yankee in King Arthur's Court,* The Boss makes use of heraldic satire quite openly and deliberately as 'a furtive, underhanded blow at this nonsense of knight errantry'. He equips knights on a quest with advertising signboards instead of tabards (Twain, ch. XVI), and turns their chivalric prowess into the professional aggressiveness of travelling salesmen. This scheme is working fine with the hat-peddling Sir Ozanna Le Cure Hardy, who is wearing a stovepipe hat instead of a helmet, and who forces all knights he bests in a joust to replace their crested helmets with plug hats from the hat-boxes that festoon his saddlebow (Twain, ch. XXI). Another one of The Boss's questers, Sir Madok de la Montaine, bears a sign board with letters of shining gold: USE PETERSON'S PROPHYLACTIC TOOTHBRUSH, and on his shield the 'quaint device of a gauntleted hand clutching a prophylactic toothbrush' (Twain, ch. XX), a charge rather reminiscent of the crest of Guivret le Petit, the armoured arm holding a brush, in the 'Armagnac' armorial.

Though there is a superabundance of humorous details in T. H. White's *The Once and Future King,* there is only one funny reference to a 'canting' device, the couple of elbows in flowing sleeves marking the tent of Sir Ulbawes, in the camp before Bedegraine (White: 111:9).

As to be expected of such an outrageous spoof, in the film *Monty Python and the Holy Grail,* heraldry is made good use of as satire. The armorial devices of the crest of the Knight of the Red Herring, and the *chicken regardant* on the shield of Sir Robin the Not-Quite-So-Brave are quite straightforward fun, but sometimes the tongue-in-cheek device is surprisingly subtle, such as when the chorus line of high-kicking knights at Camelot bears surcoats *argent, a chevron sable,* the arms of de Wanton (Foster 201)! In the array of knights and men-at-arms before the final battle – patterned after the grim host of the Teutonic Knights in Eisenstein's *Alexander Nevsky* – a white shield with a black cross (the arms of the Teutonic Knights) is placed in the middle of the front rank.

In another Arthurian film, *The Black Knight,* the bizarre helmet crests invented by the miniaturist who illustrated the sumptuous master copies of King René d'Anjou's *Livre des Tournois* (Paris, Bibliothèque nationale, MSS. fr. 2692, 2693) were skilfully used to enhance the glittering pageantry of the tournament. In the parade of knights entering the lists, the very first knight bears as his crest a dog's head with a bone in his mouth, followed by a mermaid and a unicorn side by her side – very much like the juxtaposition of the arms of Mandin l'Envoisie and Gringalais le Fort, in the armorial appendix to King René's *Livre* – and behind these two come a candlestick and a pair of black-stockinged legs (René 54-55, 60-61; Richards 76)!

Naturally, subtle as well as outrageous examples of humorous heraldry are to be found in the book that was intended to deliver the deathblow to all romances of chivalry, *Don Quixote de la Mancha.* Of the hero's three *noms de guerre* the first one, *Quixote,* is the term for a thigh defence (not exactly the most heroic element of a knight's armour, and also practically obsolete by Cervantes's time). His second and best-known name, *the Knight of the Rueful Countenance,* was given to him in a flash of inspiration by Sancho Panza, who then had to convince his master that it would be unnecessary to have a sorry figure painted on his shield (Cervantes I, ch. XIX). Don Quixote's third name, however, *the Knight of the Lions,* which he adopts (Cervantes II, ch. XVII) after his happily terminated adventure of the lions (who refuse to leave their cage and prefer ignoring him to fighting him) is a persiflage of the arms: *Or, two lions combatant azure* and surname, *Knight of the Lions,* of

Amadis de Gallia, the main hero of Iberian spinoffs of the Matter of Britain.

The crowning glory of quixotic heraldry are the arms of the champions seen among the two armies that to the unimaginative Sancho are just two flocks of sheep on collision course (Cervantes I, ch. XVII). Here Don Quixote recognizes not only any number of extravagantly accoutred heroes, such as Pentapolin with the Rolled-up Sleeve, thus named because he was wont to go to battle with his sword arm bare, and the undaunted Brandabarbaran de Boliche, wearing as his armour a dragon's skin and as his shield a gate, which, Fame says, was the one from the temple Samson pulled down, but gives detailed blazonings, such as the arms of the victorious and never vanquished prince of New Biscay, Timonel de Carcajona, who on his murray shield displays a golden cat with the motto: MIAU, as an allusion to his lady, the peerless Miulina, daughter of Duke Alfeñiquen of Algarbe, and those of the doughty duke of Nervia, Espartafilardo del Bosque,[10] bearing on his shield the motto: RASTREA MI SUERTE (Search My Fortune) emblazoned on a field of asparagus.

Notes

1. *Sarapandratest* is Wolfram's rendering of 'tete de serpent'. A dragon's head was the actual canting crest of the kings of Aragon (d'Aragon).
2. There were two different theories about how ostrich eggs were hatched. The first simply assumed that it was done by the heat of the sun's rays, though only when the Pleiades were in the proper place (White 121). A more fanciful theory insisted that an ostrich's eyesight was so sharp and 'hot' that by just standing next to the clutch of eggs and fixing his glare on them the ostrich would not only fertilize the eggs but also hatch the young within three days (Staehelin 49-57). The belief that ostriches hide their heads in the sand in order not to see approaching danger is post-medieval.
3. Aramiz is a small town in Gascony, together with the villages Athoz and Porthoz it is located near the birthplace of the historical Charles Louis d'Artagnan, Mousquetaire du Roi under Louis XIII, and Marechal de France under Louis XIV.
4. The elephant was considered to be the embodiment of magnanimity and the non-abuse of power, because this largest of beasts contents

himself with vegetarian fare, and does not prey on other animals. His or her trunk was thought to be used for gently blowing ants and bugs out of his way, in order not to tread on them. The Owl was a badge preferred by rugged individualists, who rather prided themselves in being in opposition to all others. In the Arms and Armor collections of the Metropolitan Museum, New York, is a German tournament shield of *c.* 1500, with the image of an owl and the motto: *Wie wol ich bin der vogel has, dennoch erfret mich das*, 'Though I am hated by the [other] birds, I nevertheless rather enjoy that.' In the case of the good knight Cleir de Voie ('Clear of Way') it is the day-blindness of the owl that provides the joke.

5. Even in *The Coat of Arms,* the quarterly of the British Heraldic Society, the Fool of Arms has an occasional column 'Motley Heraldry'.
6. The German term for *cotice* is *Faden,* 'thread'.
7. Joanot Martorell was a native of Valencia, and the most important relic in the cathedral there is a late Roman agate bowl in fourteenth-century silver-gilt countings, revered and (as I was informed by the sexton) authenticated in a document signed by six archbishops as the one and only Holy Grail.
8. Chaucer's use of *charbocle* as a term of 'pierrerie' predates the *Book of St Albans* by almost three quarters of a century, but there is contemporary documentation in the arms of Sir Pryamus in the *Alliterative Morte Arthure* (11. 2521-24):

   He bare glessenande in golde thre grayhondes of sable
   With chapes and cheynes of chalke-whytte syluer,
   A charebocle in the cheefe chawngande of hewes,
   And a cheefe anterous, chalange who lykes.

   The transformation of greyhounds to griffins (Malory V, 9) is most likely due to an intermediate 'grephondes', the *charebocle* is 'chawngande of hewes' (2523), exactly because of the ambiguity of the term.
9. A protective icon on the inside of a shield, where it can be seen by the fighter to give him strength in battle, would be nothing unusual; we know it as the image of the Virgin Mary painted on the inside of King Arthur's and Sir Gawain's shields (there are also actual shields preserved with icons of St Christopher, who protects against violent

death). A secular example is the portrait of a lady painted on the inside of Erek's shield as recorded by Hartmann von Aue.
10. The names of these champions are outrageous fun in themselves: *boliche,* bowling alley; *alfeñique,* almond pap, milksop.

Select Bibliography

Berners, Dame Julia. *The Book of St Albans,* as printed at Westminster, by Wynkyn de Worde in 1496, with the Literary Researchers of the Joseph Haslewood edition of 1810. New York: Abercrombie & Fitch, 1966.

de Blangy, A. *La forme des tournois au temps du roy Uter et du roy Artus, suivie de Armorial des chevaliers de la Table Ronde.* Caen, 1897.

Brault, G. J., *Early Blazon: Heraldic terminology in the twelfth and thirteenth centuries, with specific reference to Arthurian literature.* Oxford, 1972

Cervantes, Miguel de, *Don Quixote de la Mancha.* Trans. Walter Starkie. New York: Signet Classic, 1957

Chaucer, Geoffrey, *The Canterbury Tales.* From the text of W.W. Skeat. New York: Oxford World's Classics, Avenel Books, 1985

Crompton, N. J. R., 'Mediaeval Symbolic Heraldry.' *The Coat of Arms* VIII. 60 (October 1964): 166-68. Dennys, Rodney. *The Heraldic Imagination,* New York: Clarkson N. Potter, 1975.

Dennys, Rodney, *The Heraldic Imagination*, New York, Clarkson N. Potter, 1975

Douet d'Arcq, L. C., 'Un Traitié du Blason du XV siècle.' *Revue Archéologique* XV. I (1858): 257-342.

Foster, Joseph, *The Dictionary of Heraldry: Feudal Coats of Arms and Pedigrees.* New York: Bracken Books, 1989 (reprint. of 1902 edition).

Griffith, Richard R, 'Bertilak's Lady: The French Background of *Sir Gawain and the Green Knight.' Annals of the New York Academy of Sciences,* vol. 314: 249-66.

Hinkle, William M, *The Fleurs de Lis of the Kings of France 1285-1488.* Carbondale: Southern Illinois University Press, 1991.

Malory, Sir Thomas, *Caxton's Malory: A new Edition of Sir Thomas Malory's Le Morte Darthur based on the Pierpont Morgan Copy of*

William Caxton's edition of 1485. Ed. James W. Spisak. Berkeley: University of California Press, 1983

Martorell, Joanot & Marti Joan de Galba, *Tirant lo Blanc*. Trans. David H. Rosenthal. New York: Schocken Books, 1984.

Morte Arthure, Ed. Mary Hamel. New York: Garland, 1984.

Palliser, B., *Historic Devices, Badges, and War Cries*, London, 1870.

Pastoureau, Michel *Armorial des chevaliers de la Table Ronde*. Paris: Le Léopard d'Or, 1983.

Randall, Richard H., *A Cloisters Bestiary*, New York: The Metropolitan Museum of Art, 1960.

René d'Anjou. *Le Livre des Tournois dv Roi Reni*. Paris: VERVE, Revue Artistique et Litteraire 1946 (IV. 16).

Richards, Jeffrey, *Swordsmen of the Screen: From Douglas Fairbanks to Michael York*, London: Routledge & Kegan Paul, 1977.

Sandoz, Edouard 'Tourneys in the Arthurian tradition'. *Speculum XIX* (1944): 389-420.

Scott-Giles, C. W. 'The Heraldry of Romance.' *The Coat of Arms* 11.15 (July 1953): 257-60.

______ 'Some Arthurian Coats of Arms.' *The Coat of Arms VIII*. 64 (October 1965): 332-39; IX.65 (January 1966): 30-35.

Staehelin, W.R., 'Der Vogel Strauss in der Heraldik'. *Archives Héraldiques Suisses* 39 (1925) pp 49-57.

Timpson, George F., 'Heraldry in Wolfram's *Parzival*.' *The Coat of Arms* IV. 31 (July 1957): 278-81.

Twain, Mark, *A Connecticut Yankee in King Arthur's Court*, First published 1889. New York: Washington Square Press, 1948; New York: Bantam Classics, 1981.

White, T. H., *The Bestiary: A Book of Beasts*, New York: Capricorn Books, G. P. Putnam's Sons, 1954.

______ *The Once and Future King*, New York: Berkeley Medallion Books, 1966.

Wolfram von Eschenbach, *Parzival*. Trans. A. T. Hatto. New York: Penguin Classics, 1980.

Originally published in *Quondam et Futurus: A Journal of Arthurian* Interpretations, vol. 3, no 4 (Winter, 1993) pp. 28-40.